ASTRONOMY
MADE SIMPLE

REVISED EDITION

BY

MEIR H. DEGANI, Sc.D.

CHAIRMAN, SCIENCE DEPT., STATE UNIVERSITY OF N.Y.,
MARITIME COLLEGE

MADE SIMPLE BOOKS
DOUBLEDAY & COMPANY, INC.
GARDEN CITY, NEW YORK

TABLE OF CONTENTS

CHAPTER IX

CHAPTER X

CHAPTER XI

CHAPTER XII

CHAPTER XIII

A BRIEF HISTORY OF ASTRONOMY

The history of Astronomy may be conveniently divided into three periods: the Geocentric, the Galactic, and the Universal. The first had its beginnings in ancient history, and came to a close in the 16th century. The second extends from the 17th through the 19th centuries. And the third began and continues in the present century.

THE GEOCENTRIC PERIOD

Early astronomers believed the earth to be in the center of the universe; and assumed that the sun, moon, and stars revolved about that stationary earth. Their interest, hardly scientific in our sense of the term, was mainly in practical matters, in the real and supposed relation of celestial events to those on the earth; in searching the skies for clues to good and evil omens.

Even so, remarkable discoveries were made then. The calendar was developed with great accuracy. The apparent path of the sun among the stars—the ecliptic—was carefully defined. The complete cycle of solar and lunar eclipses was determined. And as early as the second century B.C., the motion of the earth's axis was well understood.

The great figure of Nicolaus Copernicus (1473–1543) is closely associated with the end of the primitive Geocentric period in the 16th century.

THE GALACTIC PERIOD

Modern Astronomy can be said to have begun in this period. Copernicus demonstrated that the earth, far from being the center of the universe, was merely one of the planets revolving about the central sun. Hardly unique, the earth was found to be a quite ordinary planet, going through ordinary motions in an ordinary way.

Indeed the central sun itself was realized to be merely one star among the multitudes of the heavens, one among a vast galaxy of similar stars in every direction about us—some larger, some smaller, some heavier, some lighter than our sun.

In this period the approach became increasingly scientific, motivated largely by the desire to know, to understand the basic laws governing the motion of heavenly bodies, to explain what the eye saw.

Progress from the 16th through the 19th centuries resulted from the effective combination of extended observation, improved instruments, and the work of scientific genius.

Observation. Great quantities of data of fundamental importance were painstakingly gathered by careful observers, chief among whom is the great name of Tycho Brahe (1546–1601).

Instruments. The introduction of the telescope in 1610 by Galileo Galilei was, of course, a milestone in the development of the science of Astronomy; as was the later invention and introduction of the spectroscope. The two instruments complement one another: the telescope permits us to see the stars more clearly; the spectroscope analyzes stellar light, furnishing us with much information about the stars.

Genius. Like every science, Astronomy requires for its advancement the labors of great minds that are able to apply to the observed data insight, imagination, intuition, as well as great learning. Such minds were Johannes Kepler (1571–1630) and Sir Isaac Newton (1642–1727): Kepler by the discovery of the laws of planetary motion, and Newton by the discovery of the Universal Law of Gravitation.

THE UNIVERSAL PERIOD

Now it became apparent that the galaxy of stars to which our sun belongs is merely one of many galaxies—some larger, some smaller than ours. To these much of the astronomical research of the last half century has been devoted, in an effort to achieve a "complete" picture of the universe. For this attempt ever greater telescopes have been constructed.

The great theoretical genius associated most closely with this period in the public mind (although he was primarily a physicist and mathematician) is the late Dr. Albert Einstein (1879–1955).

This is the astronomic period in which we live. And it is far from concluded.

CHAPTER I

THE UNIVERSE

PART 1: BUILDING BLOCKS

INTRODUCTION AND DEFINITION

For as long as man has been conscious of himself and the universe he inhabits, he has regarded the sky with awe and wonder—a source of constant and compelling fascination. Awe and wonder generate study and science; and from its beginnings in primitive, childlike stargazing, as man sought ceaselessly to conquer ignorance and solve mysteries, there emerged finally the science of Astronomy.

Astronomy is the science of the position, motion, constitution, history, and destiny of celestial bodies. In the course of its development as a science, it has already discovered many of the basic laws governing those bodies. But it is the nature of scientific investigation that its work is never done—and here, as elsewhere, immense labors remain to be performed.

WHY STUDY ASTRONOMY?

Each in his own way and for his own purposes, professional astronomer and amateur "stargazer" alike, studies the science because it yields essential information about the universe; and that information then becomes available for numerous practical and scientific applications.

But to ask this question is like asking: "Why learn to read?" For the amateur especially, there is more even than the knowledge to be gained, or the gratification of intellectual curiosity. We study Astronomy because the intelligent, inquiring mind must ask questions and seek answers; must know "Why?" and discover "How?" And from the beginning, whenever man has looked up, there was the sky—always confronting him with seemingly imponderable problems, always challenging him to solve its mysteries.

On one level, man has stated his reaction in magic and mythology, and this is permanently embedded in the world's art, literature, and religions. On another level, he has attempted to explain the celestial phenomena perceived by his senses in scientific terms—and those explanations are the subject matter of the science of Astronomy.

THE BUILDING BLOCKS

The "earth" we live on is a planet—one of a number of planets that revolve about the sun. The unassisted eye is capable of detecting several planets, one satellite (our moon), several thousands of stars; and, several times during the year, showers of shooting stars become clearly visible.

Stars, planets, and satellites are some of the "building blocks" of the universe. The universe is composed of these "blocks" in much the same way that a community is composed of homes, churches, hospitals.

Among the distinct kinds of celestial (heavenly) bodies are planets, planetoids, satellites, comets, meteors, stars, and nebulae. These are the building blocks of the universe; the known physical universe is an immense assembly of these blocks. To the best of our knowledge, **the universe consists, primarily, of nine planets, thirty-one satellites, a vast number (billions) of stars and other classes of celestial bodies.**

PLANETS

Planets are large, solid, nearly spherical masses, revolving about the sun in nearly circular orbits. The best known to us is, of course, our own earth. All of them are relatively cool and are made visible by reflected sunlight; several can be seen at one time or another by the unaided eye. Three planets, however, can be seen only with the aid of a telescope. At first glance, planets look very much like the multitude of stars that glitter in the sky; but an observer can identify a planet as possessing one or more of the following characteristics:

A. Planets shine with **a steady** light, while stars do not. The light reaching our eyes from stars seems to change rapidly in both color and brightness. These changes in color and brightness cause the **twinkling** of the stars.
B. Planets **wander** in the heavens: A planet which at one time was close to one star may later be observed close to another star. Stars, on the other hand, seem to keep the same positions relative to one another. See Fig. 1. The very word "planet" is derived from a Greek word meaning "wanderer."
C. Planets, when observed through telescopes, appear as **small disks** of light. The greater the magnification, the larger will be the diameter of the disk. Stars, even with the largest telescope, appear only as points of light. Even in the 200-inch telescope, they appear as mere points, having no measurable diameter.
D. Planets may be found **only in a narrow strip** in the sky. Their motions are limited to the boundaries of this strip. Stars, of course, may be found in any part of the sky.

PLANETOIDS

Planetoids are small, irregularly shaped solid bodies revolving, like the major planets, about the sun, and differing from planets primarily in size. They are also known either as Asteroids or as Minor Planets. The largest planetoid, Ceres, has a diameter of 480 miles; but many of them have a diameter of only two miles. The first planetoid was discovered on January 1, 1801; many more have since been discovered. It is estimated that nearly 50,000 planetoids can be photographed with one of the large telescopes.

They, too, shine by reflected sunlight; however, because of their small surface, the amount of reflected light is very small. They cannot be seen without the aid of a telescope.

SATELLITES

Six of the nine major planets have one or more moons revolving round them. These are called satellites. The earth has only one moon (satellite), while the planet Jupiter, for example, has twelve. To date, thirty-one satellites have been discovered, the last as recently as 1951.

COMETS

Comets are celestial bodies of unique form and large size which appear from time to time. A typical comet consists of a luminous sphere, or head, connected to a long, tenuous cylinder, or tail. The head may seem as large as the sun; the tail describes an arc in the sky.

To the naked-eye observer a comet appears as motionless as the moon. Actually it moves at speeds of hundreds of miles per second. The exact speed can be determined from its changing position relative to the fixed stars.

There are approximately a thousand known comets, and several new ones are discovered every year.

The vast majority are too faint to be visible to the naked eye. Fairly great comets are rather rare; these appear, on the average, once or twice in a lifetime. The most recent of these spectacular objects appeared in December of 1947.

Of the thousand or so known comets, nearly a hundred are known to move in "closed orbits"—that is, in elongated and cigar-shaped paths. The fact that the orbit is "closed," has no beginning or end, is of great importance. Comets moving in them go round the same path continuously; many of them have been observed several times during their returns to the vicinity of the earth.

The orbits of the other 900 comets have not been definitely ascertained. It is believed that

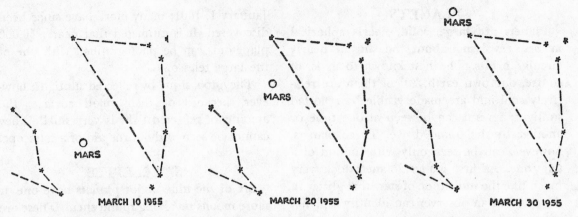

FIG. 1. Views of the same part of the sky on three different dates, March 10, March 20, and March 30, 1955. Note that the stars maintain the same relative position. The planet (Mars) has wandered considerably in that time.

most of these also move in closed orbits and hence will be seen time and again when they come close to the earth, while the rest very likely make only one appearance in the vicinity of the earth, coming, probably, from outer space, making a U-turn, and then leaving, never to be seen again.

METEOROIDS*

Meteoroids are usually tiny (about the size of the head of a pin), solid objects traversing through space. Occasionally a group of meteoroids is attracted to the earth and becomes entangled in its atmosphere. The heat resulting from this encounter consumes the object; the dust resulting from this cremation falls to the earth. Hundreds of tons of meteoric dust descend each year. On rare occasions large meteoroids manage to reach the earth before they are consumed. **The light phenomenon which results from the entry of the meteoroid into the earth's atmosphere is called meteor, or "shooting star,"** the glow of which may persist several seconds.

STARS

Stars are large globes of intensely heated gas, shining by their own light. At their surface, they reach temperatures of thousands of degrees; in their interior, temperatures are much higher.

* The revised terminology for meteoric phenomena is used here. This revision was approved by the International Astronomical Union in 1961.

At these temperatures, matter cannot exist either in solid or in liquid form. The gases constituting the stars are much thicker than those on the earth usually are. The extremely high values of their density are due to enormous pressures which prevail in their interior.

Stars move about in space, although their motion is not immediately perceptible. No change in their relative position can be detected in a year. Even in a thousand years, the stars will seem not to have moved substantially. Their pattern now is almost exactly that of a thousand years ago. This seeming fixedness is due to the vast distance separating us from them. At these distances it will take many thousands of years for the stellar pattern to undergo a noticeable change: This **apparent constancy of position accounts for the popular name "fixed stars."**

NEBULAE

A nebula is a vast cloud composed of dust and gas. The gases which compose it are extremely thin and of low temperature. Nebulae do not shine by their own light, but are made visible by the light of neighboring stars. (These are known as Bright Nebulae.) When they are so visible, they appear to the unaided eye not unlike a fuzzy star. Their actual size and structure, however, can be determined only with the aid of a telescope. Other nebulae are dark, obscure the stars beyond them, and are not visible to the unassisted eye.

PART 2: ORGANIZATION

INTRODUCTION

Thus, the universe is composed of stars, nebulae, planets, comets, and other celestial bodies. Here, the blocks are assembled to form the plan of the universe.

The planets, planetoids, satellites, comets, and meteorites revolve about a single star: the star we call the sun. Together they form the Solar System. The sun, and billions of other stars, form the community of stars known either as the Galaxy, Our Galaxy, or the Milky Way Galaxy. The universe contains many such stellar communities, or galaxies.

Stellar distance is of an order of magnitude entirely different from that of planetary distance: the former is enormously greater than the latter.

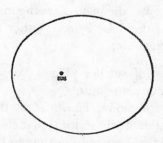

Fig. 3. Other objects, too, appear smaller with increasing distance. Note the apparent size of the distant tree.

Fig. 4. The oval curve suggests the circumference of the whole universe. The dot represents the location of the sun.

Fig. 2. The sun is just an ordinary star. All the other stars look tiny, as they are so remote that we see them only as mere points of light.

Distances between galaxies are still greater than distances between stars. In attempting to visualize unimaginable distances it is essential to use a scale. The plan of the universe on such a scale is given later in this section.

THE SUN

Although it may not seem so, the sun is just an ordinary star, similar to numerous other stars that we see in the sky.

The sun appears large to us because it is, relatively speaking, near to us. All other stars appear as small points of light in the sky because they are far away. See Fig. 2. Our interest in this star (the sun) derives from the fact that the earth receives from it both heat

and light—energy of fundamental importance in maintaining life. The oval curve in Figure 4 represents the universe and the dot the position of the sun within the universe. (Note that Fig. 4, as well as Figs. 5, 6 and 7, are symbolic representations and not figures drawn to scale.)

PLANETS

There are nine planets revolving about the sun: Mercury, Venus, Earth, Mars, Jupiter, Saturn, Uranus, Neptune, and Pluto. Mercury is closest to the sun, and at a somewhat greater distance is Venus; then, the earth; and the farthest known planet from the sun is Pluto.

The earth is 93 million miles from the sun. **This distance is often referred to as an Astronomical Unit.** Mercury is only four-tenths the earth's distance from the sun. Pluto, the most distant planet, is forty times the earth's distance. The distance of Pluto can be stated as forty times ninety-three million miles, or simply as forty Astronomical Units.

A reducing scale may help to visualize these distances. The scale that is commonly used represents the sun-earth distance as one foot long:

93 million miles equal 1 foot; or,

1 Astronomical Unit equals 1 foot.

On this scale, Mercury is four-tenths of a foot; Venus is seven-tenths; and the earth is one foot away from the sun. The farthest planet is forty feet from the sun. A circular box of forty foot radius could accommodate all the planets. The box could be quite shallow, as all the planets move approximately in the same plane.

THE SOLAR SYSTEM

The sun and the planets are the major components of the Solar System. Other members of this system are:

1. the host of smaller planets known as asteroids or planetoids;
2. the several moons, known as satellites, that revolve about six of these planets;
3. comets that appear from time to time;
4. the vast number of meteoroids.

The circle around the dot in Figure 5 represents the entire Solar System.

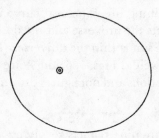

FIG. 5. The oval curve suggests the circumference of the whole universe. The dot and the small circle represent the sun and the solar system, respectively.

THE STARS

Distances to stars are immensely greater than distances to planets. Even the star nearest our own sun is at a distance of 270,000 Astronomical Units. Using the scale (one foot equals one Astronomical Unit or ninety-three million miles), the star closest to our sun would be at a distance of fifty miles.

The two units should be carefully noted. Distances between planets are stated in **feet,** while those between stars are stated in **miles.** A mental picture might help to visualize this distinction. The sun, and all the planets, could be accommodated in a circular house of forty foot radius. The closest star, by our scale, would be in a house fifty miles away. Other stars, by our scale, are at scale distances of thousands and hundreds of thousands of miles from the sun.

OUR GALAXY

These stars form a large community called Our Galaxy or the "Milky Way" Galaxy. It is estimated that the number of stars in Our Galaxy is close to a hundred billion—otherwise stated as 100×10^9, or a hundred thousand million.

The outer surface of the Galaxy is often compared either to a grindstone or to a lens.

A top view of the Galaxy would reveal its circular shape as well as the spiral design formed by the stars. A side view would suggest its similarity to a lens, namely, that it is thick in the center, and thins out toward the edges.

Again using the one foot scale, the diameter of the circle would be close to a million miles, while the maximum thickness is only about one sixth of the diameter.

Our Galaxy is represented in Figure 6.

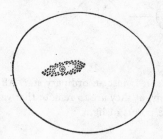

FIG. 6. The oval curve represents the circumference of the universe. Our Galaxy is indicated inside the oval. The dot and the circle represent the sun and the solar system, respectively.

OTHER GALAXIES

Ours is not the only galaxy in the universe: many have been discovered in recent years, strikingly similar to our own. The scale distances between them are from ten to twenty million miles. A highly simplified picture of the universe is shown in Figure 7.

THE UNIVERSE

The universe, then, consists of many galaxies, as galaxies consist of billions of stars.

FIG. 7. The "complete" universe consists of many galaxies. One, containing the sun, is known as Our Galaxy, the Galaxy, or the Milky Way Galaxy.

One of these, the sun, is the star around which our earth moves, as do the other planets of our Solar System.

OUTLINE OF THE UNIVERSE IN TERMS OF ACTUAL DISTANCE

The distance to the sun is 93 million miles; the distance to our nearest star, Alpha Centauri, is 25,000,000,000,000 miles, or 25 million million miles. Distant stars are inconceivably more remote.

The mile unit is of no use in dealing with the distances of stars and galaxies—instead, astronomers use the unit "light year": one light year is the distance that a beam of light travels in one year. The distance covered by a beam of light in one second is 186,000 miles; hence:

One light year =

$$186,000 \times 60 \left(\frac{\text{seconds}}{\text{minute}}\right) \times 60 \left(\frac{\text{minutes}}{\text{hour}}\right)$$

$$\times\ 24 \left(\frac{\text{hours}}{\text{day}}\right) \times 365\tfrac{1}{4} = 5,880,000,000,000 \text{ miles}$$

or six million million miles, approximately.

The star nearest the Solar System is 4.3 light years away. The diameter of Our Galaxy is about 100,000 light years; its maximum thickness is 15,000 light years. An average distance between galaxies would be approximately a million light years.

The sun is only a minute fraction of a light year from the earth. The distance to the sun may be stated as 8 light minutes.

Distances to heavenly bodies, when stated in terms of light, have an added meaning—for the sun, it implies that it takes a beam of light 8 minutes to reach the earth.

So for the stars. A ray of light from Alpha Centauri reaches the earth 4⅓ years after leaving the star.

The most distant object seen by the unaided eye is the Andromeda Galaxy—a million and a half light years away. The light entering the observer's eye has been en route for that time.

CHAPTER II

STARS WITHOUT A TELESCOPE

PART 1: THE BIG DIPPER

INTRODUCTION

Astronomy is one of the several sciences engaged in the study of nature. Much remains to be learned, and many important discoveries can still be made without the use of any equipment. The sky is the laboratory. The time is any fine, clear evening. The place is outdoors, preferably away from city lights, with an unobstructed view of the sky.

Even casual observation reveals that the stars seem to be assembled in groups. Such a group is called a constellation. Modern astronomy recognizes eighty-eight stellar constellations, many of which are of interest only to the professional astronomer. Only twenty of the eighty-eight may be considered well known—among them Orion, the Big and Small Dippers, the Dragon, and the Big and Small Dogs.

The group easiest to identify is probably

the Big Dipper. As its name implies, the stars form the outline of a dipper. It is important to become familiar with that group of stars as it is with reference to it that the locations of other constellations are most readily determined. The Big Dipper can be seen every clear evening in most of the northern hemisphere. This section deals primarily with the stars of that constellation.

THE STARS OF THE BIG DIPPER

Seven bright stars form the pattern of the Dipper. The four forming the "bowl" are known as Dubhe, Merak, Phecda, and Megrez, all Arabic names: Dubhe means "bear," Merak "loin," Phecda and Megrez, "thigh" and "the root of the bear's tail," respectively.

The stars forming the "handle" of the Dipper are known as Alkaid, Mizar, and Alioth, also Arabic names, meaning "the chief," and "the apron"; the precise meaning of the name "Alioth" is still disputed.

Close to Mizar is the small star Alcor. The Arabs called these two stars "the Horse and the Rider." The star Alcor was used by them in a test for good eyesight. See Fig. 8.

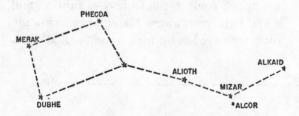

FIG. 8. The Big Dipper.

SCALE OF ANGULAR DISTANCES

Locations of stars are stated in terms of angles. The angular distance, measured in degrees, is the angle subtended by these stars at the observer.

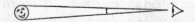

FIG. 9. The angular distance of the full moon is about half a degree.

It is of importance to be able to gauge small angles in the sky. The diameter of the full moon is about half a degree, otherwise stated more formally as: The angle subtended at our eye by the diameter of the full moon is 0.5 degree. See Fig. 9.

Another angular distance often used is the one between Dubhe and Merak—close to five degrees.

FIG. 10. The angle subtended by Dubhe and Merak at the eye of an observer is close to 5°. Ten full moons could be placed side by side in that angle.

Ten moons could be placed side by side in the distance between these two stars. See Fig. 10.

PROBLEM 1:
    Estimate the angular distance between Dubhe and Megrez.
    Answer: 10°, approximately.
PROBLEM 2:
    Find the North Star, using the following data: (See Fig. 16).
    a. The North Star is on the extension of the line joining Dubhe and Merak.
    b. It is 29° from Dubhe, and, of course, 34° from Merak.

LEGENDS

One of the early names given to this constellation was the "Great Bear" and the Arabic names meaning "thigh," "loin," etc., describe parts of the bear. See Fig. 11.

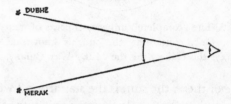

FIG. 11. The Great Bear. Note the position of the Big Dipper.

The reason for this is not known, as an observer can scarcely imagine the outline of a bear or any other animal in that constellation.

An ancient legend held that the Bear represented Callisto, a daughter of the King of Arcadia, beloved of Jupiter, who, in order to protect her, changed her into a Bear and transferred her to the skies.

Another legend held that the Great Spirit purposely put the Great Bear in the sky to act as a "calendar" for earthly bears. During the half year when the Great Bear is low in the sky, all earthly bears stay in their dens and keep warm. When the Bear is high in the sky, bears leave their dens, for summer has begun.

OTHER NAMES

The names Great Bear, Big Dipper, are still in common use. The scientific name for the constellation is the Latin translation of Great Bear—Ursa Major (*ur' sa ma' jer*). In England, the constellation is known as the "Plough," or the Wain (for wagon).

NOTE: At times the term Big Dipper is used to refer to the seven bright stars, and the term Great Bear or Ursa Major to refer to all the stars in the constellation. Usually, however, these terms are used interchangeably.

APPARENT BRIGHTNESS OF STARS

The seven stars of the Big Dipper differ materially in apparent brightness. The brightest star is Alioth; the faintest, Megrez.

Technically this is stated in terms of apparent magnitude. Alioth has the smallest apparent magnitude (1.7); Megrez, the largest (3.4).

HIPPARCHUS' CLASSIFICATION OF STARS ACCORDING TO BRIGHTNESS

The ancient Greek astronomers classified the visible stars according to their apparent brightness, into six classes. This basic classification, in the main, is still valid. To Hipparchus, who lived on the island of Rhodes in the second century B.C., goes the credit for this classification. The twenty brightest stars known to him were arbitrarily designated as stars of the **first magnitude**; and the next fifty in order of apparent brightness were designated as stars of the **second magnitude**; and so on. The designation of **sixth magnitude** was given to several hundred stars barely visible to the normal human eye. See Fig. 12. Thus a completely arbitrary classification of

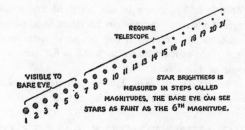

FIG. 12. The relationship between brightness and magnitude.

stars, according to their brightness, was obtained. These magnitudes are, however, only *apparent* magnitudes. Some stars are actually bright, but appear faint because of their great distance.

DECIMAL DIVISION OF APPARENT MAGNITUDES

In the 19th century, the decimal division was introduced. In this classification, a star of magnitude 5.5 has an apparent brightness halfway between that of a star of magnitude 5.0 and that of a star of magnitude 6.0. Similarly, to state that the North Star (Polaris) has a magnitude of 2.1 signifies that its apparent brightness is only slightly less than the brightness of a star of magnitude 2.0. Increasingly, the decimal method of denoting magnitudes has been applied more extensively and made more precise.

RELATION BETWEEN APPARENT MAGNITUDE AND APPARENT BRIGHTNESS

Applying results from modern psychophysics and physics (based on the psychophysical law formulated by Fechner in 1859. The law states that if a stimulus increases in a geometric progression the sensation resulting from it increases in an arithmetic progression), it was determined that magnitude 2 stars are 2.5 (more precisely, 2.512) times brighter than magnitude 3 stars. Similarly, magnitude 3 stars are 2.512 times brighter than magnitude 4 stars, and so on.

PROBLEM 3:

The star Dubhe in the constellation Ursa Major has an apparent magnitude of 2.0. An unknown star, X, has an apparent magnitude of 4.0. How much brighter is Dubhe than star X?

Solution: A decrease in one order of magnitude corresponds to an increase in 2.5 times in apparent brightness. A decrease in two orders of magnitude is the same as increase in $2.5 \times 2.5 = 6.25$ times in apparent brightness.

Answer: To the eye, Dubhe will appear more than six times brighter than the star X.

ZERO AND NEGATIVE VALUES OF APPARENT MAGNITUDE

The twenty stars originally designated as first magnitude stars were subsequently regrouped. This was necessary because some of the stars were much brighter than others. The brighter stars of this group were designated as having magnitudes of 0.9, 0.8, 0.7, etc., through 0.0 to negative numbers. The star with the greatest apparent brightness at night is Sirius. Its apparent magnitude is −1.6. On the same scale, the apparent magnitude of our sun is immensely greater: −26.7.

DETERMINING APPARENT MAGNITUDES

The method of determining the magnitude of stars by observation is rather simple. With practice, fairly accurate results (an accuracy of .1 of a magnitude) can be obtained. The method was used extensively by the German astronomer Argelander (1799–1875) and his associates in the preparation of the great star catalog, the "B.D. Catalog." (B.D. is the abbreviation of the German title of the catalog, "Bonner Durchmusterung"—"Bonn Catalog.") By this method, the observer compares the apparent brightness of a star with two or more neighboring stars of known magnitudes. Thus, a star that appears somewhat fainter than a neighboring star of 2.4 magnitude and somewhat brighter than another neighboring star of 2.6 magnitude, will be designated as having a magnitude of 2.5. In using this method it is advisable to make sure that:

1. The star to be measured and the known magnitude stars should be at about the same distance above the horizon.
2. The known magnitude stars should be as close as possible to the star to be measured.
3. One of the known magnitude stars should be somewhat brighter and the other somewhat fainter than the star to be measured.

The following table contains a list of stars of known apparent magnitude. These can be used for the determination of magnitude of many other stars.

Star	Constellation	Apparent Magnitude
Alpheratz	Andromeda	2.2
Schedar	Cassiopeia	2.5
Diphda	Cetus	2.2
Achernar	Eridanus	0.6
Hamal	Aries	2.2
Acamar	Eridanus	3.1
Mirfak	Perseus	1.9
Aldebaran	Taurus	1.1
Rigel	Orion	0.3
Capella	Auriga	0.2
Bellatrix	Orion	1.7
Canopus	Carina	−0.9
Sirius	Canis Major	−1.6
Procyon	Canis Minor	0.5
Pollux	Gemini	1.2
Regulus	Leo	1.3
Dubhe	Ursa Major	2.0
Acrux	Crux	1.1
Arcturus	Boötes	0.2
Zubenelgenubi	Libra	2.9
Shaula	Scorpius	1.7
Nunki	Sagittarius	2.1
Markab	Pegasus	2.6

PROBLEM 4:

Determine which of the two is the brighter star, Alkaid or Merak.

Answer: Alkaid is the brighter one. The apparent magnitude of Alkaid is 1.9; that of Merak, 2.4.

PROBLEM 5:

Find three stars in the Big Dipper that appear to be of equal brightness.

Answer: Mizar, Merak and Phecda have almost the same apparent brightness. Precisely, they are designated as being 2.4, 2.4, and 2.5 magnitude stars, respectively. Phecda is by a very slight degree fainter than the other two.

PROBLEM 6:

Determine the apparent magnitude of the North Star (Polaris).

Answer: Polaris is but slightly brighter than Merak, and slightly fainter than Dubhe. It is usually designated as a 2.1 magnitude star.

Note again, this refers to **apparent** magnitudes. Actually, Polaris is much brighter than our sun—in fact, nearly 1,500 times brighter. The great distance accounts for its being only a magnitude 2.1 star. Stated in terms of time, it takes light, traveling at the speed of 186,000 miles per second, 8⅓ minutes to reach earth

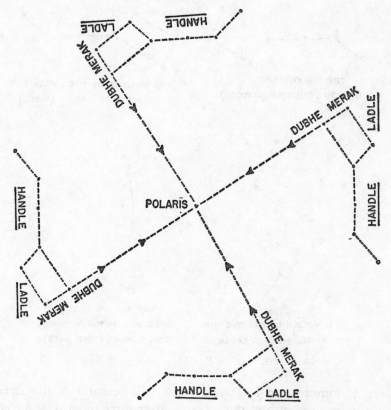

Fig. 13. In the course of approximately 24 hours, the Big Dipper completes one revolution in the sky. Only part of that circle can actually be observed, as sunlight makes it impossible to observe the stars during the daytime. This figure shows the Big Dipper at 6-hour intervals.

from the sun; and 400 years to reach earth from Polaris.

APPARENT DAILY MOTIONS OF STARS

It is common knowledge that the sun seems to rise in the East, describe an arc in the sky, and set in the West.

The stars, too, seem to move in arcs in the sky—also from the eastern to the western part of the horizon. A complete revolution takes 23 hours, 56 minutes and 4.09 seconds. This can very easily be approximately verified any clear evening with the aid of a good watch.

PROBLEM 7:

Object: To verify a complete revolution of a star. (This period is known as a "sidereal" day, or a "star-day.")

Equipment: A good watch.

Procedure:

a. Note the time at which some bright star appears just above the eastern horizon.

b. The next day repeat the procedure under (a).

Results: The experiment demonstrates that every star completes one apparent revolution in 23 hours, 56 minutes and 4 seconds.

The term "apparent" is often repeated here for good reason. The motion is really *only* apparent; it may even be considered an optical illusion. Actually it is the earth, spinning on its axis in the opposite direction, that causes the stars to seem to move as they do.

This daily rotation can also very effectively be observed by watching a constellation, such as Ursa Major.

If, when first observed, the constellation appears level with the bowl on the right:

Six hours later it will appear with the handle pointed downward;

Twelve hours after the original observation, the Big Dipper will appear with the open part of the bowl pointing downward;

Eighteen hours after the original observation, the Big Dipper will appear to have the handle pointing upward.

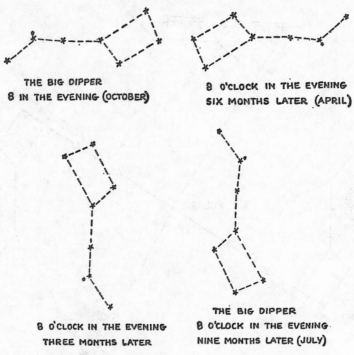

THE BIG DIPPER
8 IN THE EVENING (OCTOBER)

8 O'CLOCK IN THE EVENING
SIX MONTHS LATER (APRIL)

8 O'CLOCK IN THE EVENING
THREE MONTHS LATER

THE BIG DIPPER
8 O'CLOCK IN THE EVENING
NINE MONTHS LATER (JULY)

FIG. 14.

In any 23 hours, 56 minutes and 4 seconds, the Big Dipper can be seen in any one of those positions.

During part of that time, the sun will interfere with the observations. The faint starlight cannot be discerned in the bright sky of day.

THE APPARENT ANNUAL MOTION OF THE STARS

The fact that stars complete a revolution in less than twenty-four hours is of great importance. It signifies, of course, that the stars make more than one revolution in a 24-hour period.

The difference between 24 and the period of revolution is:

$$\begin{array}{r} 24 \text{ hours} \\ -23 \text{ hours, } 56 \text{ minutes, } 4 \text{ seconds} \\ \hline 3 \text{ minutes, } 56 \text{ seconds.} \end{array}$$

Thus, the stars begin the next revolution in the remaining 3 minutes and 56 seconds. This can be verified by observation.

A star that appears **on** the horizon, say, at 8 o'clock on a Sunday evening will be slightly **above** the horizon the following evening at 8 o'clock. Tuesday evening at 8 o'clock, the star will be still further above the horizon and a month later at 8 o'clock in the evening, the star will be substantially above the horizon.

After three months, at 8 o'clock in the evening, the star will be a quarter of a circle away from the eastern horizon. At the end of a year, the star will have completed an apparent circle.

This movement of a star is also an *apparent* movement. It is due to the **real** movement of the earth about the sun. The earth completes a revolution around the sun in 12 months.

This apparent annual movement of stars obtains for constellations as well.

Thus Ursa Major at 8 o'clock in the evening in October is close to the horizon with the bowl opening upward.

Three months later at the same time in the evening, the handle will point downward.

In April at the same time of the evening, the Big Dipper will be high above the horizon and will appear with the bowl to the left.

In July at the same time of the evening, the Big Dipper will appear with the bowl at the bottom.

Thus in a period of 365¼ days, the Big Dipper completes 366¼ apparent revolutions: 365¼ of them are due to the rotation of the earth on its axis, and one is due to the revolution of the earth about the sun.

PART 2: CIRCUMPOLAR STARS

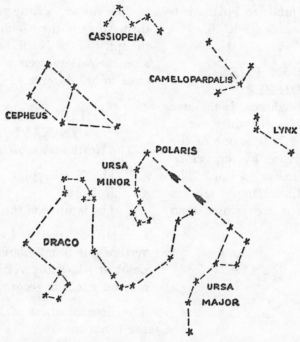

FIG. 15. The North Circumpolar Constellations.

INTRODUCTION

At any given latitude some stars appear to rise and set; **others, called circumpolar stars, are continuously above the horizon.** Circumpolar (= near the Pole) stars can be seen every night of the year, weather permitting. They would be observable during the day as well were it not for the interference of the sun, whose bright light makes it impossible to discern the faint light of the stars.

LATITUDE AND NORTH CIRCUMPOLAR STARS

The number of north circumpolar stars varies greatly with latitude, increasing with distance from the equator. To an observer at 20° N, the stars of the Big Dipper are not circumpolar—they rise and set and, part of the time, are below the horizon. To an observer at 40° N, however, the stars of the Big Dipper are circumpolar.

NORTH CIRCUMPOLAR CONSTELLATIONS

In addition to the Big Dipper, four other well-known constellations are continuously in view in latitudes North of 40°. These are the Little Dipper, Cassiopeia, The Dragon, and Cepheus. See Fig. 15.

THE LITTLE DIPPER

The best known and brightest star in this constellation is the North Star. It is easy to locate: The starting points are two stars in the

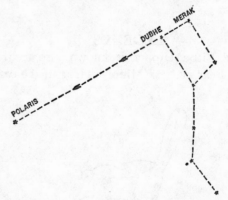

FIG. 16. Use the pointers (Dubhe and Merak) of the Big Dipper to locate Polaris. Extend the distance between Merak and Dubhe six times beyond Dubhe to find Polaris (the North Star).

bowl of the Big Dipper, Dubhe and Merak, known as "The Pointers." An extension of the line joining these two stars points to the North Star, which is also known by the names "Polaris" and "Alpha-Ursae Minoris." The angular distance from Dubhe to Polaris is 6 times the Pointer distance. See Fig. 16.

THE STARS IN THE LITTLE DIPPER

Next to Polaris in brightness is the star Kochab, or Beta-Ursae Minoris, which has an apparent magnitude of 2.2. **It is one of the 57 stars used for reference by navigators.** The Arabic "Kochab" means "a star." The other five stars in the Little Dipper are less prominent—four of them are fainter than magnitude 4. See Fig. 17.

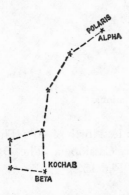

FIG. 17. The stars of the Little Dipper.

The constellation is distributed over a spread of about 20°, or four times the Pointer distance.

LEGENDS

The Little Dipper is known also as the Little Bear or Ursa Minor and, as in the case

FIG. 18. The Little Bear.

of the Great Bear, the name is entirely inappropriate. See Fig. 18.

According to a remarkable Indian legend about the Little Bear, an Indian hunting party had lost its way in the forest. In answer to their prayers, a little girl appeared to guide them safely to their homes. She proved to be the spirit of the North Star; and the hunters, after their death, were placed in heaven to be close to her, forever.

THE NORTH STAR IN NAVIGATION

The North Star is often used to determine:

1. The North point on the horizon (geographic North).
2. The latitude of the observer.

Geographic North is located by dropping a vertical line from Polaris to the horizon. The point at which the vertical line touches the horizon circle is geographic North.

The determination of latitude is based on the formula:

Latitude of any place in the northern hemisphere = Altitude of North Star at same place.

Thus, to an observer at 40° N, the star Polaris has an altitude of 40°; to an observer at 60° N, it would have an altitude of 60°; and so on.

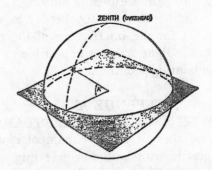

FIG. 19. The observer is at A. The altitude of the star is the angle between a line to the star and a line to the horizon. The angle is also denoted by A. When the star is close to the horizon the altitude is small; when the star is at Zenith the angle is 90°.

The altitude of a star, measured in degrees, is the angle along a vertical circle between the horizon of the observer and the star. The angle A in Figure 19 represents the altitude of the star.

THE CELESTIAL POLES

The name Polaris derives from the fact that the pole of the earth, if extended, would intersect the sky very close to this star. **This extension of the earth's axis is known as the celestial axis.**

Theoretically, the celestial axis extends an infinite distance both up and down. "Up" in this case means beyond the earth's north pole; "down," the earth's south pole. The earth's axis is only a minute part of the celestial axis. **The points at which the celestial axis pierces the sky are known as North Celestial Pole and South Celestial Pole, respectively.**

The Celestial Poles are the intersections of the extended axis with the Celestial Sphere. See Fig. 20.

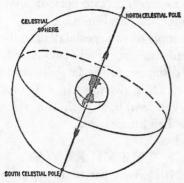

FIG. 20. The celestial axis is the extension of the earth's axis. The point where the northern part of the axis intersects the celestial sphere is the North Celestial Pole. The intersection of the southern extension of the axis with the celestial sphere is the South Celestial Pole.

The celestial sphere is a figment of imagination. No definite size can be ascribed to it. It may be assumed to have an "infinite" radius.

THE CELESTIAL SPHERE

It is helpful to imagine the stars as being permanently attached to the inside of a large, hollow hemisphere (half sphere), the edge of which extends all around the horizon. This hemisphere of visible stars is matched by another hemisphere, studded with all the stars below the horizon at that time. **The two hemispheres are joined at the horizon to form what is known in Astronomy as the "Celestial Sphere."**

It must be emphasized, however, that:

a. despite the fact that the term "celestial sphere" is often used; and,

b. despite the fact that the "celestial hemisphere" appears to be very real and definite in its geometric form; and,

c. despite the fact that many stars give the impression of being attached to the inside of this hollow sphere—

there is no such thing, in reality, as a celestial sphere. The celestial sphere is simply an **imaginary** background against which the observer sees the projection of near and distant stars. In this sense, it is often used to state positions for various stars and to describe the apparent daily motion of the stars.

Astronomy deals with two spheres: one is the earth; another, infinitely larger than the earth, is a "projection screen" upon which we see all the stars in the heavens.

It should be noted that we live on the *outside* of the real terrestrial sphere and *inside* the imaginary celestial sphere.

THE CELESTIAL EQUATOR

The points on the celestial sphere half-way between the north and the south celestial poles form the celestial equator.

Theoretically, the celestial equator is a circle of infinite radius, lying in the same plane as the earth's equator, the two circles having the same center.

Another way of visualizing the celestial equator is by imagining that the radius of the earth's equator is made increasingly large, until the circle coincides with the inner surface of the celestial sphere. See Fig. 21.

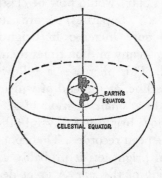

FIG. 21. The Celestial Equator. This equator is in the same plane and has the same center as the earth's equator. The celestial equator is "infinitely" larger than the terrestrial.

CASSIOPEIA AND CEPHEUS

An extension of the line through the pointers of the Big Dipper, beyond the North Star, leads to the constellations of Cepheus and Cassiopeia. Cepheus has the shape of a triangle built on a square; and Cassiopeia is somewhat similar to the letters M or W. See Fig. 22.

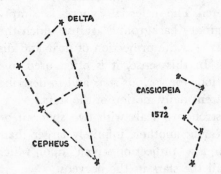

FIG. 22. The constellations Cepheus and Cassiopeia. Note that the latter appears either as a W or an M depending on whether she is below Polaris or above that star. The point marked 1572 is the location of Tycho Brahe's Star.

TYCHO'S STAR

The constellation Cassiopeia made history in 1572. On November 11th of that year, a "new" star quite suddenly appeared in that constellation, bright enough at one time to be seen in daylight. The Danish astronomer, Tycho Brahe, made a careful study of that "new" star and recorded a detailed description of its adventures. The historic star has long since lost its tremendous brightness. It is still known as "Tycho's Star."

"Tycho's Star" would now be classified as a "Supernova." **"Supernovae" are stars that quite suddenly increase in brightness tremendously**—many million times their original brightness. This increase is followed by a gradual decline, at the end of which the star retains only a small fraction of its original pre-supernova brightness. Several other supernovae have been recorded. Their phenomenal increase in brightness is probably caused by an explosion of the star. A great deal of the star's mass is lost during this cataclysm. This loss in mass may very well be the underlying reason for the fact that in its final stages the star has lost most of its pre-explosion brightness.

CEPHEIDS

Neither the brightest star nor the second brightest in Cepheus is of particular importance. Fame came to the fourth brightest star in that constellation, Delta-Cephei.

A great many stars are currently classified as "Cepheids." These are **variable-brightness stars**. Delta-Cephei's maximum brightness is two and a half times greater than its minimum. Its apparent magnitude varies from a maximum 3.7 to a minimum 4.6 in highly regular periods of 5 days, 8 hours, 47 minutes, 39 seconds.

The probable reason for this variation in brightness is pulsation. Their volume seems to increase and decrease periodically, producing changes in brightness.

Astronomy owes a special debt to these stars. The cepheids are of enormous aid in estimating distances to the farthest points in the universe. Thus, distances to neighboring galaxies are determined with the aid of these variable brightness stars.

THE MILKY WAY

The Milky Way passes through Cassiopeia and Cepheus, appearing to the naked eye as a narrow band of hazy light, stretching round the heavens. Through a telescope the nature of that hazy light becomes obvious: It is produced by an enormous number of separate stars, neighboring our sun in the Galaxy.

To the best of our knowledge, the Galaxy is similar in shape to a lens. The location of the sun in that lens is indicated in Figure 23.

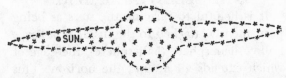

FIG. 23. A cross-section of the Milky Way. Note the similarity to a lens (except for greater thickness at the center).

The top view of the Galaxy is circular. The whitish band of light on the celestial sphere, known as the Milky Way, is due to the combined light of millions of stars that are situated along the middle plane of Our Galaxy.

Naturally, many more stars can be seen by looking along the lens than by looking across it. The light from those stars fuses to give the impression of a hazy band. Old legends tell of a flow of milk along that path in the heavens, but there is no record of its celestial source.

LEGENDS ABOUT CASSIOPEIA AND CEPHEUS

According to mythology, Cassiopeia was the beautiful but vain Queen of Ethiopia. Her husband was Cepheus, and their daughter, Andromeda. As punishment for her vanity, Cassiopeia was doomed to be transformed into a group of stars traveling eternally round the pole, watched over by her jealous husband, Cepheus.

THE CONSTELLATION DRAGON

"Draco" is the Latin name for "Dragon." This is a fairly long and curving constellation —part of it, halfway between the Big and Little Dippers; the rest coiling about the Little Dipper, ending in a group of four stars. These four stars mark the head of the Dragon. See Fig. 24.

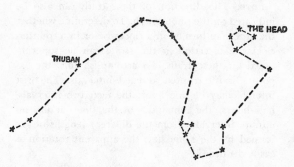

THUBAN

★ THE HEAD

FIG. 24. The constellation Dragon. Note the star Thuban in Draco. 5,000 years ago it was the North Star. The earth's axis was pointing to that star. In the year 22,000 A.D., it will again be the North Star.

THE STAR THUBAN, OR ALPHA-DRACONIS

Five thousand years ago, Thuban was the "North Star," because the North Celestial Pole was near it. At that time Thuban appeared as the only "stationary" star in the sky, all the other stars describing circles about it. Thuban was venerated by the Egyptians. At present, the North Celestial Pole is, of course,

near Polaris. The North Celestial Pole describes a complete circle once every 25,800 years. The motion of the North Celestial Pole, as well as that of the South Celestial Pole, is due to the fact that the axis of our earth precesses, i.e., describes a slender cone, once every 25,800 years.

A MAP OF NORTH CIRCUMPOLAR CONSTELLATIONS

The constellations near the North Celestial Pole are indicated on the map on page 19.

Each star in a constellation is designated by a Greek letter. The Greek alphabet starts with A, B, G, D, and not A, B, C, D.

GREEK ALPHABET (SMALL LETTERS)

α alpha	ι iota	ρ rho
β beta	κ kappa	σ sigma
γ gamma	λ lambda	τ tau
δ delta	μ mu	υ upsilon
ε epsilon	ν nu	φ phi
ζ zeta	ξ xi	χ chi
η eta	o omicron	ψ psi
θ theta	π pi	ω omega

NAMES OF STARS

Some fifty or sixty well-known stars are often called by proper names. Among these are Polaris (the North Star), and Sirius (the brightest star in the sky).

Generally, the stars are identified by Greek letters, used as prefixes to the constellation. The stars in the Big Dipper are known as Alpha-Ursae Majoris, Beta-Ursae Majoris, Gamma-Ursae Majoris, and so on. (The genitive form of the constellation is used: The genitive of Ursa Major in Latin is Ursae Majoris.)

Usually the brightest star gets the α (Alpha) prefix; the second brightest is denoted by β (Beta), and so on.* The brightest star in the constellation Big Dog (Canis Major) is known as α (Alpha)-Canis Majoris. The third brightest star in the constellation Twins (Gemini) is known as γ (Gamma)-Geminorum. If the number of bright stars in a constellation ex-

* There are exceptions to this. Thus the brightest star in the constellation Twins (Gemini) is designated β (Beta) Geminorum, while the second brightest star in that constellation is known as α (Alpha) Geminorum.

ceeds the number of Greek letters, Roman letters are also used.

This description of stars is known as the "Bayer Designation." It was first introduced in a catalog of stars published by the German astronomer Johann Bayer in 1603.

HOW TO USE THE MAP

Beginners in Astronomy often have difficulty in using a map. It is not clear perhaps how the map should be held so as to correspond with the stars in the sky. The difficulty is probably due to the fact that the observer is on the **outer** surface of one sphere (the earth) observing the stars on the **inner** surface of another sphere (the celestial sphere).

To use this map properly, imagine that it has glue on its reverse side, like a postage stamp. The map is to be pasted to the **inner** surface of the celestial sphere. The "glue" will thus "stick" to the stars. Before attaching the map, it is necessary to align it properly: Make Polaris on the map cover Polaris in the sky; and the Big Dipper on the map cover the Big Dipper in the sky. The other stars on the map will then correctly represent the real stars.

APPARENT DAILY AND ANNUAL MOTION OF THE STARS

Every star and every constellation takes part in these apparent daily rotations, and it is a great pleasure to watch the stars move in their assigned orbits.

It is an even greater pleasure to photograph the trails of these stars. Rather good photographs can be obtained with relatively inexpensive equipment. The procedure for this follows:

Object: To obtain a star-trail photograph of the circumpolar region.
Equipment:
a. A good camera.
b. Fast plate or film.
c. Flashlight.
Procedure:
a. Point camera so as to bring Polaris to center of film.
b. Focus, carefully, on Polaris.
c. Open shutter to widest aperture compatible with a good definition of the stars.
d. Expose for several hours. Four to five hours is a reasonable time.
e. Dew may form on lens. Should this happen, it must be wiped off at intervals. Do not shift the camera while wiping the lens. Careful use of a dim flashlight may help. The flashlight should never be pointed into the lens.
f. Develop the negative.

Results: The developed negative will show the trails of the circumpolar stars. Each trail will be in the form of an arc of a circle. The negative will also demonstrate that Polaris is not at the North Pole. Polaris itself describes a small arc around the Pole. The length of this arc will depend upon the duration of exposure. In six hours of exposure, the arc will be a quarter of a circle.

NOTE: The direction of these trails can also be indicated on the photograph. To determine whether the arcs were formed in a clockwise or in a counterclockwise direction, a time scale can be superimposed on these trails. To accomplish this, the exposure is interrupted at fixed intervals. The first interval may be one hour; the next two intervals, half hours; the remainder of the time, at fifteen-minute intervals. From the different lengths of arc formed by the same star, the apparent rotation is easily deduced.

PART 3: NON-CIRCUMPOLAR STARS

INTRODUCTION

The previous section dealt with the stars that can be seen every night of the year—the north circumpolar stars of the north circumpolar constellations.

The present section deals with the stars that are only part of the time above the horizon for observers in the middle latitudes. The other part of their apparent motion is below the horizon. The middle latitudes include most of the United States, Canada, and Europe. These stars can be seen at one time or another during the year, when they are above the horizon at night.

Watching the stars may be compared to watching a parade. Over a period of twelve months, the complete parade of stars can be observed. This parade repeats itself, year after year.

Becoming familiar with many of the bright

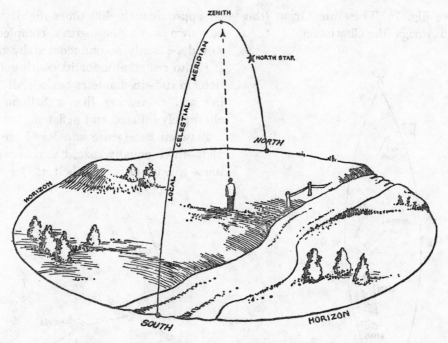

FIG. 25. The Local Celestial Meridian is an imaginary circle in the sky. It goes through the North and South points on the horizon and the Zenith. Observe the stars at about 8 P.M. near the middle of the month and in a year's time you will see the entire parade of stars pass this line.

stars is not difficult; nor is learning some of the well-known constellations. To accomplish this, you need not look for them all over the sky. An imaginary circle can be drawn across the sky and the constellations observed as they approach or cross the circle. The circle that can serve this purpose most conveniently is the "Local Celestial Meridian." This circle goes through the Zenith, and the North and South points on the observer's horizon. The **Zenith is the point in the sky directly above the observer.** Only half of this celestial meridian, of course, is above the horizon.

The Local Celestial Meridian may also be defined in terms of the terrestrial meridian. The technical definition is that the local **celestial meridian is the intersection of a plane through the earth's meridian and the sky;** the intersection itself is a circle, only half of which is above the horizon of the observer.

The best way to outline the local celestial meridian in the sky is by drawing an imaginary line through the following three points (Fig. 25):

1. North on the horizon. A simple magnetic compass will help here.

2. Zenith—the point in the sky directly above the observer.

3. The point marking South on the horizon. Use a magnetic compass.

Note that the Local Celestial Meridian will also go through Polaris, the North Star.

The parade of stars is conveniently divided into twelve parts, one part for each month.

The constellations near the celestial meridian each month are described below. A description of the stars as they appear on one evening a month will serve our purpose. If you learn how the sky looks on one evening a month, or twelve evenings a year, you will be familiar with the nightly appearance of the sky. We can begin with any month and any hour. Let us begin with February. The maps of the sky are designed to show how it will look at about 8 P.M. on the fifteenth of each month.

FEBRUARY CONSTELLATIONS

Two of the most interesting constellations can be found near the meridian on February evenings. See Fig. 26. These are Orion (the Hunter) and Auriga (the Charioteer).

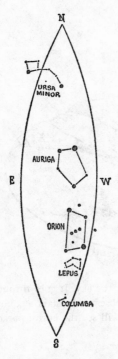

FIG. 26. February Constellations. The constellations near the Local Celestial Meridian at 8 P.M. about the middle of February. Follow instructions on how to use the map on page 26. Only the more familiar constellations are indicated. Stars of the third magnitude and brighter are shown, as well as fourth-magnitude stars that are part of the design usually associated with the constellation. The size of the dot corresponds to the brightness of the star. The larger the dot, the brighter the star.

THE STARS IN ORION

Rigel and Betelgeuse are the two bright stars in this constellation. See Fig. 27a. Rigel is the seventh brightest star in terms of apparent brightness. In reality, it is the most luminous star in Our Galaxy. If Rigel was as close to the earth as the sun and not 500 light-years away, it would appear to be 21,000 times brighter than the sun. Rigel, Arabic for "leg," marks the leg of the hunter. Betelgeuse, light orange in color, marks the shoulder of the hunter and is variously distinctive. It was the first star whose diameter was obtained by direct measurement, using an ingenious instrument known as a beam interferometer. It is one of the largest known stars, with a diame-

ter approximately 400 times the diameter of our own sun. The earth's complete orbit would be easily accommodated by this star. It is also remarkable for its continuous variations in size—its diameter periodically increasing and decreasing like a balloon that is alternately inflated and deflated.

Between Betelgeuse and Rigel are the triplets—three equally spaced second-magnitude stars—which outline the belt of Orion.

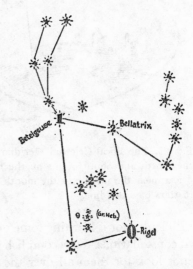

FIG. 27a. Orion (the Hunter). The number indicates the magnitude. Stars up to and including the fourth magnitude are shown. When they form part of the design usually associated with the constellation, fifth-magnitude stars are included and indicated by a five-point symbol.

An object of great interest is located in the "sword of Orion." There the naked eye observes a rather fuzzy star; closer study reveals this to be the Great Nebula of Orion, a vast mass of gas and dust in a continuous state of agitation, estimated to be 10,000 times the mass of the sun. The nebula is seen by the light of the star θ (Theta)-Orionis, which lies near the center of this vast cloud. Theta-Orionis is actually a quadruple star, the four stars forming the shape of a trapezium.

LOCATING ORION IN THE SKY

Orion is about 90° from Polaris. The constellation can easily be located by facing south and looking upward about halfway between the horizon and Zenith.

ORION IN LEGEND

There is much folklore concerning Orion. One of the legends states that Orion boasted that no animal could overcome him. He paid for this boast with his life. A scorpion sent by Jupiter killed him. The goddess Diana pitied Orion and transported him to heaven and placed him as far away from the Scorpion as

FIG. 27b. Orion is shown holding a club in one hand and a lionskin in the other. Rigel is in the leg of the Hunter. Betelgeuse, Arabic for "armpit," appears as shown. The sword is usually pictured as ending in the Great Nebula.

possible—halfway across the sky from the Scorpion.

Orion is often pictured (see Fig. 27b) as holding a club in one hand and a lion's skin in the other.

THE STARS IN AURIGA

This constellation is characterized by its clearly defined pentagon of stars. See Fig. 28.

Actually, only four of the stars belong to Auriga; the fifth star β Tauri belongs to the constellation Taurus, the Bull. Capella, the brightest star in this pentagon, ranks fifth in apparent brightness among all the stars. The Charioteer is usually pictured holding a she-goat, the star Capella representing the heart of the goat. The little triangle of stars near

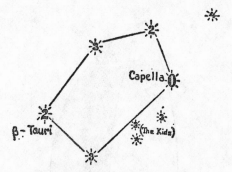

FIG. 28. Auriga (the Charioteer).

Capella should also be noted. The three stars were known to the Arabs as the "Kids."

LOCATING AURIGA

Auriga is directly overhead, about halfway between Orion and the North Star. Its pentagonal shape, as well as the brightness of Capella (apparent magnitude 0.2), helps identify this group of stars.

MARCH CONSTELLATIONS

Three most interesting constellations can be found near the meridian in March. Gemini (the Twins), Canis Minor (the Little Dog), and Canis Major (the Big Dog) adorn the sky near the celestial meridian. Constellations that were here in February have moved on. Orion and Auriga are now to the west of the meridian. See Fig. 29.

THE STARS IN GEMINI

Castor and Pollux are the two bright stars in this constellation. See Fig. 30. They are commonly known as the twins. Pollux is a giant first-magnitude star; Castor is slightly dimmer.

In scientific terminology, Pollux, the brighter star, is known as β (Beta)-Geminorum, and Castor as α (Alpha)-Geminorum. This is one of the cases in which the rule that the brightest star is designated as the α star has not been followed. (Some astronomers think that at the time of the original classification, Castor was actually brighter than Pollux.)

In Greek mythology, Castor and Pollux were the sons of Leda and Jupiter and the brothers of Helen of Troy. The Arabs affec-

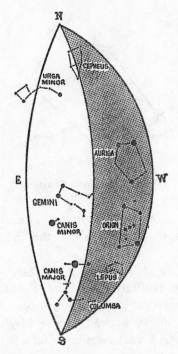

FIG. 29. March Constellations. The prominent constellations near the Local Celestial Meridian are Gemini, Canis Minor, and Canis Major. The February constellations, shown here in light shade, have moved on toward the western horizon. See the notes under Fig. 26.

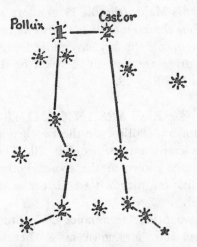

FIG. 30. Gemini (the Twins). Pollux's magnitude is 1.2 and Castor's is 1.6. Castor is actually a double star: the brighter component has an apparent magnitude of 2.0; the fainter component has an apparent magnitude of 2.9.

tionately referred to them as "the Peacocks"; to the Hindus they are known as the "Twin Deities."

And yet they are **not** twins. The two stars, though seemingly neighbors in the same part of the sky, are in reality widely separated. Castor is much farther from our earth than is Pollux.

THE STARS IN CANIS MINOR

The bright star in the Little Dog constellation is Procyon. It has an apparent magnitude of 0.5, with a characteristic yellowish hue, rising half an hour before Sirius, the bright star of the Big Dog. The name "Procyon" is derived from two Greek words meaning "before the dog." See Fig. 31.

FIG. 31. Canis Minor (the Little Dog) is a very small constellation. Procyon, the eighth-brightest star, is one of the nearest stars to earth, only 11.2 light years away.

THE STARS IN CANIS MAJOR

Here is the brightest star in the night sky: Sirius, with an apparent magnitude of −1.6. See Fig. 32. Its apparent brightness is due

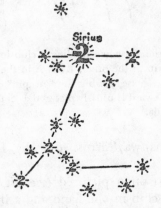

FIG. 32. Canis Major (the Big Dog).

both to its intrinsic brightness—it is 27 times more luminous than our sun—and to its closeness to our Solar System. It is 8.6 light years away. Sirius is the closest star that can be seen from most parts of the United States. In the southern states, stars can be observed that are closer to the earth than Sirius.

As famous as it is, Sirius has a still more remarkable companion, the "Pup": Sirius and the Pup together form a Binary Star. (**Two stars revolving around a common center of gravity are called a "Binary Star."**) The Pup is only 1/10,000 as bright as Sirius. Its claim to fame is due to its unusually high density, caused by a large mass contained in a fairly small volume. The mass of the Pup is estimated to be 250,000 times the mass of the earth. Its diameter is a mere three times that of the earth. One cubic inch of the Pup's matter would weigh a ton.

LEGENDS ABOUT THE DOGS

Orion being the "Hunter," it was natural to regard the "Dogs" as his property. Both the Big and the Little Dog follow closely on Orion's heels in the sky.

There is a beautiful legend about Icarius and the faithfulness of his dog Mera. Mera stood by his master during his lifetime and after he was murdered. According to the legend, the gods rewarded Mera's faithfulness by placing him among the stars, and he became "Canis Minor."

LOCATING THE TWINS AND THE DOGS

The Twins cross the celestial meridian close to the Zenith. Canis Major crosses close to the south point of the horizon; Canis Minor is about halfway between the Big Dog and the Twins.

Various aids are used to identify individual stars. It is helpful to know that Betelgeuse in Orion, Sirius in Canis Major, and Procyon in Canis Minor form an equilateral triangle. Each side in the triangle subtends an angle of 25°, or about five times the pointer distance.

Another guiding line is often used to locate Sirius: an extension of the "belt stars" in Orion to the southeast points to Sirius.

APRIL CONSTELLATIONS

Leo (the Lion), Leo Minor (the Little Lion), and Hydra (the Sea Serpent) are near the meridian in April. The Twins and the Dogs are now west of the meridian. The Hunter and the Charioteer are close to the western horizon. See Fig. 33.

THE STARS IN LEO

The stars that belong to Leo, the larger of the two lions, form the design of a sickle fol-

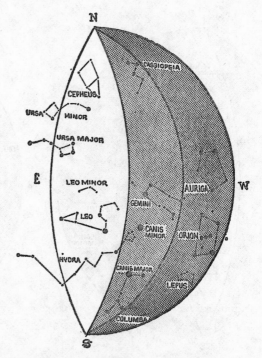

FIG. 33. April Constellations. Leo, Leo Minor, and Hydra are among the prominent constellations near the Local Celestial Meridian. The March constellations, shown in light shading, have moved to the west, and the February constellations (Auriga and Orion) are now close to the western horizon. See the notes under Fig. 26.

lowed by a triangle. See Fig. 34. In mythology, this constellation represented the lion slain by Hercules as the first of his twelve chores. The bright star at the bottom of the sickle

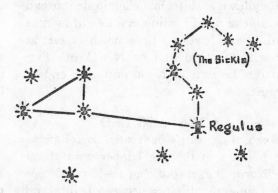

FIG. 34. Leo (the Lion). Regulus, with a magnitude of 1.3, is 71 light years away from the sun. It is receding from earth at an approximate rate of 5000 miles per hour. Regulus is nearly 100 times more luminous than the sun.

is Regulus, the Little King. This name was bestowed on the star by Copernicus. The star is also known by a variety of other names, such

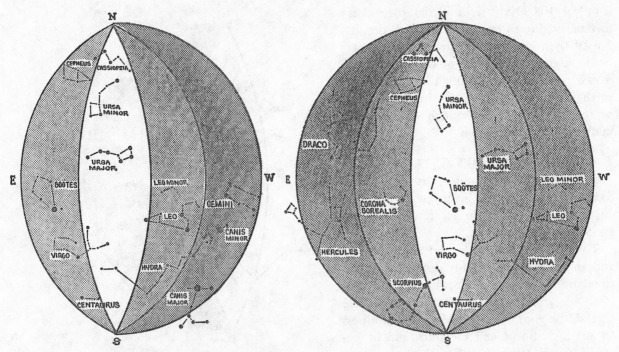

FIG. 35. May Constellations. Prominent near the Local Celestial Meridian are three of the circumpolar constellations: Ursa Minor, Ursa Major, and Cassiopeia. The April constellations, in light shading, are to the west of the meridian and the March constellations (Gemini, etc.) are well on their way toward the western horizon. To the east, in light shading, are Boötes, Virgo, and Centaurus. See the notes under Fig. 26.

FIG. 36. June Constellations. Boötes and Virgo are prominent, close to the Local Celestial Meridian. The April constellations (Leo, etc.) are well on their way toward the western horizon. Corona Borealis and Scorpius are in the lightly shaded segments and will be near the Local Celestial Meridian in July. Hercules, in the heavily shaded segment near the eastern horizon, will be near the Local Celestial Meridian in August. See the notes under Fig. 26.

as "the King," "the Mighty," "the Hero," and "the Ruler."

Regulus is a white, first-magnitude star and is visible at middle latitudes for eight months of the year. It rises a little north of east at about 9 P.M. local time on New Year's Eve, and can be seen at night until the end of August.

LOCATING LEO

Regulus can easily be located by following the pointers in the Big Dipper, away from the North Star, through an angle of 35°, or seven times the distance between Dubhe and Merak, the pointer stars.

THE SEA SERPENT

This constellation stretches more than a quarter of a circle across the sky. The head of the serpent is near Canis Minor, its tail nearly 100° away, close to the constellation Libra. The stars in this constellation are

faint: the brightest is a second-magnitude star named Alphard, which means "the solitary one." It is a red star located in the heart of the Serpent.

According to an old legend, the Sea Serpent was a rather peculiar creature. It had many heads and the ability to replace them. As one head was cut off, two new ones grew in its place.

MAY CONSTELLATIONS

High in the sky is Ursa Major (the Big Dipper). See Fig. 35. The pointers cross the meridian close to the Zenith. The bowl of the Dipper is open downward and the handle stretches to the east. Ursa Major, being a circumpolar constellation, was described in detail earlier.

JUNE CONSTELLATIONS

Boötes (the Plowman) and Virgo (the Virgin) are the two constellations to be observed this month. Each has one bright star to help identify it. See Fig. 36.

While Boötes is crossing the meridian near the Zenith, Virgo is halfway between the Zenith and the southern point of the horizon.

Close to the southern horizon, several stars belonging to the constellation Centaurus can also be seen. The brightest stars of this constellation are never above the horizon in middle latitudes. They can be seen in latitudes close to the equator and southward.

THE STARS IN BOÖTES

Of the eight clearly visible stars in Boötes, α (Alpha)-Boötis, commonly known as Arcturus, is of particular interest. See Fig. 37. A

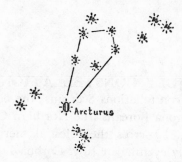

FIG. 37. Boötes (the Plowman or the Herdsman). Arcturus is about 80 times brighter than the sun. It is a giant star with a low temperature and a low density.

bright reddish star, it is one of the few stars mentioned in the Bible. In 1933 the light coming from Arcturus—focused on a photoelectric cell—was used to open the Chicago World's Fair. At the time it was thought that Arcturus was 40 light years from the earth, and hence a ray of light would have been on the road since 1893, the year of the previous World's Fair in Chicago. More recent computations indicate that Arcturus is actually 38 light years away.

Arcturus is the fourth-brightest star visible in middle latitudes (app. mag. 0.2) and is the sixth-brightest star seen anywhere in the sky. It is also one of the fastest moving of the bright stars. Its speed is estimated to exceed 80 miles a second. Because of its distance, it will take Arcturus more than eight hundred years to move half a degree on an arc across the sky. Eight hundred years from now Arc-

turus will be closer to the constellation Virgo by half a degree, a distance equal to the apparent diameter of the moon.

LOCATING BOÖTES

The handle of the Big Dipper is often used to help locate Arcturus, the bright star in Boötes. The arc described by the handle is extended about 30° (six times the pointer distance); the extended arc leads to Arcturus.

THE STARS IN VIRGO

The bright star in the constellation is Spica. See Fig. 38. It is a beautiful white star, rising a little to the southeast in March, and remaining visible, in middle latitudes, throughout the summer. Legend has it that Spica represents an ear of wheat, held in the hands of the Virgin, reminding the farmer that planting time has arrived.

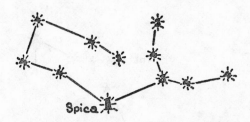

FIG. 38. Virgo (the Virgin). Spica, with an apparent magnitude of 1.2, is the bright star in this constellation. In ancient times Spica was known as the "Star of Prosperity," and temples were built in its honor.

Two important circles on the celestial sphere—the celestial equator and the ecliptic—intersect near Spica. **The ecliptic is the apparent circle described by the sun on the celestial sphere.**

The point where the equator and ecliptic intersect is called the Autumnal Equinox. The sun is at that point on or about September 23.

LOCATING VIRGO

The handle of the Big Dipper and Arcturus are often used as aids to locate Spica, the bright star in Virgo. The arc of the handle, when extended through Arcturus, points to Spica.

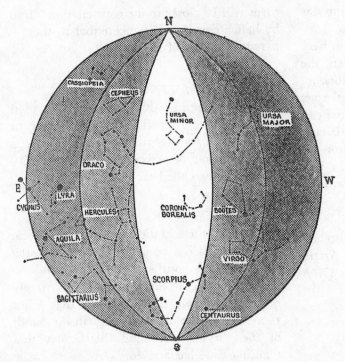

FIG. 39. July Constellations. Corona Borealis and Scorpius are prominent near the Local Celestial Meridian. The June stars, in light shading, have passed the meridian and are on their way to the western horizon. The August stars, in light shading, and the September stars, in heavy shading, are to the east of the line. See the notes under Fig. 26.

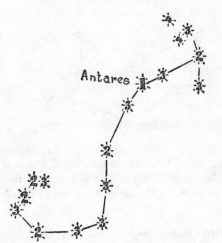

FIG. 40. Scorpius (the Scorpion). Scorpius is one of the twelve constellations of the Zodiac. The sun is in this constellation late in October and early in November. Antares, the bright star, has an apparent magnitude of 1.2.

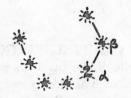

FIG. 41. Corona Borealis (the Northern Crown). The α (alpha) star is known as the "Pearl of the Crown." Navigators call it Alphecca.

JULY CONSTELLATIONS

The constellations Scorpius (the Scorpion) and Corona Borealis (the Northern Crown)—see Fig. 39—cross the celestial meridian in the early evening in July. Corona Borealis is near the Zenith, while Scorpius is near the southern horizon. The stars in Scorpius appear to form an outline of a scorpion and the stars in Corona Borealis suggest the outline of a crown.

THE STARS IN SCORPIUS

The bright star is Antares, one of the few bright and distinctive red stars. See Fig. 40. A giant of a star, its diameter is about 300 times larger than that of the sun.

THE STARS IN CORONA BOREALIS

The constellation is composed of seven stars in the form of a semicircle. See Fig. 41. Six of the seven principal stars are of fourth magnitude. The star in the middle is of the second magnitude and is known as the "Pearl of the Crown."

CORONA BOREALIS IN LEGEND

Legend has it that this crown once belonged to the beautiful Ariadne, wife of Theseus, who was one of the many Athenians

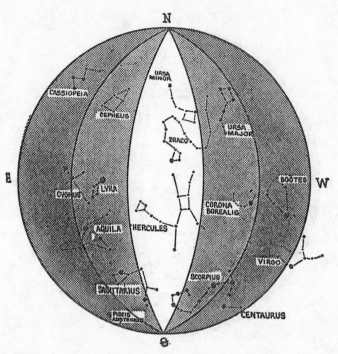

FIG. 42. August Constellations. Hercules is near the Local Celestial Meridian. The July constellations, in light shading, and the June constellations, in heavy shading, are in the western sky. The September constellations, in the light shading, and the October constellations, in the heavy shading, are to the east of the meridian. See the notes under Fig. 26.

destined to be a sacrifice to the Minotaur, the ferocious half man, half bull that inhabited a famous labyrinth near Crete. Theseus, with the aid of Ariadne, killed the monster. Ariadne supplied her lover with a sword and a spool of thread. Unwinding the thread, Theseus penetrated the labyrinth and accomplished his mission. Then, retracing his steps with the aid of the thread, he escaped. The story, however, has an unhappy ending. The marriage of Theseus and Ariadne did not last long. Theseus deserted his wife. The god Bacchus, to console Ariadne, presented her with the crown, which after her death was placed in the sky.

Again, this constellation is merely an effect of chance. No two of the seven stars are moving in the same direction or at the same speed. The two stars α (Alpha)- and β (Beta)-Coronae are moving in opposite directions and have nearly exchanged places in the past fifty thousand years. In another fifty thousand years the constellation will no longer bear a resemblance to a crown.

AUGUST CONSTELLATIONS

The constellation Hercules (the Kneeler)—see Fig. 42—is overhead. It follows in the footsteps of Boötes and Corona Borealis, which have already passed the meridian and are on their way to the western horizon.

THE STARS IN HERCULES

The interest in this constellation is not due to the brightness of its stars. There are no zero, first, or second magnitude stars in this

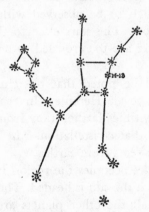

FIG. 43. Hercules (the Kneeler). The brightest stars in this constellation are of the third magnitude.

constellation. The several bright stars that seem to form the letter "H" are all of the third magnitude. See Fig. 43. There are, however, two major reasons for great interest in Hercules:

1. It contains one of the finest globular

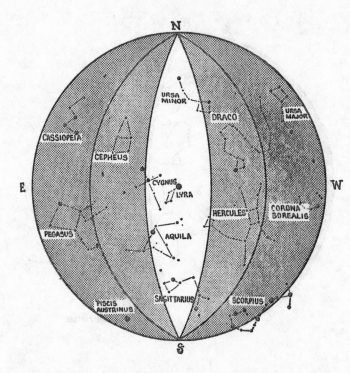

Fig. 44. September Constellations. Cygnus, Lyra, Aquila, and Sagittarius crowd the Local Celestial Meridian. Corona Borealis, in the heavily shaded zone, is near the western horizon. Pegasus, which is near the eastern horizon, will be discussed with the November constellations. See the notes under Fig. 26.

clusters. This is the cluster that is generally known by its number in the Messier catalog—M13. It is barely visible to the unaided eye on a clear, moonless night, appearing there as a hazy star of the sixth magnitude. Telescopic magnification reveals this hazy spot of light to be a closely packed cluster of stars. More than 50,000 stars in the cluster are bright enough to be observed with present-day telescopes. The stars close to the center of the cluster are too crowded to be counted separately.

It should be noted that the cluster only appears to be in Hercules. In reality it is many, many times farther away from us than the stars in that constellation. The cluster is 34,000 light years from earth.

2. Hercules occupies the region in the sky toward which the sun is headed. The sun, the earth, and all the other planets are moving as a unit through space at the rate of 12 miles a second. Every second the whole solar system moves 12 miles closer to that region in the sky.

SEPTEMBER CONSTELLATIONS
The meridian is again crowded with wonderful constellations. See Fig. 44. Lyra (the Lyre) and Cygnus (the Swan) are close to the Zenith. Sagittarius (the Archer) is close to

south on the horizon. Aquila (the Eagle) is halfway between the Archer and the Lyre.

THE STARS IN LYRA
The bright star in the Lyre is Vega. See Fig. 45. It is a zero-magnitude star, the fourth-

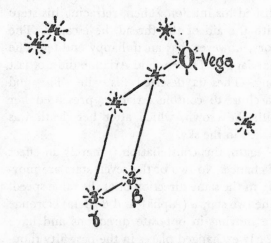

Fig. 45. Lyra (the Lyre). Vega, the bright star, has an apparent magnitude of 0.1. In 1850, Vega became the first star to be photographed.

brightest of all the stars. Vega was once the earth's North Star and in 12,000 years it will again be the Pole star. The axis on which our earth rotates describes a slender cone once every 25,800 years. **This motion of the** axis is known as precession and is explained in detail on page 133. The axis now points to α (Alpha)-Ursae Minoris. In the year 14,000 A.D. it will again point to Vega.

Another star of interest in this constellation is β (Beta)-Lyrae. This star changes its apparent magnitude every 12.9 days. The change in brightness ranges from 3.4 to 4.3. This variation can be observed by the naked eye by comparing β (Beta)-Lyrae with its neighbor γ (Gamma)-Lyrae. At its brightest, β (Beta) is almost as bright as γ (Gamma), apparent magnitude 3.3; at its dimmest, it is considerably fainter.

LEGENDS ABOUT THE LYRE

The constellation Lyra symbolically represents the lyre which Apollo gave to Orpheus. Orpheus was renowned in his day for being able to charm both animate and inanimate objects with his music.

After the death of Orpheus, Jupiter placed the magic lyre in the sky.

THE STARS IN CYGNUS

Cygnus, the Swan, is also known as the "Northern Cross." See Fig. 46. The Swan is usually pictured as flying south with Deneb,

FIG. 46. Cygnus (the Swan). This constellation is also known as the Northern Cross. Stars whose magnitudes are as bright or brighter than the fourth magnitude are shown. Several stars fainter than the fourth magnitude are represented by the symbol ★.

the brightest star, marking the tail; the Cross as pointing northward with the 1.3 magnitude star, Deneb, marking the head.

The flimsy, whitish Milky Way can be seen in the background of this constellation.

Another star in Cygnus, 61 Cygni, is of historical importance. It was the first star whose distance was measured. For many years it was thought that 61 Cygni, 11.1 light years away, was the nearest neighbor of the Solar System. Later measurements have shown several other stars, e.g., α (Alpha)-Centauri, and Sirius, to be much closer.

THE STARS IN SAGITTARIUS

Sagittarius, the Archer (see Fig. 47), has no very bright stars. Many astronomers believe that a line from the sun extended through

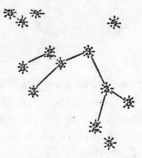

FIG. 47. Sagittarius (the Archer).

Sagittarius would point to the center of Our Galaxy.

The brightest part of the Milky Way can be found in this region of the sky.

THE STARS IN AQUILA

Aquila, the Eagle, which bore Ganymede to Mount Olympus to act as Jupiter's cup-bearer, has Altair as its very bright star. See Fig. 48. Altair is fairly close to the earth—its distance is a mere 14 light-years (or 80 trillion miles). Aquila attracted great attention in 1918

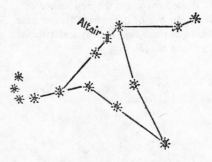

FIG. 48. Aquila (the Eagle).

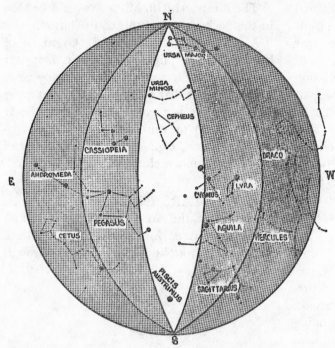

FIG. 49. October Constellations. Cepheus and Piscis Austrinus are near the Local Celestial Meridian. The lightly shaded zones indicate the September and November stars. The heavily shaded zones indicate the August and December stars. See the notes under Fig. 26.

when for a brief time a very brilliant star that reached a maximum apparent magnitude of —1.4 appeared in that constellation, then waned rapidly in brilliance. It is now restored to the faint magnitude 12.

OCTOBER CONSTELLATIONS

Cepheus, the circumpolar constellation, is now high in the sky. The celestial meridian divides it in half.

Piscis Austrinus (Southern Fish) is the other constellation near the meridian that is of particular interest. It is also known as Piscis Australis. See Fig. 49.

THE STARS IN PISCIS AUSTRINUS

Fomalhaut, a first-magnitude star, is the bright star not only in that constellation but also in this whole region of the sky. Fomalhaut was one of the four "Royal Stars" of

FIG. 50. November Constellations. Cassiopeia and Pegasus are near the Local Celestial Meridian. Near the western horizon, in the heavily shaded zone, are the September constellations. In the heavily shaded zone near the eastern horizon are Taurus and Perseus. See the notes under Fig. 26.

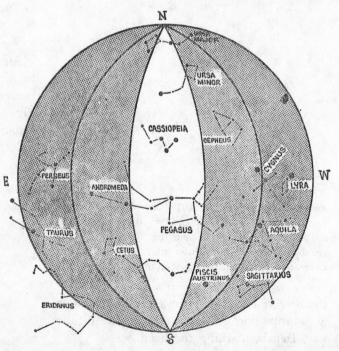

astrology. (The other three were Regulus, Antares, and Aldebaran.) In ancient astrology Fomalhaut was considered to be indicative of power and eminence.

NOVEMBER CONSTELLATIONS

Cassiopeia is now high in the sky near the celestial meridian. See Fig. 50.

Pegasus (the Winged Horse) is also along the meridian.

THE STARS IN PEGASUS

This constellation is usually identified with the aid of the Great Square of Pegasus. See Fig. 51. Only three of the stars that form the square actually belong to Pegasus. The star at the northeastern corner, Alpheratz, belongs to the constellation Andromeda. The Winged Horse, also known as the Flying Horse, generally visualized upside down in the sky, represents the horse on which Perseus rode when he rescued Andromeda from the Sea Monster.

LOCATING PEGASUS

Alpheratz, the northeastern star at the Square, can be located by drawing a line from Polaris to Caph, β (Beta) Cassiopeiae, and extending it an equal distance.

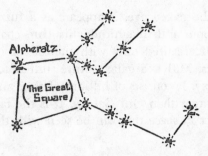

FIG. 51. Pegasus (the Winged Horse or the Flying Horse).

DECEMBER CONSTELLATIONS

Andromeda (the Chained Lady) follows Pegasus in the sky. See Fig. 52. Andromeda is closer to the Zenith than Pegasus.

Another interesting constellation at the meridian is Cetus (the Whale), which can be located about 30° above the southern horizon.

THE STARS IN ANDROMEDA

Alpheratz, the brightest star in this constellation (see Fig. 53), has an apparent magnitude of 2.1. In the Bayer classification of stars it is denoted as α (Alpha)-Andromedae.

Of great interest in this part of the sky is an object denoted scientifically as M31, or as NGC224, located near ν (Nu)-Andromedae.

FIG. 52. December Constellations. Andromeda and Cetus are near the Local Celestial Meridian. The November constellations, in light shading, and the October constellations, in heavy shading, are in the western part of the sky. The January constellations, lightly shaded, and the February constellations, heavily shaded, are to the east of the meridian. See the notes under Fig. 26.

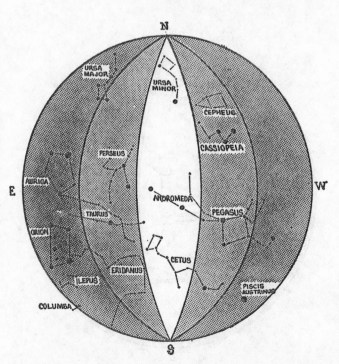

To the naked eye, it appears as a fuzzy star of about fifth magnitude; its true character can be realized only with the aid of instruments. M31 is a galaxy quite similar to Our Galaxy. It consists of billions of stars and is a bit larger than Our Galaxy. It is the farthest object in space that can be seen with the un-

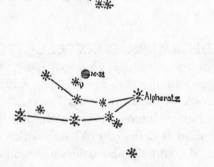

FIG. 53. Andromeda (the Chained Lady). Alpheratz marks the head of Andromeda.

aided eye. Light leaving the Great Galaxy in Andromeda reaches us after traveling through space for nearly 1,500,000 years.

Other similarities between the Great Galaxy in Andromeda and Our Galaxy are: (a) they are both surrounded by globular clusters, (b) they both contain large star clouds, and (c) large dark areas can be seen in both galaxies.

ANDROMEDA IN LEGEND

Andromeda, the beautiful daughter of Cepheus and Cassiopeia, enraged the sea nymphs by her boastful vanity. To punish her, Neptune chained her to a rock at the seashore as prey to the sea monster then ravaging the coast. Perseus came to her rescue. Just as the monster was about to attack Andromeda, Perseus magically turned the monster into a stone, saving her.

JANUARY CONSTELLATIONS

Perseus (the Champion), Taurus (the Bull), and Eridanus (the River Po), are near the meridian this month. See Fig. 54. Perseus can be seen close to the Zenith, Taurus to the southeast of it, and Eridanus stretches over a large portion of the southern sky. To the east of the meridian are Auriga, the Charioteer, and Orion, the Hunter. A new cycle of the procession of stars is about to begin.

THE STARS IN PERSEUS

There are no really bright stars in Perseus; however, the star β (Beta)-Persei is of interest. See Fig. 55. It is an eclipsing star. β (Beta)-

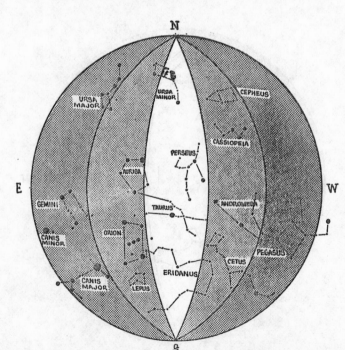

FIG. 54. January Constellations. Perseus, Taurus, and Eridanus are close to the celestial meridian. Near the western horizon, in heavy shading, are the November constellations. Near the eastern horizon, also in heavy shading, are the March constellations. See the notes under Fig. 26.

Persei, also known as Algol, the "Demon," consists actually of two stars of unequal brightness 13 million miles apart, revolving about their center of gravity. Their orbits are inclined 8° from the edgewise position relative to the earth. Every 2 days, 21 hours, the fainter star eclipses the brighter companion, and the apparent brightness of the combination is reduced to one-third its normal value—i.e., from apparent magnitude 2.2 to apparent magnitude 3.5. The eclipse of the faint companion by the bright one causes only a minute diminution of brightness.

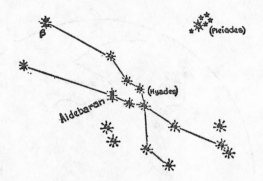

FIG. 56. Taurus (the Bull). Both the Hyades and the Pleiades are open clusters of stars. There are several hundred stars in the Pleiades cluster.

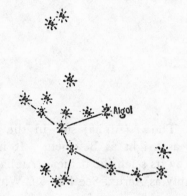

FIG. 55. Perseus (the Champion or the Hero).

THE STARS IN TAURUS

The beautiful constellation of Taurus is well known because the Pleiades form part of it. See Fig. 56. The Pleiades are a subgroup of seven stars arranged in a form of a tiny dipper. According to legend, the Pleiades, the seven daughters of the powerful Atlas, were pursued by Orion, the Hunter, and were changed into doves to escape him.

The other subgroup of Taurus is the Hyades. Sometimes the Hyades are pictured as outlining the head of the Bull, the Pleiades forming the shoulders.

The brilliant, red, first-magnitude star Aldebaran is invariably placed in the left eye of the Bull. Aldebaran means "the follower" in Arabic. It follows the Pleiades in the sky.

THE STARS IN ERIDANUS

Eridanus is one of the longest constellations in the sky. At various times in history it has been known as the King of the Rivers, the River Jordan, the River Nile, and, in more recent times, the River Po.

The source of the river is the star β (Beta)-Eridani, several degrees northwest of Rigel in Orion. From these, the constellation winds its way past Cetus, the Whale, for a total length of 130°.

Achernar, the first-magnitude star in Eridanus, cannot be observed from the middle northern latitudes. The star is only 33° from the south celestial pole and never rises above the horizon for observers north of latitude 33° N.

PART 4: SOUTH CIRCUMPOLAR STARS

This section deals with the stars that are always **below** the horizon for observers at middle latitudes. These are termed **South Circumpolar Stars**, and can be seen from the earth's southern hemisphere, and observed ideally from Australia, South Africa, or South America. See Fig. 57.

Three beautiful constellations embellish the sky "down under." Carina (the Ship's Keel) is one of these constellations; Crux (the Southern Cross), an object of great interest to the people of the Antipodes, is another. The third constellation is Centaurus (the Centaur), twice represented in the list of the Twenty Brightest Stars.

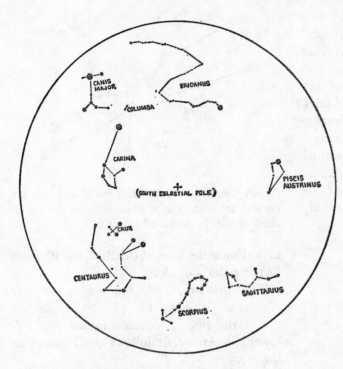

FIG. 57. The South Circumpolar Stars. There is no bright star near the South Celestial Pole. Only the more familiar constellations are indicated. Stars of the third magnitude and brighter are shown. Fourth-magnitude stars are shown only when they are part of the design usually associated with the constellations. The size of the dot corresponds to the brightness of the star. See the notes under Fig. 26.

THE STARS IN CARINA

The α (Alpha) star in Carina is Canopus, the second-brightest star in the sky. Its apparent magnitude is —0.9 as compared to —1.6

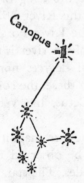

FIG. 58. Carina (the Ship's Keel). Some astronomers regard Carina as part of another constellation known as Argo.

for the brightest star, Sirius. Canopus can be seen on winter evenings in the southern regions of the United States. It crosses the local celestial meridian about the same time as Sirius. See Fig. 58.

THE STARS IN CRUX

The Southern Cross is generally considered to be the most beautiful constellation in the sky. The brightness of the four stars is greatly enhanced by the compactness of the constel-

lation. The α (Alpha) star in the Cross is nearly as bright as Betelgeuse. It is known either by its scientific name α (Alpha)-Crucis, or simply as Acrux. See Fig. 59. While these stars cannot be seen from most parts of the United States, they can be observed from its southernmost areas. The Southern Cross can be seen at its highest point from parts of Florida and Texas. Seeing the Cross is a mem-

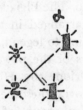

FIG. 59. Crux (the Southern Cross).

orable experience: the beauty of the constellation itself is enhanced by its background—the band of faint light known as the "Milky Way."

The Southern Cross does not, however, photograph very well. The top and right-hand stars of the Cross have a yellowish tint and appear faint; the resulting picture lacks all similarity to a cross.

Three of the four stars comprising the Southern Cross, together with a number of fainter stars near the Cross, form a cluster.

These stars are all approximately the same distance from the Solar System. They are moving away from us, describing parallel tracks, at an average speed of 15 miles per second. The stars are also similar in their physical characteristics: they are all very hot, among the hottest known.

It is a widely held belief that the stars in this cluster had a common origin. According to this theory, they were all created from one "chunk" of matter in the remote past. In time, relatively small velocities with respect to each other caused them to separate and form their present pattern—a pattern of individual stars receding continuously along parallel lines from the Solar System.

THE STARS IN CENTAURUS

Both α (Alpha) and β (Beta) Centauri have apparent magnitudes of less than 1. This is not their only distinction. α-Centauri is the closest known stellar neighbor—a mere 4⅓ light-years from the Solar System. At one time it was thought that one of the faint stars close to α-Centauri was closer. That faint star, 2° away from α-Centauri, was named Proxima Centauri. The word "Proxima" signified its proximity to us; but further investigation challenged its closeness. To the best of our knowledge, both α-Centauri and Proxima Centauri are at equal distances from the Solar System.

To navigators the world over, α-Centauri is known as Rigil Kentaurus, the "leg of the Centaur."

Several degrees from α-Centauri is β-Centauri. These two stars serve as pointers in the southern hemisphere. A line through α and β points to the northernmost star of the Southern Cross. See Fig. 60.

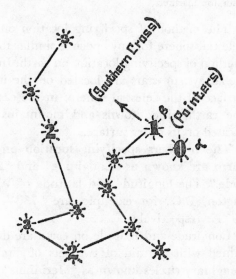

Fig. 60. Centaurus (the Centaur). When the line from α to β is extended, it points to the Southern Cross.

The closeness of β-Centauri to α is only apparent. The beta star is nearly fifty times more distant than the alpha star. The distance to β-Centauri is more than 190 light years.

CHAPTER III

ELEMENTS OF NAVIGATION

INTRODUCTION

Stars have addresses: The location of every star is specified by a pair of numbers which fit only that star. One of these numbers is known as the **"Sidereal Hour Angle"** of the star; the other, the **"Declination of the Star."**

In the case of Vega, the numbers are 81 and

39. The Sidereal Hour Angle and the Declination of Acrux are 174 and —63, respectively.

NOTE: These addresses change very slowly with time. Hence, to be very accurate, it is necessary to specify the date, known as epoch, when the star has the particular sidereal hour angle and declination. The slight changes in these numbers are due to the phenomenon known as "precession of the equinoxes," which in turn is due to precession of the earth's axis. Due to these phenomena, the vernal equinox, the point from which the sidereal-hour angle is measured, moves continuously westward.

The sidereal hour angle and declination of stars and other heavenly bodies are listed in various catalogs and almanacs, among them the American Nautical Almanac, published annually by the United States Naval Observatory, to provide astronomical data for mariners.

The method of specifying location on the celestial sphere for any epoch is similar to the method of specifying location on earth. In the stellar system, stars are located on the inner surface of the celestial sphere; in the case of the earth, cities, towns and mountains are located on its outer surface.

The numbers specifying location on the earth are known as "Longitude" and "Latitude." The longitude and latitude of Washington, D.C., for example, are 77° W and 39° N, respectively.

Longitude and latitude on earth are determined with the aid of two sets of circles—**imaginary circles known as "Meridians" and "Parallels of Latitude."**

Similar sets of circles are drawn on the celestial sphere, in reference to which they are often called **"Hour Circles,"** and **"Parallels of Declination."** An understanding of this system of circles, both on the earth's (terrestrial) sphere and on the celestial sphere, is essential.

PARALLELS OF LATITUDE

The points on the earth's surface, half-way between the North Pole and the South Pole, form the global equator. The equator thus divides the earth into two hemispheres, the Northern and the Southern. See Fig. 61.

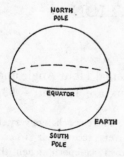

FIG. 61. The equator divides the earth into two hemispheres.

Each hemisphere can be further subdivided by drawing circles parallel to the equator which are known as "Parallels of Latitude" and are designated by numbers in the Northern Hemisphere, beginning with zero at the equator and ending with 90° N at the North Pole. The parallels of latitude in the Southern Hemisphere are denoted by the suffix "S"; thus, the latitude of the South Pole is 90° S.

The parallels of latitude are used in stating any point's angular distance, in degrees, from the equator. See Fig. 62. This distance is

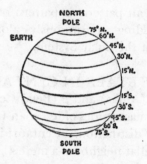

FIG. 62. Parallels of Latitude. They indicate the angular distance from the equator.

known as the "Latitude" of that point—thus, Key West has a latitude of 25° N, Washington, D.C., 39° N, and Paris, France, 49° N. This can also be stated by saying that the angles subtended by these points and the equator at the center of the earth are 25, 39 and 49 degrees, respectively. The latitudes are stated to the nearest degree. When greater accuracy is desired, the angles are stated in terms of degrees, minutes and seconds of arc. For Washington, D.C., the more accurate latitude figure is 38 degrees, 53 minutes, and 51 seconds of arc, more compactly written as 38° 53′ 51″.

MERIDIANS

The other set of circles usually drawn on a globe are called "Meridians of Longitude." Unlike the parallels of latitude, they are all of equal size, each circle passing through both the North and the South Poles. See Fig. 63.

Since the meridians are of equal size and are otherwise equal in importance, the map makers had to designate one of these as being the prime meridian, in reference to which all the others are marked. In 1884, it was decided, by international agreement, to designate the one passing through Greenwich, England, as the prime meridian, which is also known as

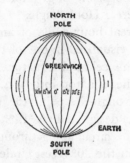

FIG. 63. Meridians. The "zero" meridian passes through Greenwich, England. These lines indicate longitude on the earth.

the "zero" meridian, i.e., longitude 0°. The meridians to the west are marked 1° W, 2° W, and so on, to 180° W. The meridians to the east are designated 1° E, 2° E, and so on, to 180° E. 180° E and 180° W are, therefore, the same longitude.

THE CELESTIAL SPHERE

This sphere has already been discussed. It has been shown that this sphere serves as a background upon which the stars are projected. The observer sees all the stars as if they were attached to the inside of a vast spherical surface. The celestial sphere is concentric with the terrestrial one, and is infinitely larger. No definite value is assigned to its radius, **as the sphere is merely imaginary.**

The two spheres not only have a common center, but also a common axis and a common equatorial plane.

The Celestial Axis extends indefinitely beyond the earth's North Pole and South Pole. **The points of its intersection with the celestial sphere are termed North Celestial Pole and South Celestial Pole.**

The Celestial Equator is an extension of the terrestrial one; both are in the same plane but the radius of the celestial equator, which divides the sphere into two halves, is infinitely larger. See Fig. 64.

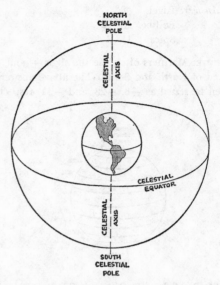

FIG. 64. The Celestial Sphere. We live on the *outside* of the terrestrial sphere. The stars appear to an observer as if attached to the *inside* surface of the Celestial Sphere.

The Celestial Axis is merely an extension of the earth's axis beyond the North and South Poles of the earth.

The Celestial Equator is an extension of the terrestrial equator.

PARALLELS OF DECLINATION

Each half of the celestial sphere can be further subdivided: one method is to draw circles parallel to the equator. **These circles are called "Parallels of Declination."** In the Northern Hemisphere, they are designated by number, starting with zero for the celestial equator and ending with 90° N declination for the North Celestial Pole.

Similar numbers are given to the parallels of declination in the southern half of the celestial sphere. The designations here run from 0° at the equator to 90° S declination at the South Celestial Pole.

These parallels of declination on the celestial sphere serve a purpose similar to that of the parallels of latitude on the terrestrial sphere. They are used to state the angular distance between any object in the heavens and the equator; and this distance, in degrees of angle, is known as the declination of the object. See Fig. 65.

PROBLEM 7:

Using a Star Catalog, or an Almanac, find the declinations of the following stars: Rigel, Pollux, and Spica.

Answer: Rigel   8° S
          Pollux 28° N
          Spica   11° S

NOTE: Mariners often use the signs + and − instead of North and South. The above answers will then be stated as −8, +28, and −11, respectively.

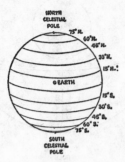

FIG. 65. Parallels of Declination. These circles on the celestial sphere are similar to parallels of latitude on the terrestrial one except for the fact that they are to be visualized as drawn on the inside surface of the sphere.

Parallels of Declination are used in stating the declination of a star on the Celestial Sphere, that is, the angular distance between a star and the Celestial Equator.

HOUR CIRCLES

The earth's meridians of longitude also have a counterpart on the larger sphere, on which they are known as Hour Circles, passing through the North and South Celestial Poles. They are all of equal size and importance. By international agreement, one of these was chosen as the prime hour circle.

The hour circle so designated is the one that goes through "the First Point of Aries" (the Greenwich of the sky). The First Point of Aries is a point on the celestial equator denoted by the symbol ♈. Our sun, in its apparent movement in the sky, crosses the equator at that point as it moves from the southern to the northern celestial hemisphere. When the sun is at that point, days are equal in length to nights everywhere on earth. (The prime hour circle is also known by the formidable name, the Equinoctial Colure.)

The other hour circles are marked as follows:

1. Eastward, by astronomers, in either degrees of angle (0° to 360°) or, more often, in units of time (0ʰ to 24ʰ). The number of degrees or hours that a celestial body is east of the prime hour circle is known as the "Right Ascension" of that body.

2. Westward, by navigators, in degrees (0° to 360°). The angle that a celestial body is west of the prime hour circle is known as the "Sidereal Hour Angle."

The sidereal hour angle of any circle can easily be visualized in one of two ways:

A. Along the celestial equator. The circles divide the equator into arcs. The circle going through the point 15° West of zero is, then, designated as 15° West Hour Circle, the circle going through 30° West of zero in the 30° West circle, and so on. See Fig. 66.

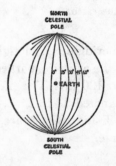

FIG. 66. Hour Circles. These are similar to meridians on the surface of the earth.

Hour circles are used to denote the angular distance of a heavenly body from the zero-hour-circle. These angular distances are similar to longitudes on the terrestrial sphere.

Note, though, that we are looking at the inside of the celestial sphere, and 15° is to the left of 0°.

B. From a vertical view. At the Poles, a different view of the circles is obtained. Those at the North Pole, say, appear to be straight lines emanating from the Pole, and are, of course, vertical views of these circles. See Fig. 67. The line representing the Equinoctial Colure is denoted as 0; all the other lines are designated with reference to that circle.

At any given epoch (time), every star has a well-determined sidereal hour angle; this angle changes very slowly with time. Thus, the sidereal hour angle for Sirius, in the year 1900, was 259°49′, and in the year 1950 it was 259°15′.

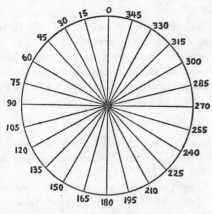

FIG. 67. A vertical view of the hour circles. Looking directly up to the North Celestial Pole, the hour circles appear as straight lines emanating from that pole.

PROBLEM 8:

Using a Star Catalog or an Almanac, find the sidereal hour angle for the following stars: Betelgeuse, Dubhe, and Arcturus.

Answer: Betelgeuse 272
Dubhe 195
Arcturus 147

PROBLEM 9:

Object: To plot the stars of Ursa Major, Ursa Minor, and Cassiopeia on a Star Chart.

Equipment:

a. A Polar Chart. See Fig. 68.
b. A list of declinations and sidereal hour angles for the stars in the three constellations.

Results: Part of a Circumpolar Star Chart.

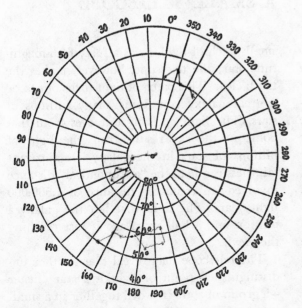

FIG. 68. Polar Chart to be used to plot three of the circumpolar constellations.

LIST OF DECLINATIONS AND SIDEREAL HOUR ANGLES FOR THE STARS IN PROBLEM 9

	S.H.A.	Declinations
Ursa Major	195	62
	195	57
	184	54
	176	58
	167	57
	160	55
	154	50
Ursa Minor	137	74
	128	72
	114	76
	123	78
	105	82
	90	87
	330	89
Cassiopeia	359	59
	350	56
	346	60
	339	60
	332	63

EFFECT OF LATITUDE ON VIEW OF THE SKY

It has been stated that the view of the sky changes with the latitude of the observer. This change can easily be explained with the aid of the terrestrial and celestial spheres. Figure 69 describes the view as seen by an observer at 40° N (about the latitude of New York).

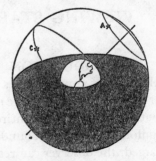

FIG. 69. Effect of Latitude. The orbit of star A is completely above the horizon in this latitude. This star can be seen in the sky every night of the year. The orbit of star B is completely below the horizon in this latitude. It cannot be observed from this point on the earth. Star C is part of the year above the horizon at night, and during the rest of the year is below the horizon at night. The relative number of stars in each group varies with terrestrial latitude.

The heavily lined circle here represents the horizon as seen by that observer. The straight line is the axis about which the celestial sphere makes its apparent rotation, inclined 40° to the horizon. All the stars within 40° of the Pole are continuously above the horizon. For an observer at 30° N, all the stars within 30° of the Pole are classified as circumpolar; for an observer at 18° N all the stars within 18° of the Pole are circumpolar, and so on. This can also be stated in terms of declinations. For an observer at 40° N, all the stars having declinations between 50° and 90° N are continuously above the horizon. For an observer at 30° N, the same is true for stars having declinations between 60° and 90° N, while for an observer at 18° N this will be true for all the stars having declinations between 72° and 90° N.

PROBLEM 10:

The geographical latitude of an observer is 43°. Which stars are north circumpolar in that latitude?

Solution: All the stars within 43° of the North Pole are north circumpolar at that latitude. The declinations of these stars are between the limits of 90° and (90 − 43 =) 47° N.

Answer: All stars having a declination larger than 47° N are north circumpolar.

PROBLEM 11:

The latitude of an observatory is 47° N. How far south can stars be observed?

Solution: An observer can see stars as far beyond the equator as 90° minus his latitude. At this observatory, stars are visible which are (90 − 47 =) 43° south of the equator.

PROBLEM 12:

At which latitude will Capella be a north circumpolar star? The declination of Capella is stated as +46 or 46° N.

Answer: At any geographical latitude north of 44° (say north of Portland, Maine) Capella is constantly above the horizon.

PROBLEM 13:

An observatory is 25° N. Which stars can never be seen at that observatory?

Answer: All the stars having declinations of 65° S to 90° S.

PROBLEM 14:

Which stars are north circumpolar at the equator?

Answer: There are no circumpolar stars at the equator. At any time of the year, an observer sees half of all the visible stars in the sky. Six months later, the other half of the sky is in view.

CHAPTER IV

VIEWING STARS WITH A SMALL TELESCOPE

INTRODUCTION

The telescope, of course, makes possible a far clearer view of the sky; and the excitement it contributes is immense. An entire new perspective unfolds: The very boundary of the sky is enlarged; the observer can reach farther into the universe. The Milky Way, until now a flimsy, thin, whitish background, becomes an almost infinite number of colorful stars, forming a multitude of geometric patterns.

A fuzzy small point of light, which had seemed a relatively unimportant object in the sky, is actually a galaxy consisting of billions of stars. The faintness of the light is due entirely to its vast distance from the observer. An illustration is provided by the Great Galaxy in Andromeda: the eye sees it as a small patch of light, or as a fuzzy fifth-magnitude star; the telescope, however, makes the truth clear. This patch of light turns out to be a great galaxy containing many billions of stars. The light entering our eyes from that point in the sky results from the light of billions of stars in the galaxy. Its apparent faintness is due to the "astronomical" distance involved—an estimated distance of 1,500,000 light years. The light that left the galaxy a million and a half years ago is just reaching the earth.

The telescope may reveal that another undistinguished point of light is a **star cluster —a group of stars crowded together in a small volume in space.** There are many such clusters in our galaxy, many of them containing tens of thousands of stars. **Those clusters that appear to have a spherical shape are known as Globular Clusters. Others, not so closely packed, are called Open Clusters.**

Many objects that appear to be normal-variety stars are, in fact, double stars, the two usually very close to one another. The distance between their centers is often about the size of the diameter of the larger star. The stars revolve continuously about a point in space—**the point is the center of gravity of the double star. Two such close stars are known as a Binary Star or Binary System.**

The brighter of the two is known as the **"Primary Star,"** while the fainter is known as the **"Companion Star."** In some cases, the stars eclipse one another; such a binary is known as an **Eclipsing Binary,** an **Eclipsing Binary Star,** or as an **Eclipsing Variable Star.** The light that reaches us from such a binary star is not constant in intensity. When the two stars are side by side, as seen from the earth, light reaches the observer from both stars and the binary is at its brightest. When one of the stars moves in front of the other, the binary appears to be dimmer.

Another group of variable-light stars is known as the Cepheids. These stars seem to pulsate, increasing and decreasing their size alternately. The brightness of the Cepheids increases as their size increases, and the brightness decreases as they diminish in size.

Some objects that look like fuzzy stars are in reality **nebulae, that is, clouds of gases and dust**—their true nature revealed by telescopic observation.

There are two kinds of telescopes: Refracting and Reflecting.

A Refracting Telescope consists of an objective and an eyepiece. The objective is the lens that is pointed toward the object, the observer's eye is placed next to the eyepiece. The objective forms an image of the distant object, the eyepiece magnifies that image.

The Reflecting Telescope's objective is a mirror, rather than a lens.

Telescopes are rated according to the dimensions of the clear diameter of the objective—the aperture. The largest Refractor in the world, at the Yerkes Observatory, Williams Bay, Wisconsin, has a 40-inch aperture. The largest Reflector, at the Mount Palomar Observatory in California, has a mirror 200 inches in diameter. For amateur work, a 3-inch Refractor or a slightly larger Reflector is ideal. Fairly good telescopes are now available at reasonable prices, or may easily be constructed by the amateur hobbyist. (Instructions for building a Refractor and a Reflector will be found in the Appendix.)

SELECTED LIST OF OBSERVATIONS

Numerous interesting observations can be made with the aid of a small telescope alone. These include large numbers of:

A. Double and multiple stars in all parts of the heaven;
B. Variable stars;
C. Star clusters;
D. Nebulae; and
E. Galaxies.

Of particular interest are the Variable Stars, which change periodically in brightness. A great deal of further information is necessary to solve the mystery of their behavior. The giant telescopes are usually engaged in other projects and hence are seldom turned on these stars. Amateur astronomers are doing important work in providing information about them.

A selected list for observation of the variable stars—as well as the groups A, C, D and E—is contained in the following: first, objects of interest in the North Circumpolar Constellations; then a description of the objects that are near the local meridian every month of the year.

The day is about the middle of the month. The hour is about eight or nine o'clock in the evening, local time.

NORTH CIRCUMPOLAR CONSTELLATIONS

a. **Ursa Major.** The star Mizar, at the middle of the handle, is a double star: the brighter component has an apparent magnitude of 2.1; the fainter star, 4.2. This was the first of the double stars to be discovered, in

1650. The angle they subtend at an observer is 15 seconds of arc. Subsequent Spectroscopic research showed that the brighter star of this binary system is in itself a double, thus making Mizar a triple star. See Fig. 70.

FIG. 70. Ursa Major. The star Mizar is a double star. Its two components have apparent magnitudes of 2.1 and 4.2. Both are greenish white in color—a good double to watch with a low-power telescope.

The location of the Owl Nebula, M97, is also indicated.

Another object of interest in the Big Dipper is the Owl Nebula. It is a round large cloud known by catalog numbers M97 or NGC3587.

The first catalog of nebulae and star clusters was compiled by the French astronomer, Messier, in 1781. The list contains 103 objects, more than half of which are star clusters. (M97 means object 97 in the Messier catalog.)

A New General Catalog, containing a comprehensive list of nebulae and clusters, was published in 1888 in England, and two supplementary lists were later added to it. Most nebulae and star clusters are commonly known by their number in that catalog. Thus, Messier 97 is object number 3587 in the New General Catalog.

b. **Ursa Minor.** Polaris, Alpha-Ursae Minoris, is a double star. The two companions differ greatly in apparent brightness. One of the stars in this binary system has an apparent magnitude of 2.0, while the value of the other star is 9.0. A 3-inch telescope and good atmospheric conditions are needed to see the faint companion, which is located below the bright one in November, and above it in May. See Fig. 71.

c. **Cassiopeia.** Cassiopeia is rich in double stars, star clusters, and other objects for telescopic observation. The Alpha star in Cassiopeia as well as the Eta, Iota and Sigma stars are doubles. The Sigma star has a particularly

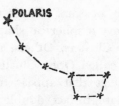

FIG. 71. Ursa Minor. Polaris, the North Star, is a double. The bright companion is blue, and has an apparent magnitude of 2.0; the dim partner is also bluish, its magnitude a dim 9.0. A 3-inch telescope is needed to resolve this binary system.

beautiful color combination. One of the stars is very blue; the other is green. See Fig. 72.

One of the most beautiful star clusters (designated as number 7789 in the New General Catalog) is located in Cassiopeia. Its great beauty has been universally extolled.

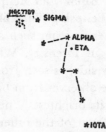

FIG. 72. Double stars in Cassiopeia. The Alpha Star is a double that can be resolved with a 1-inch telescope. The bright companion is yellowish in color, having an apparent magnitude of 3.0; the dim companion is a 9.0 apparent magnitude star, bluish in hue.

The Eta star can also be resolved with a fairly small telescope.

d. **Cepheus.** Delta-Cephei is a double star. The brighter component is the historically important Variable Star, which gave its name to the whole class of stars known as Cepheids.

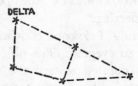

FIG. 73. The Delta star in Cepheus is a double star. The brighter companion varies in magnitude from 3.7 to 4.6; the dim partner is a 7.5 apparent magnitude star, blue in color.

The companion star to Delta-Cephei is a 7.5 magnitude star. It is bluish in color and can be seen even with a 1-inch telescope. See Fig. 73.

FEBRUARY OBSERVATIONS

Near the celestial meridian at about eight or nine in the evening are the constellations of Orion and Auriga.

a. **Orion.** The most remarkable object in this constellation is, no doubt, the Great Nebula. It is invariably thought to be the most wonderful object in the sky; and it is visible to the unaided eye. Its real beauty, however, can only be appreciated with the aid of a telescope. The larger the telescope, the better. The Great Nebula in Orion is also known by its catalog numbers M42 or NGC 1976. It is greenish in color and fairly irregular in form.

Orion is rich in double stars. Over seventy of these stars are in the constellation, among them Rigel and Delta Orionis. There are also multiple stars. Theta Orionis has already been mentioned. This object appears to the unaided eye as a single star. The telescope reveals the object to be actually composed of four distinct stars which form a compact unit in the shape of a trapezium. See Fig. 74.

FIG. 74. Orion. Note the Great Nebula. Its mass is estimated to be 10,000 times that of the sun.

Rigel is a double star. The bright component has an apparent magnitude of 1.0; its color is yellowish-white. The companion is an 8.0 apparent magnitude of orange hue.

Theta Orionis is a multiple star. The four companions have apparent magnitudes of 4.0, 10.3, 7.5, and 6.3. The four individual stars form the outline of a baseball diamond or the geometrical form of a trapezium.

b. **Auriga.** The Alpha-star, Capella, itself is a binary, but this cannot be determined with the aid of a telescope alone. The binary character of Capella shows up in spectroscopic studies of the star: **such double stars are known as Spectroscopic Binaries.** The two companions of Capella are of about equal mass and are similar in their physical charac-

teristics. The period of one revolution about their common center of gravity for each star is 104 days.

Beta-Aurigae, too, is of special interest. It is an Eclipsing Binary. The two companions revolve in a plane that is inclined only slightly to the line of sight. They mutually eclipse one another at every revolution. The period of a complete revolution is 3 days, 23 hours, and 2.5 minutes.

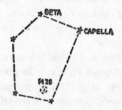

FIG. 75. Auriga. Beta-Aurigae is an Eclipsing Binary; the two companions are of equal size and brightness. Note the very beautiful M38 star cluster.

A particularly beautiful star cluster is to be found in Auriga. M38 or NGC 1912 is usually described as having the shape of an "oblique cross with a pair of large stars in each arm." See Fig. 75.

MARCH OBSERVATIONS

a. **Gemini.** M35 is the object to observe. It is a star cluster of most interesting design. Two streams of small stars run parallel on each side of the cluster.

The star Castor (α-Geminorum) is a three component star. Two of these form a binary system with a period of revolution of 300 years. The third component completes one revolution in about 10,000 years. Spectroscopic studies seem to indicate that each of these components is itself a double star. Castor is thus probably a unit consisting of six stars. See Fig. 76.

b. **Canis Major.** Mention has already been made that Sirius is a double star. The companion of this star was described earlier in some detail.

Not far from Sirius is the scattered star cluster M41 (or NGC 2287), which can be seen by the unaided eye. Fairly good detail can be obtained with a 3-inch telescope. The stars

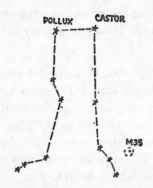

FIG. 76. Gemini. The star cluster M35 can be seen, under excellent weather conditions, by the naked eye. Even a small telescope brings out the extreme beauty of this cluster.

The star Castor is known scientifically as Alpha-Geminorum, although Pollux is in number one place as far as apparent brightness is concerned.

The three known components constituting the star Castor have apparent magnitudes of 2.7, 3.7, and 9.5. It is quite possible that each of the three stars is in itself a double.

form two distinct groups, joined by a red star in the center. See Fig. 77.

c. Canis Minor. The bright star Procyon is a remarkable binary. Its companion is one of the lightest stars known, its mass being less than one quarter the mass of the sun. The star

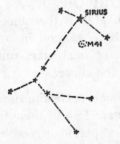

FIG. 77. Canis Major. The apparent magnitude of the companion of Sirius is 8.4.

Note the M41 cluster. It can be seen by the unaided eye. The red star in the center of the cluster can easily be observed with a small telescope.

is also extremely faint. It gives only 1/100,000 as much light as Procyon does, and cannot therefore be seen through a small telescope. See Fig. 78.

FIG. 78.

APRIL OBSERVATIONS

a. Leo. The bright star Regulus is a double; the companion is a faint 8th magnitude star. It is quite possible that Regulus is an "optical" and not a true double star. **An Optical Double consists of two stars that appear close because they are in line of sight of a terrestrial observer but are really at a great distance from one another, along that line.** The stars in an optical double do not, of course, rotate about any common center of gravity as true double stars do. Gamma-Leonis is a true double star. It is acclaimed as one of the finest double stars in the heavens, best observed when not quite dark, or in moonlight. The bright star of this binary system (apparent magnitude 2.6) has a golden tint; the fainter star (apparent magnitude 3.6) is greenish in color. The companions rotate fairly slowly about their center of gravity, a complete revolution lasting more than a thousand years.

A well-known variable star is of interest in this constellation—the long period variable, R-Leonis. At its maximum brightness, visible then to the naked eye, it is a red magnitude 5 star. At its minimum light intensity, when it is observable only with a good telescope, it is a tenth magnitude star. See Fig. 79.

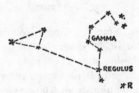

FIG. 79. Leo. Regulus is probably an optical double. The two stars appear close because they lie along the same line of sight for a terrestrial observer. A side view of these stars would reveal the true distance between them.

Gamma-Leonis is the double to observe in this constellation. The two companions have apparent magnitudes of 2.6 and 3.6.

The variations in brightness of R Leonis can easily be observed with a small telescope. A complete period lasts 310 days, while the change from fifth to tenth magnitudes alone takes 144 days.

R-Leonis forms an equilateral triangle with two nearby stars of apparent magnitudes 9.0 and 9.6.

The changing brightness of the variable can be estimated in relation to the two neighbors.

JUNE OBSERVATIONS

a. **Boötes.** Many interesting double stars can be observed with the aid of a small telescope. A partial list of these would include the stars Pi, Delta, Iota, Kappa, Xi and Epsilon. The last double is particularly beautiful: one of its components is a bright yellow; the other is a faint green. See Fig. 80.

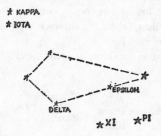

Fig. 80. Boötes. The two components of Epsilon-Boötis have apparent magnitudes of 3.0 and 6.3. The brighter star is distinctly yellow; the dimmer is greenish in color.

Xi-Boötis is also a double star; the two components are yellow and purple-red, respectively. The yellow companion is the brighter, its apparent magnitude is 4.7; the red star has an apparent magnitude of 6.6.

The information for the other objects follows:

		app. magn.	color			app. magn.	color
Kappa	{	4.6	white	Pi	{	4.9	white
		6.6	blue			6.0	white
Iota	{	5.0	yellow	Delta	{	3.6	yellow
		7.5	white			8.0	blue

b. **Virgo.** This constellation is rich in nebulae, for which reason this region of the sky has been called "the Field of the Nebulae." Several hundred of these clouds have been discovered in Virgo.

A double star is also of interest. It is the third brightest star in the constellation, Gamma-Virginis. In 1756 the angular distance between the two components was 6 seconds of angle. In 1836 the two stars were so close together that they could not be distinguished by the largest telescopes. In 1936 the separation between the stars was again 6 seconds of angle. A complete revolution of these stars, lasting 180 years, had been under observation. See Fig. 81.

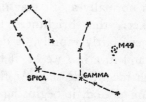

Fig. 81. Virgo. Gamma-Virginis is a famous double star. Its period of revolution is 180 years, and it has been under observation for nearly that length of time. Both components are alike in color (yellow) and in brightness (3.7).

JULY OBSERVATIONS

a. **Scorpius.** The bright red star Antares is a double. The companion is 3 seconds of angle distant from the bright star. A 4-inch telescope is needed to distinguish this binary system. Other doubles in Scorpius are the stars Beta- and Nu-Scorpii.

Several interesting star clusters are also observable. The one catalogued as Messier 80 is one of the richest in the number of stars it contains. See Fig. 82.

Fig. 82. Scorpius. Antares is a binary. The bright 1.2 red member of the system has a green companion of apparent magnitude 5.2.

The stars Beta Scorpii and Nu-Scorpii are also doubles in field glasses, and small telescopes. The Nu star is actually a quadruple star, as can be seen with a 4-inch telescope.

		app. magn.	color			app. magn.
Beta	{	2.0	yellow			
		6.0	green	Nu	{	4.2
						6.7
						7.0
						8.0

M80 is a cluster, rich in stars, globular in shape.

Many novae have appeared in this region of the sky, the first having been observed more than 2,000 years ago.

b. **Corona Borealis.** An interesting variable star can be observed in the middle of the crown. It is normally a 6th magnitude star, and may keep this brightness for many months. Then, fairly rapidly, it declines in brightness; and in a few weeks, it becomes a 14th or 15th magnitude star. At the end of the minimum period, it begins again to become a 6th magnitude star. See Fig. 83.

FIG. 83. Corona Borealis. An object of great interest to amateur astronomers is the star marked R in this constellation. It is an Irregular Variable Star. It is normally a 6th magnitude star, barely visible to the unaided eye. The periods of normality are interrupted from time to time, when the star dims to a magnitude 14 or 15 star. It is one of the highly enigmatic stars in astronomy.

AUGUST OBSERVATIONS

a. **Hercules.** The Great Star Cluster in Hercules, M13, NGC 6205, has already been described. The outer stars of the cluster are resolved into separate units even with a small telescope. But it takes a large instrument to see the full majesty of this globular cluster.

Several fine double stars in this constellation are of interest. Alpha-Herculis is one of these, as are Rho and Gamma-Herculis. The Delta star in this constellation looks like a double, but is only an optical double. The two stars are actually moving in different directions, and in several thousand years will be widely separated. See Fig. 84.

SEPTEMBER OBSERVATIONS

a. **Lyra.** The Beta star in this constellation was earlier described. It is one of the variable stars that can be observed by the unaided eye. Telescopic observations indicate that it is a multiple star, probably consisting of six components. The apparent magnitude of the individual components ranges from 3.0 to 14.3.

There are several other multiple stars in Lyra. Zeta-Lyrae consists of five stars forming a single unit.

The bright star, Vega, in this constellation is

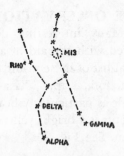

FIG. 84. Hercules. Alpha-Herculis is a beautiful binary. The bright star (apparent magnitude 3.0) is intensely yellow, while the dimmer companion (app. magn. 6.1) is very blue.

The vital data for Gamma-, Delta-, and Rho-Herculis follow:

	app. magn.	*color*		*app. magn.*	*color*
Gamma	3.8	white	Rho	4.0	green
	8.0	lilac		5.1	green
Delta	3.0	green			
	8.1	gray			

The feature of the constellation is M13, the Great Globular Star Cluster. It is barely visible to the unaided eye, resembling a fairly hazy 6th magnitude star. It takes at least a 5″ telescope to perceive its real beauty, and a much larger telescope to realize the full scope of its majesty.

The cluster probably contains more than 50,000 stars, many of them as bright or brighter than our own sun.

also a double star. The companion to Vega is a faint 10.5 magnitude star. While Vega is a blue-whitish star, the companion has a distinct orange hue.

Epsilon-Lyrae is a double double star. The main double can be seen without optical aid by persons of excellent eyesight.

Each star in the main double is resolved into two components with the aid of a telescope. The four stars in Epsilon-Lyrae have the apparent magnitude of 5.1, 6.0, 5.1 and 5.4.

The Ring Nebula, M57, is so called because of its similarity to a smoke ring when observed with a 5″ or 6″ telescope.

Larger telescopes reveal its greater similarity to a soap bubble than to a flat ring.

The nebula derives its illumination from a 15th magnitude star located at its center.

M57 is one of a large group of Planetary Nebulae: the adjective "planetary" refers to their slight resemblance in shape to terrestrial planets. See Fig. 85.

FIG. 85. Lyra. The Ring Nebula is an object of great interest to astronomers. It can be seen fairly well nearly halfway between Beta- and Gamma-Lyrae with a 3″ telescope.

To see its true annular shape a telescope of at least 5″ is needed.

Beta-Lyrae is a most interesting star. It consists of at least six companions of magnitudes 3.0, 6.7, 13.0, 14.3, 9.2, and 9.0. The variation of brightness of this composite star from 3.4 to 4.5 can be detected by the unaided eye.

Zeta-Lyrae consists of two bright stars (apparent magnitudes of 4.2 and 5.5) and three faint companions.

Vega is a double, the faint companion being a 10.5 magnitude star with a distinct orange color.

Epsilon-Lyrae is a double double. One of the doubles, Epsilon[1], consists of a 5.1 magn. star green-white and a 6.0 magn. star blue-white. The other double, Epsilon[2], consists of a 5.1 magn. star white and a 5.4 magn. star very white.

b. **Cygnus.** This is the most marvelous region of the sky for an amateur observer.

The Milky Way separates into two great parallel branches in Cygnus; a multitude of stars, star clusters, and occasionally dark gaps can be seen there. The region is probably one of the richest in stars in all the sky.

Cygnus has also an unusually large number of variable stars. Several novae have appeared in this constellation in the last three centuries.

Double stars, too, are plentiful in Cygnus— one of which is Beta-Cygni. It is one of the most beautiful of all double stars, with contrasting colors of gold and blue. See Fig. 86.

c. **Sagittarius.** The presence of the Milky Way in this constellation results in much beauty—abounding with globular clusters, and open star clusters, formed nebulae and diffuse nebulae.

M17, "The Horse-shoe Nebula"—a large cloud of gas and dust, of arched form—is one of the few that can be observed with a small power telescope. Many interesting stars provide the lighting for the nebula.

That part of the sky also contains a very fine globular star cluster, M22, the individual stars of which are faint. Typical magnitudes are

FIG. 86. Cygnus. Beta-Cygni is probably the most beautiful of all the double stars. The two companions can be seen even with a magnification of 20 times of a 2″ telescope. The bright yellow star is of apparent magnitude 3.0, while its bluish partner is a dim 5.3.

10, 11, etc. The sum total of all their light is great, making the cluster visible to the unaided eye. See Fig. 87.

FIG. 87. Sagittarius. M17, the Horse-shoe Nebula can be observed even with a small power telescope.

M22 (or NGC 6656) is one of the finest known globular clusters.

d. **Aquila.** Of interest to observers is the variable star Eta-Aquilae. It changes from a bright 3.7 to a faint 4.5 magnitude and vice versa every 7 days, 4 hours, and 12 minutes.

There are also many fine doubles in Aquila. Altair, the bright star of the constellation, is one of these. Its companion is a magnitude 10 star at an angular distance of 2.5 minutes of angle from Altair. See Fig. 88.

FIG. 88. Aquila. Eta-Aquilae is a cepheid variable. Its maximum brightness is 3.5 apparent magnitude.

Alpha-Aquilae, or Altair, is a double star.

NOVEMBER OBSERVATIONS

a. **Pegasus.** Many interesting doubles can be observed here. A fine contrast of colors is to be seen in the binary system of Epsilon-Pegasi. The bright star (magnitude 2.7) is yellowish in color; its companion (magnitude 8.7) is a clear violet. The two are more than two minutes of angle distant from one another. See Fig. 89.

Fig. 89. Pegasus. Epsilon-Pegasi is a double star. The bright (2.7) companion is yellowish in color; the dim partner (8.7 apparent magnitude) has a violet hue.

DECEMBER OBSERVATIONS

a. **Andromeda.** The Great Galaxy, M31, seen in the background of this constellation was earlier described. Its first observers considered it to be a cloud, or a nebula, and reference to the "Queen of the Nebulae" dates back more than a thousand years.

With low telescopic power, this galaxy leaves the impression of a bright elliptical object. The true nature of this grand spiral of billions of stars is revealed only by a large telescope. See Fig. 90.

Fig. 90. Andromeda. The Great Galaxy in Andromeda is also known as the Great Nebula in Andromeda. Its Messier number is M31; it is item number 224 in the "New General Catalog." It is likely that it greatly resembles our own Milky Way Galaxy.

b. **Cetus.** The chief object of interest is the long period variable Omicron-Ceti, the star also known as Mira, "the Wonderful Star." It varies in brightness from a second magnitude to a faint 10th magnitude star. Its period is highly irregular, an average of 330 days.

The star has been under study for more than 350 years, and its brightness is still being studied by amateur observers. See Fig. 91.

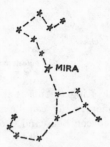

Fig. 91. Cetus. Mira, or Omicron-Ceti, is a long period variable. The star is distinctly red in color, of the giant variety of stars.

JANUARY OBSERVATIONS

a. **Perseus.** The eclipsing variable star, Beta-Persei, has been earlier described. Its light intensity varies from a bright 2.3 magnitude to a faint 3.5 magnitude, repeating every 2 days, 20 hours and 48 minutes. The changes in its brightness are very regular, remaining most of the time at its brightest, the decrease taking 4½ hours. The star then returns very rapidly to the 2.3 magnitude. Also known as Algol, it is a classic example of an eclipsing binary. Both stars have been studied at length and reasonably accurate data concerning them are available. The brighter has a diameter of 1,250,000 miles, and a mass ⅜ths that of the sun. The fainter has a diameter of 1,450,000 miles. The stars are very close to one another, the distance between their centers being about 3,000,000 miles. They revolve about their common center of gravity, completing a revolution in 2 days, 20 hours, 48 minutes. The plane of their orbit is not quite in our line of sight; it is inclined nearly 8° to that line. The eclipse is partial. When the star appears at its dimmest, less than half of the brighter component is eclipsed. Observations of Beta-Persei can be made by the unaided eye.

Another object of interest in Perseus is a double star cluster. The two close clusters can be seen with the aid of a telescope just beyond Eta-Persei, in the direction of Cassiopeia. See Fig. 92.

b. **Taurus.** The seven stars in this constel-

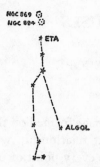

FIG. 92. Perseus. The variations of Algol can be observed by the unaided eye.

Eta Persei is a double star. The bright component has an apparent magnitude of 4.0, the dimmer of 8.5. The colors of the two are very distinct; the bright one is very yellow, the dim—very blue.

The double cluster NGC 869 and NGC 884 are of great interest. They are located beyond the star Eta Persei in the direction of Cassiopeia, and are visible to the naked eye. The pair is one of the most beautiful clusters of stars in the sky.

lation, known as the Pleiades, or the Seven Sisters, are an object of great interest to the amateur astronomer. To the unaided eye, seven stars are visible, but even a small telescope aids in detecting more than a hundred. On a photographic plate, there are thousands of stars. The stars in the Pleiades group appear to be enveloped in a tenuous nebula, the

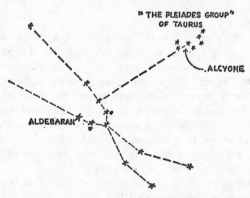

FIG. 93. Taurus. The brightest star in the Pleiades group of this constellation, Alcyone, is a triple star in small instruments, and a quadruple star when observed with large telescopes.

Aldebaran, the brightest star of the whole constellation, has as a companion an 11.2 magnitude star.

latter being illuminated by the light of these stars.

Taurus also contains many double and multiple stars. The bright star Alcyone in the Pleiades subgroup is a quadruple star. The brightest star in the constellation, Aldebaran, is accompanied by an 11.2 magnitude, orange-hued star, which can be seen under good atmospheric conditions with a 3-inch refractor. See Fig. 93.

SOUTH CIRCUMPOLAR OBSERVATIONS

In the constellations that are not visible in middle northern latitudes, there are many objects of interest to telescopic observers.

Alpha-Crucis is a double star. The Alpha star of the Centaurus constellation is a triple star, the three components having magnitudes of 0.3, 1.7, and 11.0, respectively. Formerly the 11.0 magnitude star was considered to be the nearest star (the sun excepted), and was mistakenly named Proxima Centauri (the near one in Centaurus), but this notion has been corrected by subsequent research. All three components revolve about a common center, each in turn being closest to the Solar System.

The skies "down under" are also rich in clusters and nebulae. One of the closest globular clusters of stars is listed as number 104 in the New General Catalog—an almost perfectly round ball, closely packed with a countless number of magnitude 12 and fainter stars.

A "must" object for observations are two galaxies close to the South Celestial Pole. These galaxies have been known for centuries by the names Greater Magellanic Cloud and Lesser Magellanic Cloud: both can be seen by the unaided eye. The larger galaxy extends over an angular distance of 7 degrees; the smaller subtends an angle of 4 degrees at the eye of the observer. Strong moonlight obliterates the smaller galaxy, but the Greater Magellanic Cloud remains visible even in strong moonlight.

CHAPTER V

TELESCOPES AND THEIR USES

PART 1: THE REFRACTING TELESCOPE

INTRODUCTION

All that is known about the stars is derived from the light reaching the earth from them. A detailed analysis of that light supplies much information about the chemicals contained by the star and the temperature prevailing on its surface. From careful study of the light, data are obtained about the mass and velocity of the star.

Vital to this research is the telescope, which aids the astronomer in three distinct ways: (a) by gathering the light emanating from a star, thus making the star appear brighter—this property of the instrument is called the **Light Gathering Power;** (b) by bringing out details, e.g., separating the components of a double star—this property is called the **Resolving Power;** and (c) by magnifying, or "enlarging" the section of sky under observation—this is the **Magnifying Power of the telescope.**

There are two major classes of telescopes: Refracting Telescopes, and Reflecting Telescopes. This section is devoted to the refracting telescope—its composition, properties, and characteristics.

THE PROCESS OF "SEEING"

Human beings "see" as a result of the light emanating from an object falling upon the light-sensitive inner lining of the eye, the retina. Thus, part of the light emerging, say, from the flame of a candle finds its way through the pupil of the eye, to the retina, which converts the light into a nervous impulse. The optic nerve then transmits these impulses to the brain, producing the sensation of vision.

Non-luminous objects, such as books and chairs are seen by light reflected by them— the reflected sunlight, or artificial light, reaches the observer's retina.

The visual image formed on the retina is on a point to point relationship with the object observed. Thus every point of the flame must illuminate one, and only one, point on the retina.

This idea may be clarified by an example.

Let the object under observation be a luminous arrow, AB. The light emitted by a given point of this arrow, say point C, goes off in all directions in space. A small part of that light enters the observer's eye. The part that enters the eye is in the form of a cone.

To produce clear vision, all the light in the cone must converge on a single point in the retina—a task performed by the crystalline lens in the eye, located just inside the pupil. The point on the retina is the image of the point C on the object—hence, C'.

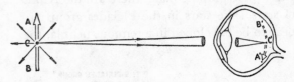

Fig. 94. The Process of Seeing. AB is a luminous arrow, every point of which is a minute source of light.

The light emanating from one of these points (point C) goes off in all directions (7 rays of light are indicated). Some of that light enters the observer's eye. The rays so entering form a cone. The crystalline lens in the eye converges all the rays to one point C', on the retina. C' is the image on the retina of point C on the object. Every other point on the arrow will form a similar image on the retina.

The sum total of all the points on the retina produces the complete image A'B'.

Images of all the other points of the object are formed on the retina in a similar manner, accumulating to form the image of the luminous arrow, A'B'. See Fig. 94.

The lens makes use of the curvatures of its surfaces to perform its task. To see how this is done, let us follow two of these rays on their route from point C to point C'. Ray No. 1, emanating from point C, is refracted at the front surface of the lens, goes through the lens, and is refracted a second time on crossing the rear surface of the lens, falling on the retina at point C'.

This refraction is similar to the refraction (the breakage) that a ray of light undergoes in passing from air into water, or from water into air; or in passing through a glass prism. See Fig. 95.

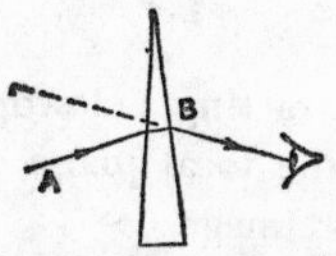

FIG. 95. Refraction of a Light Ray on going through a thin prism.
The direction of the ray is changed once on going from air (A) into glass. The direction is changed again on going from the glass into air (B).

Ray No. 2, emanating from point C, undergoes similar experience: (a) It is refracted at the front surface of the lens. (b) It passes through the lens. (c) It is refracted a second time on crossing the rear surface. To obtain a clear image of point C, Ray No. 2 must intersect Ray No. 1 at the retina. The lens in the eye adjusts its curvatures to assure the two rays intersecting at the precise point.

Similarly, all other rays emanating from point C on the object, and entering the eye through the pupil, meet at point C'. See Fig. 96.

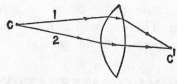

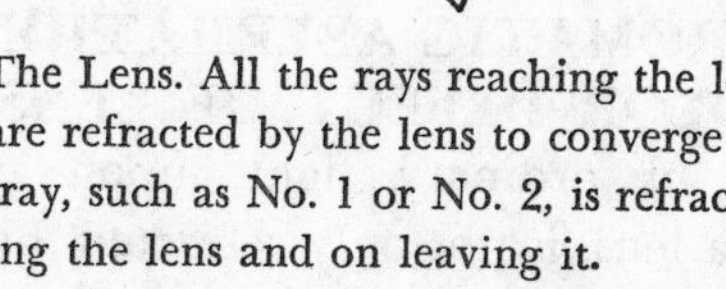

FIG. 96. The Lens. All the rays reaching the lens from point C are refracted by the lens to converge at point C'. Each ray, such as No. 1 or No. 2, is refracted both on entering the lens and on leaving it.

TRACING OF LIGHT RAYS

Mathematical equations can be used to compute the exact route traced by each ray from C to C'. The solutions of these equations are often lengthy and tedious. There are, however, several rays, the routes of which can be traced without any difficulty. Two of these are: (a) the ray that starts out from point C parallel to the axis of the lens, and (b) the ray that starts out from point C and passes through the center of the lens.

The ray starting at C, parallel to the axis of the lens on the left, will pass through the focus of the lens on the right. Its route is marked by the letters C, D, E, and Focus (in Fig. 98).

A Focus of a lens is the point on the axis where all the rays parallel to the axis meet. See Fig. 97.

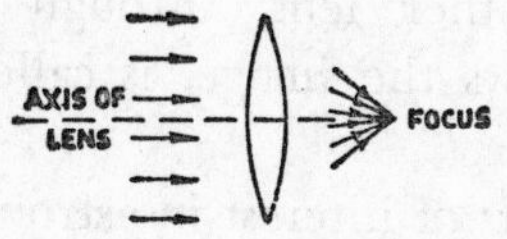

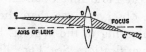

FIG. 97. The Focus of a Lens. The focus is a point on the axis of a lens where all the rays parallel to the axis meet. (Only part of the paths of the rays is shown.)

The other ray whose route can easily be traced is the one that starts from C and passes through the center of the lens O. If the lens is fairly thin, this ray will follow a straight line through O. The point of intersection of the two rays is denoted by C'. All the other rays, the routes of which are more difficult to trace, will also meet at point C'. C', then, is the image of Point C. See Fig. 98.

FIG. 98. Tracing of Light Rays. The routes of several light rays emanating from a luminous point C can easily be traced. Two such rays are shown in this figure.
All other rays emanating from point C will also go through point C'.
Point C' is the image of point C.

Other points on the luminous arrow produce corresponding points on the retina, the sum total producing the "seeing" of the arrow.

All that has been said about the crystalline lens in the human eye holds true for the glass lens used in telescopes. There is, however, an important difference between the two. The eye lens is able to change the curvature of its surfaces. This changes the distance from the focus to the lens. In the case of a glass lens, the focus is fixed.

A SIMPLE
REFRACTING TELESCOPE

The simplest kind of a refracting telescope consists of only two lenses. The one that is exposed to the object (the star, moon, etc.) is called **the Objective.** Its function is to produce an image of the object under observation. The other lens, through which the observer views the image, is called **the Eyepiece.**

The objects of interest in astronomy are, as a rule, at great distances. The light entering the objective from each point of the object is in the form of parallel rays, the image produced by these rays forming in the focal plane.

The focal plane is a plane passing through the focus, perpendicular to the axis of the lens.

The image produced by the first lens is called the "First Image."

The function of the eyepiece is to magnify the first image. To achieve magnification, the eyepiece is placed so that the first image is just inside its focus—i.e., between the eyepiece and its focus, very close to the focus.

Note that the Final Image subtends a larger angle at the observer's eye than did the object. The enlarging of the angle is known as Angular Magnification. See Fig. 99.

One of the primary functions of a telescope is to produce angular magnification.

PROBLEM 15:

An object subtends an angle of 20° at the eye of an observer. The Final Image subtends an angle of 80°. Find the angular magnification.

Answer: The magnification is 4 times.

The simple type of astronomical telescope described, composed of two lenses, will be used only for small values of magnification. Such a telescope may be used for magnifica-

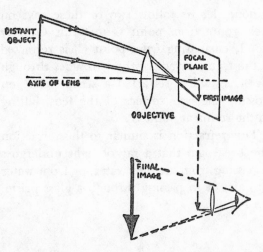

FIG. 99. A Simple Refracting Telescope. The objective forms an image in the focal plane of the lens. This is known as the First Image.

The eyepiece (shown here in the lower part of the picture as actually *in line* with the objective lens) forms the Final Image which is a magnification of the First Image.

tions up to 10 times **for each inch** of diameter of aperture of the objective. Thus, if the aperture of the objective has a diameter of 2.38″, the telescope will be used for angular magnification of 20 to 25 times. The "aperture" of an objective is the transparent part of the objective. It does not include part of the edge of the lens that is cemented to the holder, through which light cannot pass.

To obtain higher magnification (say 40 to 60 times) per inch of diameter, the objective lens will have to be designed so as to remove two common defects. These defects are known as "aberrations" and are usually present in simple lenses. One of these is known as **Chromatic Aberration;** the other as **Spherical Aberration.** The eyepiece, too, will have to be of a more complex design.

CHROMATIC ABERRATION
(COLOR DEFECT OF LENS)

A ray of ordinary light, upon passing through a lens, is not only refracted, but also dispersed into its component colors. This is a highly undesirable feature of the lens. Every ray of "white" light entering the lens from the left is dispersed into a small rainbow of colors.

The term "white light" signifies the ordinary light given off by the sun, stars, etc. This light is actually a combination of all the colors of a rainbow, well mixed. The lens "unmixes" the colors, as each color included in this white ray of light is refracted at a slightly different angle.

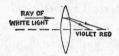

FIG. 100. Chromatic Aberration. The violet component is refracted most, while the red component of the white light is bent least. All the other colors are intermediate between these extremes.

From Figure 100, it can be seen that the violet component of the white ray of light is refracted the most; and the red part of the white ray, the least. As a result of this difference in refraction, the violet components of the light will focus closer to the lens than will the red parts.

The "trouble" caused by this defect is obvious. The point to point relationship no longer holds. Rays emanating from one point in the object no longer converge on one point of the image. Each color of the original light produces its own point on the image. For each point on the object, there will be as many points on the image as there are colors. The images of the different points on the object will overlap and eradicate all detail.

This defect of the simple lens, by which light of different colors fails to arrive at the same focus, is called Chromatic Aberration.

To reduce the effects of chromatic aberration, lenses are now made from two component parts, cemented together with Canadian balsam or airspaced to form one unit. See Fig. 101.

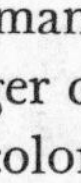

FIG. 101. A Compound Lens. Such a lens consists of two (or more) components cemented together with transparent Canadian balsam, or airspaced. Chromatic aberration can be greatly reduced by a proper choice of the quality of glass for each component.

One component is in the form of a converging lens; the other, a diverging lens.

A converging lens is thicker at the center than at the circumference. Its function is to converge rays of light, that is, to bring the rays closer. A diverging lens is thinner at the center than at the circumference. Its function is to diverge rays. See Fig. 102.

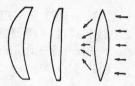

FIG. 102. Three Types of Converging Lenses. Any lens that is thicker in the middle than at the edges is a Converging Lens. As its name implies such a lens converges rays of light going through it.

The converging lens is produced from crown glass, a very serviceable material for refracting light, dispersing white light into colors only slightly.

The diverging lens is made from flint glass, which is much better for dispersing light than for refracting it. This lens nullifies the dispersion that was produced by the converging lens; it does not, however, remove all the refraction that was produced by the first lens. See. Fig. 103.

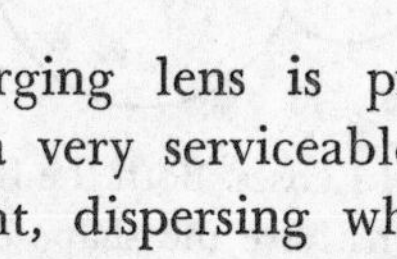

FIG. 103. Three Types of Diverging Lenses. Any lens that is thinner at the center than at the edges is a Diverging Lens. As its name implies such a lens diverges light rays going through it.

As a result the light is refracted, but not dispersed, thus eliminating chromatic aberration.

This compound lens is known as an "Achromatic" or a "Color-Free Lens," and is commonly used for objective lenses in telescopes.

A compound lens is actually "color free" for only *two* colors, say green and red or blue and violet. The two colors chosen for perfect focusing are determined by the use to which the telescope will be put. Green and red are best for an objective used primarily for visual purposes, as the human eye is most sensitive to colors at the red end of the spectrum. An objective in a telescope designed primarily for photographic work will have the compound lens calculated to bring blue and violet to the same focus, as common photographic emulsions are sensitive at the blue end of the color spectrum.

SPHERICAL ABERRATION (SHAPE DEFECT OF LENS)

This is a defect of lenses with spherical surfaces. See Fig. 104. Most lenses have such

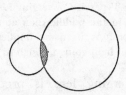

FIG. 104. Spherical Lenses. Both the front and the rear of an ordinary lens have the shape of a portion of a sphere. Such lenses cause a defect in the image known as Spherical Aberration.

surfaces. Both the front and back surfaces of these lenses are portions of spheres. Light cannot properly be focused by such a lens. The light rays passing close to the edges of such lenses are refracted more than light rays passing through the center. Thus, the rays marked **A** on Fig. 105 come to a focus

FIG. 105. Spherical Aberration. Light ray A through the lens close to its edge is refracted more than light ray B.

Parallel rays do not converge to one focus.

This defect has nothing to do with the color of light.

Spherical Aberration is present even when the light is monochromatic.

closer to the lens than the rays marked B. Again, the point to point relationship is no longer valid, and the result is a blurred image.

This defect is entirely independent of chromatic aberration; spherical aberration may be present even when there is no dispersion.

The defect is adjusted by making each face of the lens paraboloid in form rather than spherical. A paraboloid lens is curved less at the edges than at the center, and converges parallel rays to a single sharply defined focus.

CORRECTED OBJECTIVES

Achromatic objectives can now be designed to remedy spherical as well as chromatic aberrations. The components of such a lens need not have paraboloid surfaces, but instead can use spherical surfaces. There are two steps in its design: To begin, the lens maker chooses the spherical curvatures and type of glass needed for each component of the achromatic lens. Then, he employs available scientific data to choose the proper combination of curvatures to eliminate the spherical aberration.

In one such design the converging lens is made of crown glass. The radii of its spherical surfaces are in the ratio of 2 to 3; and the diverging lens is made of flint. One of its sides is a plane; the other side is constructed to fit the surface with shorter radius. This compound lens has no spherical aberration and is also corrected for chromatic aberration.

As a telescope objective the three-lens "Apochromat" lens is by far superior to the ordinary achromatic lens. In an apochromatic lens, three or more colors are focused simultaneously, rather than two colors, as with the ordinary achromatic lens. The former is also entirely free of spherical aberration.

EYEPIECES

The eyepieces of most telescopes consist of two lenses—one, the field lens; the other, the eye lens. The observer's eye is placed next to the eye lens. The two lenses are permanently mounted in a draw tube that can be moved forward and backward inside the main tube of the telescope.

The chief purpose of the field lens is to collect the light rays from the objective and direct them toward the usually smaller eye lens. The primary purpose of the eye lens is to magnify.

Many eyepieces have been designed and marketed in recent years; of these the three most useful are the Huygenian, the Kellner, and the Orthoscopic.

The quality of an eyepiece is determined by:

a. Make
b. Focal length
c. Apparent field

A complete description of a typical eyepiece would, for example, be: Huygenian, 27 millimeter focal length, apparent field of view 50°; or: Kellner, 40 mm. focal length, and apparent field of view 40°.

> NOTE: A. The focal length refers to the whole eyepiece, that is, the combination of field lens and eye lens.
> B. The apparent field of view is just that— the angle subtended by the diameter of the circular view, seen through the eyepiece. See Fig. 106.

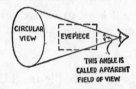

FIG. 106. Apparent Field of View. Looking through the eyepiece the eye sees a circle of light. The angle subtended at the eye by the diameter of that circle is called the Apparent Field of View. This angle is a constant for any eyepiece.

The angle that the diameter of the view subtends at the observer's eye is constant for each eyepiece, whether it is used with a telescope or independently.

THE HUYGENIAN EYEPIECE

This eyepiece consists of two plano-convex lenses, the convex sides away from the eye. See Fig. 107. A typical eyepiece of 25 mm. focal length may consist of an eye lens 12 mm.

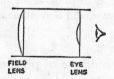

FIG. 107. The Huygenian Eyepiece. Such an eyepiece consists of two plano-convex lenses spaced about an inch apart. The plane side of each lens is toward the eye.

diameter, 16 mm. focal length, and a field lens 26 mm. diameter, 48 mm. focal length, with a spacing of 32 mm. between the lenses.

Good Huygenian eyepieces have an apparent field of view of 50°, and are used primarily when such large angles are needed. The Huygenian eyepieces are often not too well corrected for optical defects; consequently, their use is limited to low magnifications.

THE KELLNER EYEPIECE

This eyepiece, which is an improvement of a prototype known as the Ramsden eyepiece, is very popular for medium range magnifications. The eyepiece consists of a plano-convex field lens, the plane side facing the objective, and a smaller diameter achromatic eye lens.

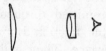

FIG. 108. The Kellner Eyepiece. This eyepiece consists of a plano-convex field lens, the plane side facing the objective, and an achromatic eye lens.

A typical Kellner eyepiece of 25 mm. focal length would consist of a field lens 28 mm. diameter, 41 mm. focal length, and an achromatic eye lens 18 mm. diameter, 32 mm. focal length, with a separation of 20 mm. between the lenses. See Fig. 108.

The earlier Ramsden eyepiece had no correction for chromatic aberration; and it looked like this (Figure 109):

FIG. 109. The Ramsden Eyepiece.

THE ORTHOSCOPIC EYEPIECE

This eyepiece is one of the best eyepieces now available, certainly for high magnifications. It consists of a field lens of three components, and a single plano-convex eye lens. The three components of the field lens are a double concave flint lens cemented in sandwich style between two double convex crown lenses. The single plano-convex eye lens is located close to the field lens and has its plane side next to the eye. The lens is corrected for both chromatic and spherical aberrations, and produces a brilliant image in normal proportions. See Fig. 110.

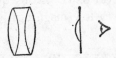

FIG. 110. The Orthoscopic Eyepiece. The field lens consists of three components, crown glass, flint glass, and crown glass, glued together with Canadian balsam. The eye lens, very close to the field lens, is plano-convex in shape, the plane side being next to the eye.

COATING OF LENSES

Only part of the light entering the telescope is actually transmitted through the several lenses; a sizeable fraction is *reflected* from each optical surface. These reflections from curved surfaces produce troublesome secondary images, and reduce materially the brilliance and clarity of the desired image.

In recent years, this shortcoming has been reduced by coating the glass surface with a thin transparent film, usually of magnesium fluoride, so as to produce interference between the light waves reflected at the top of the coating and the light waves reflected from the bottom, thus eliminating the reflected light.

Interference is one of the characteristic properties of waves. This phenomenon may take place when two waves are present. If the two waves are "out of step," by half a wave length, interference will take place.

This can be further clarified with the aid of a diagram. Let A be a wave moving from left to right in water; B a similar wave moving in the same direction.

If the waves are "out of step" by half a wave length, the troughs of one wave will fall in the same spots as the peaks of the other wave, cancelling each other. The result will be—calm: One wave interfered with the other and both were cancelled. See Fig. 111.

Many light phenomena are explained by the theory that **light is a wave motion,** that so-called rays of light are merely lines that in-

dicate the direction in which the light waves are moving.

One of the proofs of the wave theory of light is that light waves interfere.

Often, interference is an undesirable quality; however, in lens coating, it is highly desirable. The light wave reflected by the lens follows a wave reflected by the top of the coating and is cancelled out by it.

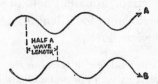

FIG. 111. Interference. A and B are two identical waves moving from left to right. They are not in step, i.e., their crests do not correspond, nor do the troughs. In this particular case they are out of step by half a wave length; the crests of B come half a wave length after the crests of A. These two waves going through water simultaneously will leave its surface perfectly calm; the troughs of one wave will cancel out the crests of the other.

This can be seen in Figure 112. Let the light wave reflected from the top of the coating be denoted by A; and the light wave reflected from the lens, by B. If one wave is at a maximum while the other is at a minimum, the two will interfere with one another. This interference will remove the troublesome reflected light. See. Fig. 112.

FIG. 112. Coating of Lenses. Wave A is reflected from the top of the coating layer, wave B from its bottom (i.e., from the lens itself). The thickness of the coating is adjusted so as to bring about interference between these two waves, and thus eliminate the troublesome reflection.

The coating must be of precisely the right thickness—one-quarter of a wave length of the light used. The thickness of the film is usually designed to remove the yellow-green reflections to which the human eye is most sensitive.

A set of lenses properly coated may increase the brightness of the image as much as 30%.

THE THREE POWERS OF THE TELESCOPE

Telescopes have three functions to perform:

1. To increase the apparent brightness of the object. This increase in brightness depends on the light gathering power of the telescope.
2. To bring out detail that cannot be seen with the unaided eye. How well a telescope performs this function depends on the resolving power.
3. Magnify the object, or make it appear that the object is closer. How well a telescope performs this function depends on the magnifying power of the telescope.

THE LIGHT GATHERING POWER OF A TELESCOPE

The most important function of a telescope, probably, is to gather a large quantity of light from a star. The telescope "squeezes the light together" into a beam narrow enough to enter the pupil of the eye. See Fig. 113.

OBJECTIVE

FIG. 113. Light Gathering Power of a Telescope. All the rays that go in through the large objective come out through the small eyepiece.

This concentration of lights increases greatly the apparent brightness of the object.

The light gathering power makes it possible to see stars of magnitude higher than 6, the stars that are too faint to be seen by the naked eye. This light gathering power depends only on the objective lens—it is proportional to its area. **Or: the Light Gathering Power is proportional to the square of the diameter of the objective lens.**

At night, the pupil of the eye has a diameter of approximately ¼ inch. A telescope having an objective of 1 inch diameter admits into the eye $4^2 = 16$ times more light than does the unaided eye. A 2-inch telescope would admit $8^2 = 64$ times more light, and so on. Experience verifies this theory. Thus, with a 2-inch telescope, one can observe stars 64 times dimmer than a 6th magnitude star. These are stars classified as magnitude 10.5.

Similarly, it can be computed that:

with a 6″ objective, stars of 12.9 magnitude can be seen; and

with a 15″ objective, stars of 14.9 magnitude can be seen.

THE RESOLVING POWER OF A TELESCOPE

This power of the telescope also depends only on the size of the objective. The resolving power is intimately connected with the clarity with which details can be seen. A point of light that appears to the naked eye to be a single star, turns out, when greater detail is obtained, to be a unit consisting of two or more neighboring stars. The greater the resolving power of the telescope, the clearer will be the detail; with low resolving power, there is much overlapping and merging. It is important to have a clear understanding of that power.

Consider two pinpoints of light—say, two candles. At a distance of several feet, the two will appear as separate and distinct sources of light. At a greater distance, the two will merge into *one* relatively fuzzy point of light. Experiment shows that the pinpoints of light can no

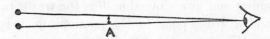

A

FIG. 114. Resolving Power of a Telescope. When the angle A subtended at the eye by two points of light is less than 6 minutes, the eye ceases to note them as two distinct points. This can also be stated by saying that at angles smaller than 6′ the eye is unable to resolve the object it sees into separate units.

longer be separated when the angle A subtended by them at the eye is less than about 6 minutes of angle. Otherwise stated: **The resolving power of the normal eye is 6′ of angle.** See Fig. 114.

The inability to separate points subtending

an angle smaller than 6 minutes is due to a basic property of light, known as Diffraction. Due to diffraction, a point of light on the object does not become a point of light on the retina, but a small disk; for each object point, there is an image disk. This disk, commonly called a "spurious" image, or a "diffraction pattern," has finite dimensions and a rather complex structure. It has a bright center, surrounded by alternating dark and light rings, the light rings decreasing rapidly in brightness toward the edge of the disk.

Thus, the light emanating from point C does not form in reality a point C′ but rather a "spurious" image C′ on the retina. See Fig. 115.

If a second point of light E (not shown in the figure) is closer than 6 minutes of angle to point C, the spurious image due to it, E′, will materially overlap C′. The brain is no longer able to distinguish two separate points. The eye cannot resolve E from C.

Fig. 115. Spurious Image. Light emanating from a point C does *not* converge to a point C′ on the retina, as is usually assumed for the sake of oversimplification. The counterpart of every point of light on the retina is a minute system of concentric light and dark circles.

The "point to point" relationship between object and image oversimplifies the truth. In reality, it is a point to disk relationship. It is not difficult to see that the smaller the size of these disks, the more detail will be obtained. Optical theory shows that the larger the objective lens, the smaller will be the diameter of the disk.

Optical theory, as well as practice, also shows that the resolving power of a telescope depends **only** upon the diameter of the objective. Thus, stars that appear as one unit in a small telescope may resolve into two or more close neighbors when viewed by a telescope with a larger objective.

There is a simple formula relating the diameter of the objective with the resolving power:

$$\text{Resolving Power} = \frac{5}{\text{Diameter of Objective}}$$

In this formula, the diameter should be stated in inches; the resolving power in seconds of angle.

A telescope with a 2-inch objective can resolve two stars that subtend an angle of 2.5 seconds of arc at the eye of the observer.

THE MAGNIFYING POWER OF A TELESCOPE

Telescopes magnify angles. **One of the primary functions of the instrument is to magnify the angles subtended by the objects under observation, a process known as Angular Magnification.** Thus, if without a telescope, an object subtends an angle of 3°, and when viewed through a telescope, the image subtends an angle of 45°, the magnification is 15 times. See Fig. 116.

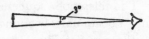

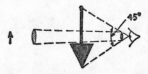

Fig. 116. The Magnifying Power of a Telescope. The object as seen by the unaided eye subtends an angle of 3°.

The image of the same object (lower figure) in the telescope subtends an angle of 45°.

The magnifying power of this telescope is

$$\frac{45}{3} = 15 \text{ times.}$$

Angular Magnification is the only magnification that a telescope performs. The increase in the angle gives the impression of nearness, thus making the image appear to be nearer than was the object.

PROBLEM 16:

The moon subtends an angle of approximately ½ a degree of angle at the observer's eye. When viewed through a telescope, the moon's image subtends an angle of 4°. Compute the angular magnification.

$$Answer: \frac{4}{\frac{1}{2}} = 8 \text{ times.}$$

The magnifying power of a telescope depends both on the focal length of the objective lens and on the focal length of the eyepiece.

The angular magnification of a telescope is stated by the simple formula:

$$\text{Angular Magnification} = \frac{f_{eyepiece}}{f_{objective}}$$

"$f_{objective}$" represents the focal length of the objective. This distance is usually stated in inches or millimeters. "$f_{eyepiece}$" represents the focal length of the eyepiece, the distance usually stated in the same units as the $f_{objective}$. **Focal length of a lens is the distance from the focus to the center of the lens.**

(The image in most telescopes appears inverted. A star, even with the highest magnification obtainable, appears as a point of light. The fact that it is inverted is of no importance.)

The formula for magnification seems to indicate that there is no limit to magnification, that any desired magnification, say a million times, can be obtained in three ways:

(a) By making the focal length of the objective large. This implies a lens that is only a little thicker at the center than at the edges.

(b) By making the focal length of the eyepiece small. In practice, this would mean that the lens would have to be much thicker at the center than at the edges.

(c) By combination of (a) and (b).

The indications of the formula are correct. Theoretically, there is no limit to possible magnifications.

There are, however, four important limitations to the use of high values of magnification:

1. Magnification decreases the clarity of the picture by increasing the size of the spurious image. The higher the magnification, the greater the decrease in the clarity and distinctness of the picture. **It does no good to force magnification beyond the resolving power of the telescope.**

2. Increase in magnification causes decrease in brightness of the image. The same quantity of light is spread out over a larger area with resulting faintness of image.

3. Increase in magnification decreases the actual field of view of the sky. On doubling the magnification, the angular diameter of the view is cut in half.

The relation between magnification and actual field of view is illustrated in Figure 117 (A), (B), and (C). In all three views the telescope pointed in the same direction.

With low magnification, the tops of two houses and a large portion of the sky were in the field of view. (A)

With higher magnification, only the tower of one of the houses can be seen through the telescope. (B)

With still higher magnification, one window occupies the whole view. (C)

The technical term "Field of View" is often used in connection with telescopes. **By definition, it is the ratio of two other quantities inherent to every telescope.** These quantities are: (a) The Apparent Field of View of the Eyepiece, and (b) The Angular Magnification of the Telescope.

$$\text{Actual Field of View} = \frac{\text{Apparent Field of View of Eyepiece}}{\text{Magnification}}$$

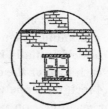

FIG. 117. (A) Left (B) Center (C) Right.

The Apparent Field of View is a fixed quantity for each eyepiece, information that the manufacturer usually supplies with the product, in terms of degrees of angle. Magnification can easily be determined by dividing $f_{objective}$ by $f_{eyepiece}$.

PROBLEM 17:

The eyepiece of a telescope has an apparent field of view of, say, 40°. Its focal length is 10 millimeters. The objective has a focal length of 800 millimeters. Find: (a) the Magnifying Power; and (b) the Actual Feld of View.

Solution:

a. The Magnifying Power $= \dfrac{f_{objective}}{f_{eyepiece}} = \dfrac{800}{10}$
$= 80$ times.

b. The Actual Field of View $=$

$\dfrac{\text{apparent field of view}}{\text{magnification}} = \dfrac{40}{80} = \frac{1}{2}$ degree.

The $\frac{1}{2}$ degree means that, looking through this telescope, the observer sees a circle, the diameter of which subtends an angle of $\frac{1}{2}$ of one degree. Half a degree is approximately the angular diameter of the moon.

4. Increase in magnification increases the twinkling of the stars, and interferes materially with the observation of stars that are close together. Twinkling of stars, while very attractive to certain poets, is a source of great annoyance to an astronomical observer. **The twinkling is actually a rapid variation of the star's apparent brightness, accompanied by rapid fluctuations in its apparent position, as well as by variations in color.** These variations and fluctuations are wholly due to the effect of the earth's atmosphere on the starlight going through it; and they are greatly magnified in a large telescope. It often happens that a great telescope is rendered practically useless on a perfectly cloudless night, due to bad "seeing" conditions.

Because of these four reasons, there is a practical limit for maximum magnification. **Maximum magnification is usually kept well within 40 times for each inch of the diameter of the objective.** A 4-inch telescope would be used at the most for magnification up to 160 times.

There is also **a minimum to useful magnification, usually 4 times for every inch of diameter of objective.** If the magnification is less than this, the column of light coming out of the eyepiece will be too large to enter the pupil of the eye and some of the light will be wasted.

TELESCOPIC MOUNTINGS

One of the most important parts of a telescope, and one to which much engineering skill and ingenuity are devoted, is the mounting.

A long tube has a tendency to vibrate, making the stars "dance." A good rigid mounting greatly minimizes vibrations.

The mounting must be designed so that the telescope can be directed to any point in the sky, from the horizon to the Zenith, and to every azimuth from 0° to 360°. The simplest unit to accomplish this is a combination of vertical and horizontal axes—the telescope is attached to a fork through horizontal bearings, and thus can be rotated from horizon to Zenith through various altitudes. The fork, in turn, is able to rotate on a vertical axis through the 360° of a horizontal circle. This is the **Alt-Azimuth Mounting.** See Fig. 118.

FIG. 118. Alt-Azimuth Mounting. The telescope can be rotated about the horizontal axis A, and can thus be directed to any altitude from the horizon to the Zenith.

The telescope together with the horizontal axis can be rotated about the vertical axis B to any azimuth from 0° to 360°.

An alt-azimuth mounting is often used to obtain instantaneous values of the altitude and azimuth of stars or other heavenly bodies.

It cannot be used for long-time observations or long-exposure photography, because the stars constantly change both their altitude and azimuth. The telescope in an alt-azimuth mounting would have to be adjusted continuously for both the vertical and horizontal angle—an almost impossible job.

The Equatorial Mounting is specially designed for the purpose of keeping a star in view for long periods of time. See Fig. 119.

Fig. 119. The Equatorial Mounting. The telescope is rotated about the declination axis to the desired declination, and clamped firmly at that position. The telescope together with the declination axis rotates about the polar axis to keep the object continuously in the field of view.

Only one angle has to be adjusted continuously; this adjustment is usually performed by a small motor. In this mounting, there are also two axes, and they are also at right angles. One axis is known as the polar axis and is constructed to be parallel to the axis of the celestial sphere. The other axis, known as the declination axis, rotates about the polar axis. The telescope is attached to the end of the declination axis, and can be turned about this axis to any declination desired. Once a star of a given declination is brought into view, the telescope can be firmly clamped to the declination axis, as the declination of a star is an invariable quantity. To keep the star in view, the telescope together with the declination axis must rotate about the Polar Axis. Once this motion is properly adjusted on the motor, the telescope will follow the star continuously along its path and will have the star in its field of view at all times.

The motor must be adjusted to complete one revolution in one sidereal day.

A telescope on an equatorial mounting can also find a given star, for which the data needed are the declination and Sidereal Hour Angle. The telescope is rotated about the declination axis to the given declination and clamped in that position. The declination axis and telescope are then rotated about the polar axis to the proper Sidereal Hour Angle.

Historically, the Refracting Telescope was the first kind invented. Practically, it is still in wide use and for good reasons:

(a) The good definition obtainable with the use of lenses
(b) The wider view obtainable
(c) The smaller liability to damage from handling
(d) Its readiness for instant use

However, the Reflecting Telescope, using a mirror instead of a lens for the objective, is becoming more and more popular. Its popularity is due both to its color-correct qualities and to the fact that no light is lost by absorption in passing through glass, as well as to its relatively lower cost.

PART 2: THE REFLECTING TELESCOPE

INTRODUCTION

Newton's name is associated with the invention of this type of telescope. In the Reflector, the function of the objective lens is performed by a mirror. The incoming light is converged by a concave mirror rather than a lens. The image formed by the mirror is viewed with an eyepiece, which is basically the same as that of the refracting type of telescope. Almost everything that was said about the refracting telescope applies here. There are, however, some minor differences, and one of these is the matter of tracing of light rays.

TRACING OF LIGHT RAYS

Two of the rays starting out from each point of a luminous object can be traced along their route. One of these, ray A, leaves C in a direction parallel to the axis of the mirror, and after reflection, passes through the focus of the mirror. The other ray, ray B, leaves C in the direction of the focus. Upon reflection at the mirror's surface, this ray moves parallel to the axis.

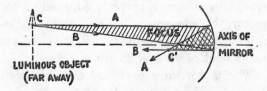

FIG. 120. Tracing of Light Rays for Objective of a Reflecting Telescope.

The routes of several rays, out of the many that emanate from luminous point C, can easily be traced.

Two of these rays are shown in this figure.

Ray A starts out parallel to axis, and is reflected by the mirror in the direction of the focus.

Ray B starts out from C in the direction of the focus, and upon hitting the mirror is reflected parallel to the axis. C' is the intersection of the reflected rays.

All other rays starting at object point C upon reflection will meet at C'.

The point of intersection of these rays (C') is where the image of C is formed. All other rays emanating from C and reflected by the mirror will meet at C'. See Fig. 120.

All other points on the object may be traced in this manner.

THE SILVERING OF THE MIRROR

Unlike the ordinary household mirror, the silver on the telescopic mirror is put on the front, or concave, side of the mirror, the glass merely acting as a support for the metal. Having the silver in front of the glass eliminates absorption. The light does not pass through the glass and does not lose part of its intensity by absorption in it.

The disadvantage is that the unprotected silver layer becomes tarnished every few months, so that the mirror must be resilvered periodically.

In recent years, an "aluminizing" process has gradually replaced silvering. It has been recently found that vaporized aluminum condensing on glass forms a brilliant surface that is in many respects superior to that of silver. The coating must be made in a vacuum; alu-

minum thus applied does not tarnish. Upon its first exposure, it becomes coated with a transparent, extremely hard, thin film of oxide of aluminum, which protects the aluminum under it from any further interaction with air.

Another superior feature of the aluminum coating is that it reflects ultraviolet light. Silver is a very poor reflector for that short-wave radiation.

Red light, however, is reflected better by silver; also, in overall reflection, silver is somewhat superior. Silver, at its best, reflects 95% of the total light; aluminum, only 90%.

LAYOUT OF OPTICAL PARTS

The mirror is placed at the lower end of the tube. The reflected light forms the image in the middle of the incoming rays. To be able to view this image through the eyepiece, it must be moved. Two arrangements that are often used were devised by Newton and Cassegrain, respectively.

In Newton's arrangement, the converging rays of light are intercepted just before the focal plane by a plane mirror. The mirror diverts the rays through the side of the tube to the eyepiece. A reflecting prism is sometimes used instead of a mirror. See Fig. 121.

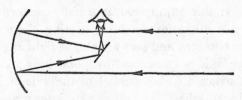

FIG. 121. The arrangement of the objective (mirror) and the eyepiece in the case of a reflecting telescope.

The mirror is at the lower end of the tube (the objective in a refractor, of course, is in the upper end).

The image produced by the mirror is amid the incoming rays. An eyepiece could not be placed there as the observer would materially interfere with the incoming light.

In the Newtonian-type telescope, the one shown here, a little plane mirror diverts the rays through the side of the tube to the eyepiece.

In a Cassegrain arrangement, a convex mirror is doing the diverting. The converging rays are intercepted by the convex mirror and brought to a focus through an opening cut in the objective. One of the advantages of this arrangement is the flexibility in the focal length of the objective mirror. A complete

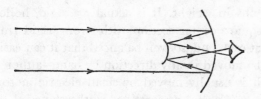

FIG. 122. The Cassegrainian Arrangement. Diverting of the image produced by the objectives is done by a small concave mirror. The converging rays reflected by the objective are reflected by this concave mirror once more and brought to a focus just beyond an opening cut in the objective.

A particular reflector may be equipped with several convex mirrors having different curvatures. The focal length of the whole telescope is altered by changing the value of the curvature of the convex mirror.

set of convex mirrors used in conjunction with the objective offers a variety of focal lengths. See Fig. 122.

Some telescopic reflectors are geared to handle both the Newtonian and Cassegrainian arrangements.

Inevitably, the small mirror or prism cuts off some of the incoming light. Relatively, the loss in light is small, a minute fraction of the total amount falling on the objective lens. The obstruction cannot be seen at the eyepiece. It does not, as one might suspect, interfere with the image.

SIMILARITIES BETWEEN REFRACTING AND REFLECTING TYPES OF TELESCOPES

Except for the objective and the arrangement for rerouting the reflected light, there are no major differences between a refracting and a reflecting telescope: the light gathering power, the resolving power, the magnifying power, and their respective formulas are identical; as are their mountings.

Each telescope has its advantages and disadvantages; each is used for the kind of research most suitable to it.

PART 3: GREAT TELESCOPES AND THEIR USES

INTRODUCTION

In his eternal search for knowledge, the astronomer designs ever larger telescopes, which enable him to see stars too faint to be seen with smaller instruments.

Larger telescopes make visible greater detail, even of remote galaxies, the study of which assists the understanding of Our Galaxy.

Thus, the astronomer hopes to answer one of the fundamental problems of his science—whether the universe has a boundary beyond which there are no stars or other heavenly bodies. And such knowledge supplies important evidence concerning the past history as well as the probable future of the universe.

THE 200″ TELESCOPE

The largest optical telescope, completed in 1948, is located on Mount Palomar, California: its objective is a mirror of 200″ diameter.

The physical principles involved in a 200″ telescope are the same as those of a small telescope. But the engineering problems that arise in making a mirror of nearly 15 tons and in the design of the complete instrument of nearly 500 tons are immense.

The basic problems of its construction and design were:

a. The choice of material for the mirror.
b. The casting and annealing process.
c. The grinding, polishing and aluminizing.
d. The design and construction of the mounting.
e. The choice of a suitable location.

a. The material used for the mirror must be hard, stony, homogeneous. It should be easy to polish and should retain the polish for a long time, expanding but little under normal variations in temperatures. All these factors are of great importance as the face of the mirror must be accurate to within about two millionths of an inch.

After testing numerous materials for suitability, the choice narrowed to two: fused quartz and a special variety of pyrex glass. Fused quartz has an ideally low coefficient of thermal expansion, five times lower than pyrex; however, the cost was prohibitive. The final choice was a variety of pyrex glass especially developed for the project.

b. The casting of the first 200″ disk took place on March 25, 1934, using large ladles to pour twenty tons of molten glass into the prepared molds—in itself a full day's work. Blasting jets of incandescent gas kept the glass both in the furnace and in the mold at a temperature of 2000° F.

Despite all the precaution and care in design, a minor accident spoiled the pouring of the first disk.

The second disk was cast on December 2nd without mishap, and after ten hours, was successfully completed. Then it was placed in the annealing oven to cool very gradually. Such a mode of cooling is important to prevent stresses and strains in the glass which might form on rapid cooling. The temperature of the oven was electrically controlled and carefully lowered by a fixed amount every 24 hours. After ten months, the disk was cooled to room temperature and was proved to be as perfect a structure as could be hoped for.

c. The grinding and polishing were done by a specially designed machine, employing a cutting abrasive against the surface of the disk.

For the initial grinding, which was to give the disk a spherical concave surface, a coarse carbide abrasive, Natalon, mixed with water, was used. Later, increasingly finer grades of abrasive were used to produce a perfect paraboloid surface.

To minimize the effect of heat resulting from the friction of grinding, the process was rather slow—four years of nearly continuous grinding and polishing were necessary to prepare the mirror for the final aluminum coating.

d. The design and construction of the mounting are evidence of the great progress engineering has made in recent years.

The polished mirror, weighing nearly 15 tons, can be pointed in any direction without the slightest sagging.

The telescope "tube" which carries the mirror so perfectly is also an imposing piece of structural design, exceeding a hundred tons in weight. It is actually a rigid, hollow square center section with strong rigid rings at each end, so well-balanced that it can easily be moved in any direction by hand—although it is usually moved by small electric motors.

e. Careful research led to the choice of the proper location.

The zone between 30° North and 35° North latitude is an ideal location. From these latitudes one can observe important areas in the southern celestial hemisphere and still have the north circumpolar stars appreciably above the horizon. This consideration narrowed the search to parts of California, New Mexico, Arizona, and other states lying within that zone.

There are many other determinants of proper location: (a) an elevation of 6,000–8,000 feet above sea level; (b) a large number of cloudless nights a year; (c) a complete absence of earthquakes or even minor tremors of the earth; (d) easy access to a large city.

Careful evaluation of various possible sites led to the choice of Mount Palomar, 80 miles northeast of San Diego in California.

There, the "Greatest Eye," as it has been called, has been engaged in the tremendous task of unravelling the mysteries of the universe.

THE GREATNESS OF THE 200″ TELESCOPE

The powers of this telescope are enormous. It gathers as much light as do a million human eyes; with its aid, one can see candlelight at a distance of 10,000 miles.

It penetrates twice as far into space—a distance of two thousand million light years—than the 100″ telescope on Mount Wilson.

THE PROGRAM OF RESEARCH

The instrument is intended to study three major problem areas: the evolution of stars; the structure of the universe; and the constitution of matter.

EARLY ACCOMPLISHMENTS

An important result was achieved in the first years of its operation. The new telescope demonstrated the previous yardstick for astronomical distances to be incorrect—the distance to the Great Galaxy in Andromeda, heretofore estimated as 750,000 light years, was fixed in 1952 at 1,500,000 light years.

PHOTOGRAPHY

Much of the "observation" is photographic: the astronomer removes the eyepiece from the telescope, attaches a photographic plate in its place, and photographs the object under observation. The objective of the telescope is thus used to form the image on the photographic plate.

Photography has many advantages over direct vision. These include the following:

a. Photographic plates can detect stars that are less than 1/6th as bright as the faintest star visible to the same telescope—primarily because the change in the chemicals of the plate is a cumulative effect: the sum total of light reaching the plate during the period of exposure. The eye sees all it can at one instant; the light energy does not accumulate on the retina.

b. A long-period exposure produces details unseen by visual observation, a result of the cumulative effect of the chemicals on the plate. Much of our knowledge of remote galaxies is yielded by the detail made possible by photography.

c. Permanency of record is especially important in studying changes in brightness and the relative displacement of stars. Some unimportant star may suddenly become prominent; the records can be examined for its past history.

d. Study at leisure. Some stars are above the horizon for rather brief periods; photographs taken then can be studied at the convenience of the astronomer.

e. Enlargements. Photographs can be magnified with the aid of a microscope, especially helpful in the mechanical task of counting stars, and of particular interest for globular clusters of stars.

f. In the study of our own Solar System, much use is made of photography. Thus, the newest member of the planetary system, Pluto, was first discovered on a photograph. Stars show up as single points while moving objects such as planetoids photograph as short lines, even in an exposure of several hours.

PART 4: THE RADIO TELESCOPE

In recent years the radio telescope has helped us to learn much about our universe. This information has been derived from a study of radio waves reaching us from outer space.

A radio telescope has a **mirror**, a **receiver**, and a **recorder**. The mirror is paraboloidal-shaped and is made from accurately machined aluminum or, in the case of larger units, from wire meshing. Its job is to focus the radio waves intercepted by it on the feeder for transmission to the receiver.

The **mirror** should be as large as possible, since radio signals are very faint. The power falling on earth from the most intense radio sources is about 100 watts, of which only 10^{-14} watts are intercepted by a giant radio telescope. One of the largest radio telescopes is a 600-foot steerable paraboloid.

The resolving power or the ability to distinguish fineness of detail is improved in direct proportion to the increase in size of the mirror. The resolving power is determined by the following formula:

$$\text{Resolving power (seconds of arc)} = \frac{10^5 \times \text{Wave length (in cms)}}{\text{Diameter of mirror (in inches)}}$$

The resolving power of a 600-ft. radio telescope for a 10 cm. wave is

$$\text{Resolving power (in seconds of arc)} = \frac{10^5 \times 10}{600 \times 12} = 138'' = 2'\,18''$$

Thus two radio sources emitting 10 cm. radio waves can just be separated by the 600-foot telescope if they are more than 2 minutes and 18 seconds of an arc apart.

The **receiver** selects a narrow band of frequencies and amplifies the power in the band. Most receivers use the type of circuits utilized in an ordinary home radio.

The **recorder** presents the receiver's output in graphic form and indicates the intensity of the signal. The amplified signal actuates the recording pen, which is in continuous contact with a moving chart.

CHAPTER VI

THE CHEMISTRY OF STARS: SPECTROSCOPY

INTRODUCTION

One of the most notable scientific advances in recent decades has been in the field of the chemistry of stars. It has been almost definitely established that the stars are made up of the same elements as those of the earth, although the relative proportions of the elements differ substantially. Thus, more than 50% of the mass of a star is usually Hydrogen; and Helium may account for almost 40% of its mass. All the other metallic and non-metallic elements account for only several per cent of the mass of the star.

These results, as well as a great deal of other information about the stars, are derived from careful analysis of the light that reaches us from the stars. **The branch of science that deals with such analysis is called "Spectroscopy," and its basic instrument is the Spectroscope.**

THE SPECTROSCOPE

The function of a spectroscope is to disperse a ray of light into its constituent colors —a process similar to the one performed by the water droplets in clouds to form a rainbow.

The dispersion of the white light, say, into its several colors is done either by a glass prism, or by a grating.

THE PRISM SPECTROSCOPE

A single ray of ordinary light, say sunlight, will be dispersed upon entering the glass of the prism into a continuous array of colors. It will be further dispersed on emerging from the prism into the air. **Such an arrangement of colors is called a spectrum.** In the case of sunlight, the spectrum will contain all the seven principal colors: violet, indigo, blue, green, yellow, orange and red. All the intermediate color transitions will also be present. See Fig. 123.

Two basic physical principles govern the dispersion into the several colors:

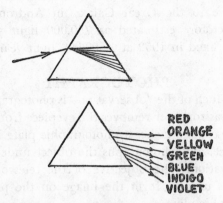

RED
ORANGE
YELLOW
GREEN
BLUE
INDIGO
VIOLET

FIG. 123. The Prism. Sunlight upon entering the prism is dispersed into a complete spread of colors, called a spectrum.

Upon coming out of the prism the colors are spread out still further.

A screen held perpendicular to these rays would show a color scheme very much similar to a rainbow.

a. **Light is a form of energy that can be thought of as consisting of waves. The** experimental evidence is that red light differs from blue light only in wave length. Red light has the longest wave length in the visible spectrum; violet, the shortest.

Wave length, as the name indicates, is the horizontal distance between crests of two adjacent waves. See Fig. 124. It is usually stated in terms of an extremely small unit of length, known as an Angstrom. One Angstrom is equal to 1/10,-000,000,000 of a meter. In these units,

FIG. 124. Wave Length. Light may be thought of as waves. Technically light is known as one branch of a very large group called Electromagnetic Waves.

As far as we know the only basic difference between violet and blue light is in wave length.

Wave length is the horizontal distance between the crests of two adjacent waves. It is often measured in one ten-billionth part of a meter (an Angstrom).

wave lengths of red light are approximately 8,000 Angstrom; the wave length of violet light is about 4,000 Angstrom.

b. The refraction suffered by light on entering glass depends on the wave length: the short wave violet is refracted more than the long wave red light. The several colors originally contained in the ray of white light are thus refracted by different amounts and hence, dispersed.

In addition to the prism, the other essential elements of a prism spectroscope are a narrow slit, a collimator, and a telescope.

The narrow slit is the gate through which the light enters the spectroscope. The slit is made fairly narrow to prevent overlapping of colors in the spectrum.

The narrow slit is placed at the focus of an achromatic lens called the "collimator," the function of which is to reroute the rays of light into parallel paths. See Fig. 125.

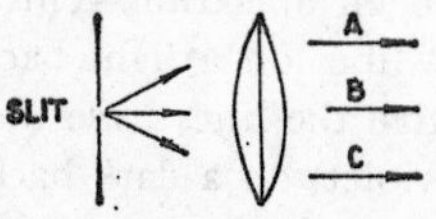

FIG. 125. The Slit and the Collimator. The slit is placed at the focus of the collimating lens (the word collimate means "to straighten out"). The diverging light rays are brought into parallel tracks by that lens.

Each parallel ray, on passing through the prism, is dispersed into the various colors. Thus, ray A produces a complete red-to-violet spectrum; similarly, ray B produces a complete red-to-violet spectrum; and so on.

The task of collecting the red components of all the rays in one place is performed by the objective of the telescope: it brings together all the dispersed red components as well as the dispersed components of the other colors, and places them side by side. The eye, looking through the eyepiece of the telescope, sees the procession of colors that is the spectrum—consisting, of course, of images of the narrow slit, each image formed by light of a particular wave length. See Fig. 126. If the light admitted through the narrow slit contains all the wave lengths, the images form a continuous succession. If some wave lengths are missing in the light entering the spectroscope, the spectrum will not be continuous. The place usually occupied by the missing wave lengths will appear black.

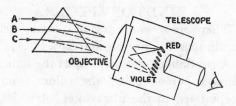

FIG. 126. The Telescope Part of the Spectroscope. Each ray is dispersed into a complete spectrum. The objective of the telescope collects all the red components into one place, all the violet components into another place. Looking through the eyepiece, an observer sees the complete spectrum of colors, from red to violet.

Some sources of light, e.g., a neon light, emit only a few definite wave lengths—the spectrum will appear as a series of bright lines separated by wide black bands. Each bright line is an image of the slit in one of the wave lengths that was present in the light.

In the above discussion, light was described variously as a wave motion, and as a ray. The wave is the correct picture; the ray is used only to indicate the direction in which the wave of light is moving.

THE GRATING SPECTROSCOPE

In a grating spectroscope, the prism is replaced by a grating—in its simplest form, a piece of glass on which a large number of parallel lines have been ruled. The more lines per inch, the better the grating: good gratings have as many as fifty thousand lines per inch. Light going through a grating will be dispersed into its various colors; the dispersion, however, in this case is not based on refraction as with the prism, but is rather due to interference between light rays that are transmitted in the spaces between the rulings.

COMPARISON OF SPECTROSCOPES

The grating spectroscope is superior to the prism spectroscope in that it gives a larger spread to the spectrum.

The prism spectroscope concentrates the

light within a narrow space, producing a brighter spectrum than does the grating spectroscope. It is used exclusively for examining the light coming from faint stars and nebulae.

KINDS OF SPECTRA

There are several kinds of spectra, such as: continuous; bright line; and dark line.

A continuous spectrum is, as the name implies, a parade of all the colors from the deepest red to the ultraviolet—of which the rainbow in the sky is a good example. In the laboratory a continuous spectrum can be produced by heating a solid, a liquid, or an opaque gas to a fairly high temperature—several thousand degrees Fahrenheit. Light from the electric lamp filament, for example, produces such a spectrum. See Fig. 127.

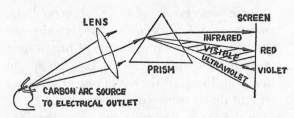

FIG. 127. A Continuous Spectrum. The visible light from a carbon arc lamp will produce a continuous spectrum with a color spread from red to violet. Note that the visible spectrum is only one part of the complete spectrum.

Beyond the visible violet, there is ultraviolet light that is invisible to the human eye; it can be detected either by a fluorescent screen or by use of photographic plates.

Beyond the visible red there is a wide region of radiation, invisible to the human eye, known as infrared.

One of the ways of detecting infrared radiation involves the use of a thermocouple. The radiation heats one junction of the thermocouple, producing an electric current in it: this current can be measured with a galvanometer.

When light emitted by a gas through which an electrical discharge is passing produces a spectrum consisting of a few isolated parallel lines, it is known as a "bright line spectrum." See Fig. 128.

The spectrum produced by hydrogen consists of only several bright lines, on a black background. See Fig. 129

Note that the shape of the "bright line" is

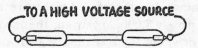

FIG. 128. Production of a Bright Line Spectrum. One of the ways of producing a bright line spectrum is to:

a. fill this tube with the gas desired (low pressure),

b. attach it to a high (several thousand volts) electric potential.

The light given off by the gas forms a bright line spectrum, when viewed through a spectroscope.

due to the narrow slit. Had the slit been in the form of a crescent, the lines would be crescent-shaped.

The characteristic color of neon signs is due to bright red and orange lines in its spectrum. See Fig. 130.

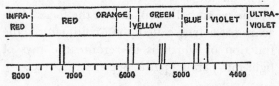

FIG. 129. Hydrogen Spectrum. This is a picture of a negative (black lines on a light background).

On the positive the lines have the colors indicated (orange, blue, violet) on a dark background.

The numbers are in Angstrom units.

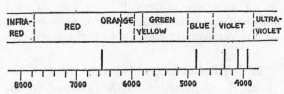

FIG. 130. Neon Spectrum. The typical color of neon signs is due to the great intensity of the red and orange lines; these lines overshadow the other colors present in the spectrum. This is a negative of the spectrum seen. On the positive the lines have the indicated colors, while the background is black.

The numbers are in Angstrom units.

Bright lines of any element can also be produced by placing a volatile salt of that element in a flame.

The spectrum due to sodium vapors shows only one visible yellow line against a dark background. On closer examination, the yellow line turns out to be a doublet, that is, two very close lines, denoted by the symbols D_1 and D_2. See Fig. 131.

It should be carefully noted that each element always gives the same pattern of lines. Each element, so to speak, has its own fingerprints, possessed by no other element. This fact is utilized in chemical analysis and in many other applied fields.

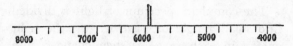

FIG. 131. Sodium Spectrum. The yellow light typical of sodium lamps is due primarily to the two very bright lines in the yellow region of the spectrum.

Spectral lines are often denoted by letters and numbers.

The two lines of the sodium spectrum are known as the D_1 and D_2 lines. The wave length of the D_1 line is 5896 Angstrom, while that of the D_2 line is 5890 Angstrom. The two lines are so close together that under poor resolution they appear as one wide line.

The numbers are in Angstrom units.

Dark line spectrum is due to absorption of light of particular wave length by relatively cool gases. The wave lengths absorbed are identical to the wave lengths that the gas would emit when properly excited.

Cool sodium vapor would remove the two yellow D_1 and D_2 lines from a continuous spectrum. See Fig. 132.

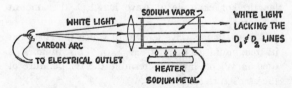

FIG. 132. Dark Line Spectrum. Ordinary light, having a continuous spectrum, would lose some of its components on going through a "cool" gas. The components lost are always identical with the ones the gas would emit when giving off light. Thus sodium vapor removes the D_1 and D_2 lines from the continuous spectrum. One way of producing such a dark line spectrum is indicated here.

The spectrum of sodium would then appear as two close dark lines on a background of an otherwise continuous spectrum. See Fig. 133.

Star spectra are of the "dark line" kind. The continuous spectrum originates at the surface of the star; the dark lines are caused

FIG. 133. A Dark Line Spectrum due to Sodium Vapor. This is a reverse of the bright line spectrum. The D_1 and D_2 yellow lines appear dark, on a background of a continuous spectrum. (Note that this is a negative and hence dark and light are reversed.)

by the relatively cooler outer atmosphere of the star.

A typical spectrum of light coming from a star is shown in Figure 134.

FIG. 134. A Typical Spectrum of a Star. Stellar spectra are dark line spectra. Some of the dark lines are due to Hydrogen, others to Helium, still others to other elements. From a careful study of these lines, the chemicals present on a star, as well as other information, are obtained.

STAR SPECTRUM

An analysis of such a spectrum would resolve the lines into several sets, each due to one of the ninety-two known elements. Thus, spectroscopy aids in determining the chemicals contained in each star and the relative proportions of these elements—determined from the relative brightness of the various sets of lines.

The analysis refers to the elements in the atmosphere of the star. It is highly probable that the composition of the interior of a star is similar to that of its atmosphere.

CHAPTER VII

PHYSICS OF THE STARS

PART 1: TEMPERATURE OF STARS

INTRODUCTION

The spectrum derived from a star's light is also used to determine the star's temperature at its surface, the layer known as "photosphere." The temperatures of stellar photospheres are very much lower than the temperatures in the interior of the stars.

Temperatures are usually stated in the Absolute (or Kelvin) scale: To change from the Absolute scale to the Centigrade scale, 273° are subtracted from the former. The temperature of the photosphere of the stars is in the thousands of degrees Absolute.

Typical temperatures of stellar surfaces are about 5,000 to 7,000° A. Extremely hot stars, like Zeta Puppis, have a temperature of 30,000° A, and there is reason to believe that some stars have surface temperatures as high as 50,000° A. On the other extreme, the coolest known star, Chi Cygni, a variable star, at the time of its minimum brightness has a temperature of a mere 1800° A, or about 1500° Centigrade.

NOTE: To change from Centigrade to the common Fahrenheit scale, multiply the former by $\frac{9}{5}$ and add 32.

The temperature of Chi-Cygni on the Fahrenheit scale would be

$$1500 \times \frac{9}{5} + 32 = \text{approximately } 2700° \text{ F}$$

COMPUTING STELLAR TEMPERATURES

In order to determine the temperature of a star from its spectrum, three preliminary steps are necessary: (a) determine the energy distribution of the spectrum; (b) find the wave length of maximum energy; and (c) use Wien's law.

a. Determination of Energy Distribution of Spectrum

The complete spectrum of light is divided into small ranges of wave length; the light energy in each range is then changed into heat energy by absorption in a black body. The value of the energy available in each narrow range of wave length can thus be determined by the rise in temperature of the black body.

The results of this work, when plotted, determine a curve such as the one in Figure 135.

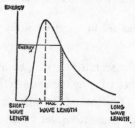

FIG. 135. Distribution of Energy in a Spectrum. The various colors in a spectrum differ greatly in their intensity, i.e., in the amount of energy contained in them.

This is a typical graph showing the amount of energy (vertical scale) that is available at any wave length. For example at wave length λ the amount is Energy$_\lambda$.

The particular wave length for which the curve has its maximum is denoted as λ_{max}. This number is used in Wien's law to determine the temperature of the star's surface.

The horizontal scale is in Angstroms. The mean wave length for each narrow range is thus used in plotting. Short wave lengths are identified as violet light; long wave lengths, red and infra-red.

The vertical scale—for which units of ergs, calories or BTU's may be used—is in energy available in these ranges of wave lengths.

b. Wave length of Maximum Energy

Of immediate interest is that for a definite wave length, this curve has a maximum. The wave length is denoted by the symbol $\lambda_{max.}$, and is used to compute the star's temperature.

c. Wien's Law

Wilhelm Wien (1864–1928) derived a simple formula relating $\lambda_{max.}$ to temperature:

$$T = \frac{289 \times 10^5}{\lambda_{max.}}$$

This formula states that the wave length for which the energy is at a maximum is inversely proportional to temperature, or, the higher the temperature, the smaller the value for $\lambda_{max.}$. This can easily be verified. When iron is heated it gives off first a dull red heat (long wave length); then, as the temperature rises, the color of the light changes to orange, yellow, and blue (short wave length).

Wien's formula enables us quickly to compute temperature of stellar bodies, once $\lambda_{max.}$ has been determined.

In the case of our sun, the wave length of maximum energy is 4700 Angstrom. The temperature of the solar photosphere is

$$T = \frac{289 \times 10^5}{4700} = 6150° \text{ A.}$$

The temperature determined in this manner is known as the "black body" temperature.

OTHER METHODS OF DETERMINING TEMPERATURES

Two other methods are often used—one involves the total area under the curve; the other, energy values taken at several wave lengths along the energy curve.

In the first case, the total energy under the curve, rather than merely the maximum, is used to determine the temperature of the sun. The value obtained is 5750° A. This value is referred to as the "Effective Temperature."

In the second case, the relative intensity of light at several different wave lengths is used. The temperature derived by this method is known as "Color Temperature." The sun's color temperature is close to 7000° A.

NOTE: 1. It is repeated here that these are the temperatures of the surface layers emitting stellar light. The temperatures in the interior of the stars are of an entirely different order of magnitude. Interior temperatures range not in the thousands but in the **millions** of degrees. These temperatures will be discussed later.

NOTE: 2. The three methods of computation give three different values for the temperature of the sun's surface; the true temperature is probably some average of these.

PART 2: STELLAR DISTANCES

INTRODUCTION

Some stars are fairly close to us; light emanating from them reaches us in a few years; the remoteness of other stars staggers the imagination.

This section deals with two methods of determining distances of stars.

DIRECT METHOD

The method used to find the distance to a star is known as triangulation. In this method, often used by surveyors, a distance such as AC is determined by measuring three quantities—the length of an arbitrarily chosen line, such as AB, and two angles, A and B. The line AB is known as a line of position. Using the line of position and the two angles, the distance AC is computed. See Fig. 136.

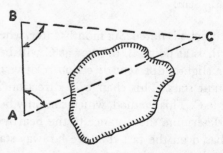

FIG. 136. Finding Distances by the Method of Triangulation. To find the distance between points A and C which may happen to be on opposite sides of a lake, say, a line of position, AB, is laid out. Knowing the length of the line AB, and the two angles A and B, it is easy to compute the desired length AC.

Standard formulas from elementary trigonometry are involved in these computations. Accuracy is obtained when the line of position is comparable in size to the distance to be determined. Thus, if AC is 2 miles, the line of position should also be about 2 miles long.

In finding distances to stars, the diameter of the earth's orbit about the sun, AB can be used as the line of position C; the angle C is measured, and the assumption is made that AC = AB.

The difficulty encountered in the case of stellar distances is that the line of position is small compared to the distances to be determined. The largest distance available to the astronomer is the diameter of the earth's orbit around the sun. Even this line of position, 186 million miles long, is only a minute fraction of the distance to one of the closer stars.

To find the angle C, the following procedure is followed:

The position of a star (see Fig. 137) close to the Solar System is observed with respect to faraway stars. When the earth is at point A, the direction in which we see the star at C relative to the direction in which we see far-

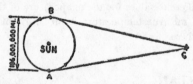

Fig. 137. Method of Determining the Distance to Nearby Stars.

away stars is noted. Six months later, when the earth is at point B, the star at C will be seen in a slightly different direction relative to the distant stars. This change in direction is the angle C. This method, which can only be used to determine the distance to the nearby stars, is based on the fact that the faraway stars do not change their relative positions in a six-month period.

NOTE 1: Distance to a star usually signifies the distance between the center of the star and the center of the sun. At times it signifies the distance between the center of the star and the center of the earth. The difference between the two, the radius of the earth's orbit, is insignificant in measuring the stellar distance.

NOTE 2: By agreement among astronomers, the radius of the earth's orbit, and not the diameter, is taken as a line of position.

NOTE 3: **The angle subtended by the star on the radius is known as the "Parallax": the more distant the star, the smaller its parallax. See Fig. 138.**

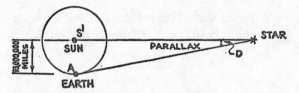

Fig. 138. The angle D in the triangle is known as the Parallax.

The parallaxes of stars are extremely small angles. Even the nearest star, Alpha-Centauri, has a parallax of only .756 seconds of angle. This is a much smaller angle than the diameter of a dime would subtend at a distance of a mile. Other stars subtend angles of .1 second and less. The direct method of parallaxes has already determined the distances of 6000 stars. The distances to the vast majority of stars *cannot* be found by this method, because the parallaxes of those stars are much too small to be measured even with the best available instruments.

Measurement of such extremely small angles is a very exacting and laborious job.

In the process of finding the parallaxes for the various stars many corrections have to be applied to the readings taken by the observer. (Some of these corrections are now automatically carried out by techniques developed in measuring parallaxes.)

Some of these corrections are due to the motion of the star; others are due to the motion of the observer; still others are due to refraction of light by the earth's atmosphere.

During the six months' interval between observations, the star itself may have moved slightly, relative to other stars. In the same interval, the whole Solar System, together with the observer, may have changed position. To obtain a reasonable estimate of the magnitude of these corrections, several sets of measurements extending over a period of several years are taken for each star under study. From measurements taken a full year apart, estimates can be made on the correction necessitated by the motions. Corrections due to the refraction of light by the earth's atmosphere have to be carefully computed, otherwise serious errors in the distance determination may be introduced. In routine parallax work several of these corrections are automatically accounted for.

UNITS OF STELLAR DISTANCES

The distances to stars are so great that the ordinary units—miles—are no longer practicable. The nearest star is 25,000,000,000,000 miles away—a number too awkward to write, to remember, or to use.

Three units are commonly used in Astronomy: (a) the Astronomical Unit; (b) the Parsec; and (c) the Light Year.

(a) The Astronomical Unit is, by definition, equal in length to the distance from the earth to the sun—93 million miles.

This unit, astronomically speaking, is a fairly small one, and is used primarily in stating distances within the Solar System. Thus, the distance of the planet Pluto is 40 Astronomical Units, or 40 × 93,000,000 miles (3,720,000,000).

(A.U. is the proper abbreviation for Astronomical Unit.)

(b) The definition of the Parsec is based on a triangle as follows:

If I, in a triangle, one of the angles is 90°; and if II, one of the legs at the right angle is 93 million miles long; and if III, the angle opposite it is one second; then, the length of the other 90° leg is equal to One Parsec. Thus, if angle B is the 90° angle, AB is 1 A.U. long, and angle D is 1 second of angle in size, then BD will have the length of **One Parsec.** See Fig. 139.

Fig. 139. Definition of a Parsec. If: I. The angle B is 90°; II. the side of AB is 93,000,000 miles long; and III. the angle D is 1 second, then: the side BD is equal in length to one Parsec.

A parsec is an extremely large distance. In terms of miles one such unit is equal to about twenty thousand billion miles.

The vastness of the parsec does not show up too well in Fig. 139, because the triangle is not drawn to scale.

When properly drawn angle A is very close to a 90° angle (it is 90° minus 1 second); the sides BD and AD are almost parallel and the point D will be far from the side AB.

One Parsec is 206,265 times as large as an astronomical unit.

PROBLEM 18:

1 parsec = 93,000,000 × 206,265 miles
Find the number of miles in 1 parsec.
= 19.2 trillion miles = 19,200 billion miles
= 19.2×10^{12} miles. *Answer*

In terms of this unit, the closest star, Alpha-Centauri, is at a distance of 1.3 parsecs. Other stars are at distances of hundreds and thousands of parsecs.

The close relationship between the parallax of a star and its distance in parsecs should be noted. One is given by the reciprocal of the other.

Thus, a star having a parallax of 0.5 second is 2 parsecs away, a star having a parallax of 0.2 second is 5 parsecs away, a star having a parallax of 0.1 second is 10 parsecs away, and so on.

(c) Another unit of astronomical distance is **the Light Year, defined simply as the distance traveled by a ray of light in a period of one year.** Knowing that the speed of light is 186,000 miles in one second, it is easy to compute that distance. 186,000 is multiplied by the number of seconds in a year:

$$186,000 \times 60 \frac{\text{seconds}}{\text{minutes}} \times 60 \frac{\text{minutes}}{\text{hour}} \times 24 \frac{\text{hours}}{\text{day}}$$
$$\times 365\tfrac{1}{4} \frac{\text{days}}{\text{year}}.$$

The answer is 5.88 trillion miles (5.88 × 10^{12} miles).

Using this unit of distance, Alpha-Centauri is at a distance of 4.2 light years; or, the light by which we see the star has been enroute for 4.2 years.

Distances in parsecs can easily be converted into distances in light years.

One parsec = 3.26 light years,
Two parsecs = 6.52 light years,
Ten parsecs = 32.6 light years; and so on.

PROBLEM 19:

Sirius is 8.6 light years away. Find its distance (a) in parsecs (b) in astronomical units, and (c) in miles.

In addition to the sun, Proxima-Centauri, and Alpha-Centauri, the following are among the stars closest to us: Barnard's Star is at a distance of 6.1 light years; Lalander's 21185, 7.9 light years away; Wolf 359, 8.0 light years away. (Barnard's Star, Wolf's Star, etc., are known by the names of the astronomers who investigated them.)

INDIRECT METHOD FOR MEASURING STELLAR DISTANCES

The vast majority of stars are beyond the reach of the parallax method; their distances have been determined by a rather indirect, although simple, method of comparing the apparent magnitude of a star with its absolute magnitude. This particular method of computing star distance is applicable to all stars for which the absolute magnitude is known or can be found. Thus it is applicable in finding distances to a certain type of star known as "cepheids"; the absolute magnitude of these stars can easily be found from the Period-Absolute Magnitude curve.

CEPHEIDS

A cepheid is a type of star whose brightness varies periodically. At the beginning of a period, its brightness increases very rapidly, for as long as several hours. That is followed by a gradual dimming which may continue for several days. This cycle is then repeated.

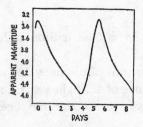

FIG. 140. Cepheids. The variation in the apparent magnitude of Delta-Cephei is shown. The maximum brightness of this particular cepheid is 3.3; at its dimmest it has an apparent magnitude of 4.5. The complete cycle repeats every 5 days and 8 hours.

See Fig. 140. The cepheids are very punctual and regular in their variation. The change in brightness from minimum to maximum is usually not very great; a change in one magnitude, say from 5.3 to 4.3, is a fairly representative value.

The first cepheid known was the delta star in Cepheus—hence the derivation of its name. Since the discovery of the first cepheid in 1784, hundreds of similar stars have been discovered.

Cepheids are discussed under Variable Stars. The aspect of immediate interest is the fact that

a. the absolute magnitude of these stars can easily be found (from the Period-Absolute Magnitude Curve), and

b. knowing the absolute magnitude, and the average apparent magnitude (the latter is obtained from direct observation), the distance to the star can be determined.

To find the distance of a cepheid, the following method may be used:

1. Determine the period of a cepheid.
2. Use Period-Absolute Magnitude Curve to find absolute magnitude of the star.
3. Observe average apparent magnitude of the star.
4. Substitute average magnitude and absolute magnitude in formula and find the distance.

ABSOLUTE MAGNITUDE

The apparent magnitude of a star depends upon both its intrinsic brightness and its distance.

To be able to compare intrinsic brightness of different stars, it is necessary to eliminate the dependence upon distance.

The concept of Absolute Magnitude does just that. In this concept it is assumed that all the stars were removed from their real location to a new place, exactly 10 parsecs away from the terrestrial observer.

Naturally, stars that are brought closer to the terrestrial observer will appear brighter, while stars that had to be "pushed" to the 10 parsec line will now appear dimmer. **The** new magnitude that will be assigned to the stars when they are 10 parsecs away is known as **Absolute Magnitude**. Most stars are at distances greater than 10 parsecs; the sun, however, with an apparent magnitude of −26.7, when moved to a distance of 10 parsecs, would have an absolute magnitude of +4.8. It would then appear as one of the fainter stars, and would be invisible to observers with below-average vision.

PERIOD OF CEPHEIDS AND ABSOLUTE MAGNITUDE

A remarkable relationship has been discovered between the period of a cepheid and its absolute magnitude.

The discovery dates back to the research in 1908 of Miss Henrietta Leavitt at the Harvard College Observatory concerning cepheid stars in the Small Magellanic Cloud. The Small Magellanic Cloud as well as the Large Magellanic Cloud are in reality galaxies—close neighbors to Our Galaxy.

The clouds named after the Portuguese navigator appear to the naked eye as two faint patches of light. They cannot be seen from the United States as they are within 20° of the South Celestial Pole.

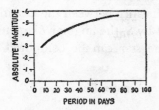

Fig. 141. Period-Absolute Magnitude Curve. The curve shows the relationship between the absolute magnitude of a cepheid and its period.

The absolute magnitude is directly read off the curve, once the period of the star is known.

The period of a cepheid is obtained from direct observation of the star.

The important result of the discovery made by Miss Leavitt is that **all the cepheid stars** having the same period have the same absolute magnitude. Stars having long periods have high values for absolute magnitude; short-period stars, low values.

This relationship can best be expressed in the form of a graph, in which absolute magnitudes are plotted on the vertical axis and the period, on the horizontal. See Fig. 141.

Magnitudes, in case of variable brightness stars, are taken to be the mean of the maximum and minimum values.

DETERMINATION OF DISTANCE WITH ABSOLUTE MAGNITUDE

Given (a) the absolute magnitude of a star, denoted by M, and (b) the apparent magnitude of a star, denoted by m, it is easy to compute the distance.

The formula applying in this case is $M = m + 5 − 5 \log D_{ps}$. D_{ps} stands for the distance in parsecs.

This formula can also be written as

$$\text{Log } D_{ps} = \frac{1}{5}(m − M) + 1$$

Example: The absolute magnitude, M, of a star is 0.60.

The apparent magnitude of the same star is .14.

$$\text{Log } D_{ps} = \frac{1}{5}(.14 − .60) + 1 = .91$$

Using a table of logarithms to the base 10, one finds that $D_{ps} = 8.1$ parsec.

This indirect method of determining distance is a splendid example of progress in science. First came several seemingly unrelated discoveries; later, connection among these was established and a powerful new method resulted. In this instance, first the cepheids were discovered; then, the relationship between period and absolute magnitude —leading to a novel way of determining distance to remote bodies.

PART 3: SIZE OF STARS

INTRODUCTION

Stars are of various sizes; the smallest known one, with a diameter of a mere 4,000 miles, is technically identified by its catalog number AC + 70° 8247. (Astrographic Catalog, star No. 8247, 70° North declination.)

The largest known star, Epsilon-Aurigae B, has a diameter nearly 3,000 times that of the sun. (The sun's diameter is 864,000 miles.)

The diameter of a star cannot be measured directly with the aid of a telescope. Even in a large telescope, stars appear simply as points of light, having no measurable diameter.

SIZE OF STARS AS DETERMINED BY THE INTERFEROMETER

An ingenious method—based on light interference—has been used in recent years to measure the diameter of stars. This method actually measures only the angular diameter; but this is not a drawback, since the true diameter can easily be computed once the angular diameter *and* the distance of the star have been determined.

The angular diameter is the angle subtended by its diameter at the observer's eye.

The method, originally suggested by Michelson, was used as early as 1920 at Mount Wilson. The interferometer attached to the upper end of the 100-inch telescope consists basically of a beam of structural steel carrying four mirrors: the two outer ones, A and D, can be moved along the beam to a maximum separation of 20 feet; the two inner ones, B and C, are fixed.

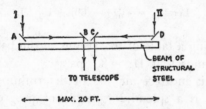

FIG. 142. A Michelson Interferometer. The mirrors I and II are moved in unison inward or outward until the dark and light fringes, seen through the eyepiece of the telescope, disappear. The angular diameter of the star is easily computed once this particular distance between the mirrors has been determined.

The function of the moving mirror is to get two beams, I and II, from the same star separated by as large a distance as possible (length of steel beam).

The function of the fixed mirrors is to divert both beams into the telescope. See Fig. 142.

It has been pretty well established that two such beams, coming, so to speak, from two different regions of the same star would produce interference. The image of the star in the telescope will no longer be a point of light, nor a spurious round diffraction disk, but a set of very fine bright and dark fringes, which appear somewhat like the teeth of a comb.

It has been determined theoretically and proven experimentally that for a certain separation between the moving mirrors, the fringes disappear. At that distance, if the star is large, the bright fringes caused by one half

FIG. 143. The image of a star as seen through the combination of Telescope and Interferometer.

The star appears as a little disk covered by alternating light and dark fringes.

For one and only one setting of the moving mirrors the fringes disappear, and the disk is equally bright throughout.

of the star overlap the dark fringes caused by the other half. At this separation of the mirrors, the image appears equally bright throughout. See Fig. 143.

If this distance between the moving mirrors is denoted by S, the angular diameter (Figure 144) of the star can be computed from the formula:

$$\text{Angular Diameter} = 12S$$

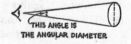

FIG. 144. Angular Diameter is the angle subtended by the diameter of a circle at the observer's eye.

The distance S must be stated in centimeters; the answer for the angular diameter is in seconds of angle.

This method is applicable only to the largest, nearest, and brightest stars. Fewer than 20 stars have had their angular diameters measured by the interferometer method. Small angular diameters would require mirror separations in hundreds of feet. However, even the few that have been measured are important as they verify the diameters of stars computed from less direct methods.

Among the stars that were measured with the interferometer are Betelgeuse, Arcturus, and Aldebaran: their angular diameters are .047″, .020″, and .020″, respectively.

As the distance to these stars is known, their linear diameter can be computed by multiplying the angular diameter by the distance. The diameter for Betelgeuse is equal to 420 times the diameter of the sun. The linear diameters for Arcturus and Aldebaran are 23 and 36 times the diameter of the sun.

SIZE OF STARS AS DETERMINED FROM LUMINOSITY

Another method for determining diameters of stars is based on the relationship between Luminosity, L, Temperature, T, and Diameter of a star, D.

Luminosity is a measure of a star's true brightness. It is usually stated in multiples or sub-multiples of the sun's brightness. The most luminous star is one in the Large Magellanic Cloud, known as S Doradus. Its luminosity of 600,000 means that it is 600,000 times brighter than our sun; that is, if the sun and S Doradus were placed at equal distances from us, say, one parsec, the latter would appear 600,000 times brighter. It also means that it sends 600,000 times as much light per second towards the earth as does the sun.

The intrinsically faintest known star is the companion to BD + 4° 4048. (Star No. 4048 in the Bonn Catalog of stars. Its declination is 4° N.) Its luminosity is only about $\frac{1}{500,000}$ that of the sun.

The luminosity of a star depends on two factors: (1) The size of the star; and (2) the amount of visible radiation it emits from each square mile of surface, which in turn depends on the surface temperature.

The formula relating the three is:

$$D = \left(\frac{5750}{T}\right)^2 \cdot \sqrt{L}$$

D is in units of the solar diameter.

T is the temperature of the surface of the star in degrees Absolute; and L is, as usual, in terms of sun's brightness.

5750 is the effective temperature of the sun's surface (photosphere).

PROBLEM 20:

Sirius has a luminosity of 27, and a temperature of 9800° A. Find its diameter.

Substituting the given data in the formula, get

$\left(\frac{5750}{9800}\right)^2 \cdot \sqrt{27} = 1.8$ times the diameter of the sun.

It should be noted that brightness of stars can be stated in various ways. Three distinct measures are often used: (a) Apparent Magnitude, (b) Absolute Magnitude, and (c) Luminosity.

The values of these for the five stars that appear brightest to us are given in the following list.

Star	Apparent Magnitude	Absolute Magnitude	Luminosity (Sun = 1)
Sirius	−1.58	+1.3	30
Canopus	−0.86	−3.2	1900
Alpha Centauri	+0.06	+4.7	1.3
Vega	+0.14	+0.5	60
Capella	+0.21	−0.4	150

This list shows that if these stars were all placed at a distance of 10 parsecs (to obtain absolute magnitude), Canopus would be by far the brightest star.

The list also shows that Vega is twice as luminous and Capella five times as luminous as Sirius.

PART 4: STELLAR MASSES AND DENSITIES

INTRODUCTION

The stars show only small variations in mass. The vast majority have masses between one-fifth and five times that of the sun.

The range is also limited. The heaviest known star HD 698 (star number 698 in a catalog of stellar spectra, prepared at Harvard University and named after the great American scientist Henry Draper) has a mass 113 times that of the sun. One of the lightest known stars is Krueger 60B, with a mass only 1/7th that of the sun.

At present, there is no direct method of finding the mass of a star. There are, however, several indirect methods; one of these can only be used in the case of pairs of stars known as visual binaries.

MASS OF VISUAL BINARIES

A binary is a pair of stars which, like the earth and moon, revolve about a common center of gravity. **If the two stars of the pair are separately visible, the pair is called a "visual binary."** Some 20,000 visual binaries are now known.

The principle involved in finding the mass of a binary is based on Kepler's Harmonic Law, which can be expressed in terms of a simple formula relating the sum of the two masses, the distance between them, and the period of revolution.

The formula is: $M + m = \dfrac{p^2}{a^3}$

where M + m is the sum of the two masses expressed in units of the sun's mass; p, the time needed for the line joining the stars to complete one revolution (which should be stated in years); and a, the mean distance between the two stars (in Astronomical Units). Both the distance, "a," and the period, "p," are determined by direct observation; the mass of the binary system, M + m, is computed with the aid of the formula.

To compute the masses of the individual stars in the pair, additional observations must be made. These concern the absolute motion of each star in the binary system about the common center of gravity. The heavier partner will describe a small ellipse about this center, while the lighter will describe a larger one. From the sizes of these ellipses, the ratio of the two masses is determined, which, with the sum of the masses, is all that is needed to determine the mass of each star.

If the sum is, say, 8 solar masses, and the ratio is 3 to 1, then their individual masses are 6 and 2 times that of the sun.

PROBLEM 21:

The sum of the masses, M + m, for Alpha-Centauri and Proxima-Centauri is 1.96.

The ratio between the masses is 1.23. Find the mass of Alpha-Centauri and the mass of Proxima-Centauri.

Answer: The mass of Alpha-Centauri is 1.08 times the mass of the sun. The mass of Proxima-Centauri is 0.88 times the mass of the sun.

Masses can also be determined for another type of binary system known as "spectroscopic binaries."

A spectroscopic binary is a pair of stars that appear as a single unit even in a large telescope. The true character of the unit shows up only in a spectroscopic study. The spectrum (see Doppler principle) indicates that the unit consists of two stars which are alternately approaching and receding, their motion being similar to the two masses of a rotating dumb-bell. There are more than a thousand known spectroscopic binaries.

Capella, the fifth star in apparent brightness, is a spectroscopic binary. The mass of the brighter member is 4.18 and that of its companion, 3.32 times the sun's mass.

MASS OF STARS OF HIGH SURFACE GRAVITY

This method to determine the mass of a star is applicable to cases of stars that have a very high surface gravity. Large values of gravitational force are present in two kinds of stars; one of them is known as White Dwarfs, the other—Trumpler Stars. The high surface gravity in the White Dwarf type is due to the fantastically high values for the density of the matter composing these stars.

White Dwarfs have a fairly normal value for mass but a greatly sub-normal (hence the name, "dwarf") value for volume. The Trumpler Stars (named after their discoverer, Robert Julius Trumpler) are of normal size but have a very high value for mass.

The masses of these stars can be computed with the aid of Einstein's General Theory of Relativity.

According to this theory, light undergoes a slight change in its wave length upon departing from a star having a high value of gravitational pull at its surface. Every light wave length is slightly increased on departure. This shift of all the wave lengths of the spectral lines to the red is known as the "relativistic shift," and is usually extremely small, though measurable. The measured values are used in computing the masses of the stars producing these shifts in the wave lengths.

DENSITIES

Density, as usual, is determined by dividing the mass by the volume. The quotient indicates how closely the matter of which the star consists is packed.

Stars vary greatly in density, primarily because of the wide range of volumes.

It strains the human imagination even to try to visualize the extreme values in star densities. One of the high density stars is the "Pup," the companion of Sirius. In mass it is equal to the sun; however, its volume is only $\frac{1}{30,000}$ as great. Since the average density of the sun is 1.5 times that of water, the average density of the Pup is 50,000 times that of water. A tablespoon of this substance would weigh a ton! And the Pup is not the densest star known.

This distinction is now held by the smallest star, AC + 70° 8247 (star number 8247 in the Astrographic catalog, 70° N declination). The present estimate of its density is 36,000,000 times that of water. A tablespoon of this substance would weigh 720 tons!

On the other extreme, there are stars that have densities less than $\frac{1}{1,000}$ of that of air. The density of these is less than the density of an ordinary vacuum obtainable in the laboratory. They are often called, in fact, "red-hot vacuum." The largest known star, Epsilon-Aurigae B, has also the distinction of having the smallest density. The value given for it is $\frac{1}{100,000,000}$ that of water.

PART 5: STELLAR MOTIONS

INTRODUCTION

It is now fairly common knowledge that the "fixed" stars move, and do so at rather high speeds; and that in the course of, say, a century, these movements will change but slightly the shape of the constellation. The fact that these high speeds have not materially disarranged the constellations is, of course, due to the great distance of the stars; and also to the rather brief period of time (in astronomic terms) that the stars have been under systematic observation.

The measurement of stellar speeds requires great precision, and is further complicated by the motion of the observer. Not only does the star move, but the observer, too, participates in motion: (a) daily revolution of the earth about its axis; (b) slight changes in direction of the earth's axis; (c) annual rotation of the earth around the sun; (d) the movement of the sun and the whole solar system in space. These motions cause displacements of the stars, called "common motions," which have, of course, nothing to do with the real movement of the stars.

Common motions must be subtracted from the total displacements of stars to obtain the true motions.

The true speed of a star, known as space velocity, is computed from its two components: one is in line of sight and is known as the radial velocity of the star; the other is perpendicular to the line of sight and is known either as cross motion or tangential velocity.

RADIAL VELOCITY

The value for this velocity is determined from the spectrum of the star. The computation makes use of a basic principle in Physics, known as the **Doppler Principle, according to which the spectrum of an approaching source of light has all its wave lengths shortened.** The change in each wave length, denoted by Δλ, is given by the formula

$$\Delta\lambda = \lambda \cdot \frac{V}{c}$$

In this formula:

λ is the original wave length of the light,
V is the relative velocity of approach, and
c is the velocity of light.

In the formula, c and λ are known. The shift in the wave lengths can easily be measured and the relative velocity of approach computed. The same formula applies to the recession of a star, in which case the shift is towards the longer wave length. The lines, instead of appearing in their normal place in the spectrum show up in new positions; the new positions of all the lines are closer to the red end of the spectrum.

In practice, photographic methods are used in this kind of work. Two spectra are photographed simultaneously on one plate, one above the other. The spectrum of the star under study is placed together with a comparison spectrum, usually one due to iron. If the star has no radial velocity, the iron lines in the stellar spectrum will coincide with the lines in the comparison spectrum. These lines will be arranged in both spectra in identical patterns.

In the case of a star having radial velocity, the lines will be displaced. The value of this displacement Δλ for any line of wave length λ is obtained directly from the plate. These values when substituted in the Doppler Formula, indicate the radial velocity of the star.

PROBLEM 22:

One of the lines due to iron in the comparison spectrum has a wave length of 5270 Angstrom. On the stellar spectrum, the same line is displaced towards the blue end of the spectrum by .527 Angstrom. The velocity of light is 3×10^5 kilometers per second. Find the radial velocity of the star.

Solution: $\quad \Delta\lambda = \lambda \cdot \dfrac{V}{c} \quad$ or $\quad V = \dfrac{\Delta\lambda}{\lambda} \cdot c$

$$V = \frac{.527}{5270} \cdot 3 \times 10^5 = 30 \text{ km/sec.}$$

Answer: The radial velocity is 30 km/sec, or 18 miles per second. The star is approaching us at that rate, since the displacement is towards the blue end of the spectrum.

The greatest radial velocity known is 547 km/sec., or 340 miles per second, possessed by star CD−29° 2277 (Cordoba Catalog Star 2277, declination 29° S).

TANGENTIAL VELOCITY

The tangential velocity of a star is also known as Cross Motion, referring to the velocity of a star in a plane perpendicular to the line of sight. It is usually stated in miles per second or in kilometers per second.

Tangential velocity cannot be found directly; it is obtained by multiplying the angular velocity of the star by its distance. It is common to call that **angular velocity "Proper Motion,"** and to state its value in seconds of angle per year.

PROPER MOTION

The greatest proper motion is exhibited by Barnard's Star (named after its discoverer, Edward Emerson Barnard, 1857–1923). The star traverses about 10.5 seconds of angle each year, and will move ½ degree (angle subtended by the moon) in about 180 years. Most stars are too remote to manifest measurable proper motions.

Out of 25,000,000 stars that have been investigated to date, fewer than ⅓ of 1% have shown evidence of proper motion.

The task of studying so large a number of

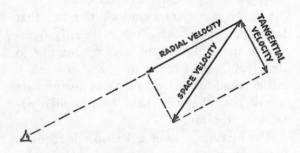

FIG. 145. Space Velocity.

a. The velocity of the star in line of sight, i.e., radial velocity, is determined with the aid of Doppler's formula.

b. The velocity perpendicular to line of sight is obtained by multiplying the angular velocity of the star by its distance.

c. The true velocity of the star in its motion through space given to scale, by the diagonal of the rectangle having radial and tangential velocity for sides.

stars is greatly simplified by using photographic methods together with a special kind of microscope known as a "blink" microscope. Photographic pictures are made of large regions of the sky at intervals of thirty years. The two pictures are then viewed through a blink microscope. There is a device in the microscope to illuminate alternately one and then the other view, in rapid succession. Stars that have moved as much as 6″ in those thirty years seem to blink, while all the others remain steady.

As indicated above, the product of proper motion, times the star distance, gives the tangential value of the stellar velocity.

SPACE VELOCITY OF STARS

Knowing the radial and tangential components, it is easy to find the true space velocity of the star. The velocity is the diagonal of a rectangle of which the radial and tangential velocities are the sides. See Fig. 145.

The highest known space velocity of a star is 660 km/sec., or 410 miles per second.

PART 6: STELLAR SPECTRA

INTRODUCTION

On a clear night, some 5,000 stars are visible to the naked eye; through a small telescope, millions; and through the Mt. Palomar telescope, billions of stars are visible. It is estimated that the number of stars in Our Galaxy alone is close to a hundred billion, and there are probably more than two billion galaxies in the universe.

A question naturally arises from the above:

Does any organizing principle govern that multitude of stars? Can the stars, like flowers or birds, be grouped into classes, each class with its own typical characteristics?

A good start towards answering this question was made in March 1913 by Professor H. N. Russell, of the Princeton Observatory.

The first weeks of March of that year were very unfavorable for astronomical observations; the skies were overcast most of the time and any kind of observatorial work seemed impossible. But Professor Russell made excellent use of this time. The result of his labor is a famous diagram, known as the Russell Diagram, which indicates a. that stars, like flowers or birds, can be grouped into several distinct classes (e.g., main sequence stars, white dwarfs, red giants, etc.); and b. that the stars we see are, like flowers or birds, in various stages of development—some are in their early youth, while others are approaching extinction. The vertical axis in the Russell diagram is graded in luminosities; the horizontal axis, in spectral classes. Luminosity is a measure of a star's true brightness, and is usually stated in multiples of the sun's brightness. The meaning of spectral classes is explained below.

SPECTRAL CLASSES

When spectra of many stars are analyzed, it is found that they can be naturally grouped into several classes. The present classification is based on extensive research pursued at Harvard College Observatory, involving a comparative study of spectra from more than 300,-000 stars. Ten distinct classes are recognized and are denoted by letters: O, B, A, F, G, K, M, R, N, S.

These letters have been chosen rather arbitrarily and the best way to remember the first nine is by the jingle: Oh, Be A Fine Girl, Kiss Me Right Now. The last letter has several versions: Smack . . . Sweetheart . . . etc.

Sub-divisions of each of these classes are recognized and designations like B2, K5, G8, etc., are used for them. K5 stands for a spectrum with characteristics half-way between K and M.

The stars Sirius and Vega are class A stars, while the star Altair is designated as A5. Class A spectra are emitted by white stars having surface temperatures of nearly 12,000° A. Characteristics of class A stars are: a. very strong dark lines due to hydrogen; b. no helium lines; c. very few and weak lines due to metals. See Fig. 146.

Other classes, too, have well-defined char-

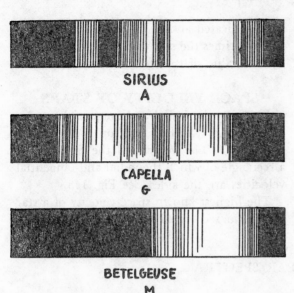

FIG. 146. Sirius is a class A star. Spectra emitted by these stars have:

    a. wide lines due to hydrogen,

    b. no lines due to helium, and

    c. very few and very thin lines due to metals.

Capella and our own sun are class G stars. Spectra emitted by these stars contain many lines due to iron and other metals. Two lines due to ionized calcium are quite eminent, while the lines due to hydrogen are much less outstanding than in class A stars.

Betelgeuse is a class M star. Low temperature lines are strong—that is to say, spectral lines that can be produced by low temperature sources of light are prominent in this spectrum.

High temperature lines, like those which require a hot electric spark for their production in the physics laboratory, are either very weak or entirely missing.

Whole bands of lines due to titanium oxide are present in spectra of class M stars.

acteristics. The characteristics of the groups may be summarized as follows:

    a. Helium lines are present in classes O and B, reaching their maximum in B2 and fading out before reaching class A.

    b. Hydrogen is the only element present in all ten series. The lines are strongest in spectra of class A.

    c. High temperature metallic lines make their first appearance in class A, rising to maximum strength in class G. (The sun is a class G star.)

    d. Low temperature metallic lines become evident in class G and rise to great prominence in class M.

    e. Titanium oxide bands are prominent in class M stars. (Betelgeuse and Antares are class M stars.)

    f. Broad absorption bands of carbon and carbon compounds are present in spectra of class N.

    g. Class S stars are identified by the presence of bands due to zirconium oxide.

SPECTRAL CLASSES AND SURFACE TEMPERATURES OF STARS

One of the incidental but important uses of this classification is to determine stellar temperature. The variation from class to class is due, to a very large degree, to the temperature of the surface of the star. Thus, class G spectra come from stars having surface temperatures of 6000° A, Class B-23000°, Class M-3200° A, and so on. As a matter of fact, the surface temperature of any star is easily determined by a glance at its spectrum—the values thus derived are fairly accurate estimates. The relationship between spectral classes, temperature, and color is given in the table for classes O through M (above).

THE RUSSELL DIAGRAM

Each star is indicated by a point. The position of the point is determined by the star's luminosity and spectral class. A careful plot of these points brings out two very important features of this diagram (Figure 147):

    a. The vast majority of the stars fit within a narrow band that runs from the upper left-hand corner to the lower right-hand corner of the diagram. It is known as the Main Sequence, and the stars belonging to it, including our sun, are known as Normal Stars, or Main Sequence Stars.

Spectral Class	O	B	A	F	G	K	M
Temperature (in degrees Absolute)	25000	23000	10000	7000	6000	5000	3200
Color	very blue	bluish-white	white	yellowish white	yellow	orange	red

FIG. 147. The Russell Diagram. On a complete diagram there are several thousands of dots. Each dot represents the luminosity and the stellar spectrum of one star. The values of absolute magnitude may be used instead of the values of luminosity for the vertical scale. Similarly the surface temperature of the star may be used instead of the spectral class for the horizontal scale.

The dot representing our sun is indicated in the proper place; the sun has an absolute magnitude of 4.8 and is in the G spectral class.

Stars brighter than +1 absolute magnitude are classified as giants; all the other stars are classified as dwarfs.

Many astronomers define a dwarf star as any star on the Main Sequence or below it.

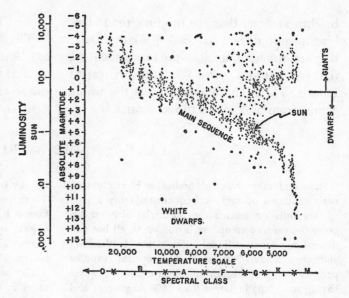

b. The marked regularity in the Main Sequence has two very important exceptions. The dots for two well-defined types of stars fall far from the Main Sequence. One set of dots is scattered in the upper right-hand side of the diagram. These are stars having high luminosity, but low temperature, and are called "Red Giants." (The star Capella belongs to this class.) The other set of dots off the Main Sequence are concentrated in a small region in the lower left-hand side of the diagram. These are stars with low luminosity, but high surface temperatures. They are appropriately called "White Dwarfs." The Pup (companion of Sirius) is a classic example of a White Dwarf.

THE NORMAL STARS

The fact that these stars are assembled along a narrow band and not distributed in a disorderly manner all over the diagram suggests a close relationship between them. The stars in this sequence are presumably similar in most of their characteristics. Their spread along the sequence is most likely due to differences in masses, the more massive stars being the more luminous.

The mass of a star is closely connected with its luminosity. The relationship between the two can be derived from purely theoretical considerations. Figure 148 indicates graphically this relationship. It is known as Mass-

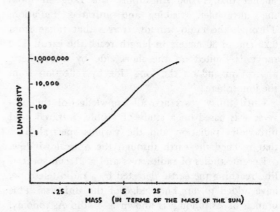

FIG. 148. Mass-Luminosity Law. Great luminosity of a star attends great mass.

The numbers on the horizontal scale are in terms of the mass of the sun (e.g., 5 times the mass of our sun).

The numbers on the vertical scale are in terms of luminosity (e.g., 100 times as luminous as our sun).

Luminosity indicates the total amount of light emitted by the star in the direction of a terrestrial observer.

Luminosity Law. **Thus the more massive the star, the more luminous it will be.** To be exact, the mass of the star determines only the light emanating *per unit area* of the star. The total amount of light leaving the star depends on the mass of the star and on its size.

The stars of high luminosity occupying the upper portion of the diagram are known as Giants. The low luminosity stars are called Dwarfs. The dividing point between Giants and Dwarfs is based on absolute magnitude of brightness. Stars that are brighter than absolute magnitude +1 are called Giants; those that are dimmer than absolute magnitude +1 (i.e., magnitudes +2, +3, etc.) are called Dwarfs. The Main Sequence runs the whole gamut from blue giants to red dwarfs.

THE ABNORMAL STARS

The stars off the Main Sequence are known as "Abnormal" or "Peculiar" stars. These stars as well as other "peculiar" stars, such as novae and supernovae, are the subject of the next chapter.

PART 7: RADIO ASTRONOMY

Stars and other celestial bodies emit electromagnetic radiation of various frequencies. Only a part of this radiation reaches the terrestrial observer because the earth's atmosphere is opaque to all but two limited ranges of radiation, the "Optical Window" and the "Radio Window." The optical window permits the transmission of electromagnetic waves having wave lengths larger than 3000 Angstroms and smaller than 10,000 Angstroms; this range includes the ultraviolet, visible, and infrared radiation. Through the radio window, waves that range from 0.25 cm. to 30 meters in length reach the earth. The range is limited on the short side by atmospheric absorption and on the long side by reflection from the ionosphere.

Until thirty years ago all knowledge of the universe was based on a study of visible, infrared, and ultraviolet radiation and the various spectral lines that reached the earth through the optical window.

Recent studies of radiowaves and a 21 cm. spectral line reaching the earth, detected by a radio telescope, have added to our knowledge of the universe. This branch of Astronomy is known as Radio Astronomy.

Research in Radio Astronomy has been devoted mainly to the study of **intensity distribution, discrete sources, the 21 cm. hydrogen line and solar and planetary emission.**

a. Intensity distribution. Several surveys of the intensities of radio waves in the sky have been made.

b. Discrete source. There are about 2000 points in the sky from which very intense radiation is emitted. These points, formerly called radio stars,* are now known by the term "discrete sources." In most cases objects other than stars are responsible for these waves. These points are the most intense discrete source.

The second most intensive discrete source is located in Cygnus and is known as Cygnus A. Photographs show that the source is associated with a collision between two spiral galaxies.

Another intense discrete source is associated with the Crab Nebula in Taurus. The Crab Nebula resulted from an exploded supernova in Taurus.

c. The 21 cm. hydrogen line. Neutral hydrogen atoms can emit radiation of 21 cm. wave lengths when the electron spin changes its orientation. With the aid of this spectral line and a knowledge of the Doppler principle, the distribution and motion of the hydrogen present in interstellar space—in Our Galaxy and other galaxies—can be studied.

d. Solar and planetary emission. The sun is an intense radio emitter, particularly during a period of sunspots and flares. Research on the relationship between these emissions and the ionosphere is being pursued. Planets such as Jupiter also emit radio signals.

* The first true radio star that we are able to see and listen to at the same time was discovered early in 1961. It is a sixteenth-magnitude star, known as 3C-48, in the constellation Triangulum.

CHAPTER VIII

THE NATURE OF STARS AND INTERSTELLAR SPACE

PART 1: "PECULIAR" STARS

INTRODUCTION

Several types of stars are called "Peculiar Stars," among them the White Dwarfs, Red Giants, Cepheids, RR Lyrae Variables, Long Period Variables, Novae and Supernovae. Their peculiarity is due to some abnormality in brightness: less than normal in the case of white dwarfs; continuous change in the case of cepheids, for example.

THE WHITE DWARFS

In color, these stars are similar to the white stars of spectral class A. Their luminosity, however, is extremely small. Many white dwarfs have a luminosity less than $\frac{1}{100,000}$ that of a normal class A star. This is not due to lack of mass, as they compare well in this respect with the mass of the sun. Their faint luminosity is due to their small size. Naturally, stars with fair-sized mass and small volume have high values of density. These high values were already noted in the consideration of the red shift in the light leaving these stars; it was noted there that a tablespoon of matter of a white dwarf would weigh tons.

Theoretically, there is a limit to the mass of the white dwarf: one cannot be greater than five times that of the solar mass; in fact, the heaviest known white dwarf has a mass of 3½ times that of the sun.

Theory also suggests a relationship between the mass of the dwarf and its diameter—namely, **the larger the mass, the smaller the diameter.**

Fewer than 200 white dwarfs are now known; and their origin is far from completely understood. They are no doubt much more numerous than we have thus far observed; but their small luminosity makes them invisible at any great distance.

THE RED GIANTS

On the Russell diagram, these as well as stars classified as Red Super-Giants appear diagonally opposite the White Dwarfs. These stars, particularly of the Super-Giant variety are of extremely large volume. Some of the latter are big enough to accommodate much of the Solar System. Their masses are 5, 10, or more times the mass of the sun, their bulkiness being due to the unusually small densities. The star Arcturus is classified as a Red Giant, while Antares is a star typical of the Super-Giant variety. The temperature of these stars is approximately 2000° A. Most of the radiation

emitted by them is in the red and in the infrared.

THE CEPHEIDS

Mention of this group of stars was already made in connection with stellar distances. It has been noted that a cepheid is a star whose brightness varies periodically.

Cepheids and other variable stars are named following a fixed set of rules: the first variable star discovered in any constellation is given a prefix, R (e.g., R-Leonis); the second bears the prefix S; Z is followed by RR, then by RS, RT, etc.; RZ by SS, ST, and so on. AA follows ZZ in that scheme, until QZ. As no combinations with the letter J are made, this scheme allows for 334 variables in any one constellation. Additional variable stars are denoted by a much simpler scheme: V335, V336, etc.; e.g., V357-Cygni.

Periods of cepheids range from a small value of 1 hour and 28 minutes for CY-Aquarii to 45 days and 4 hours for SV-Vulpeculae.

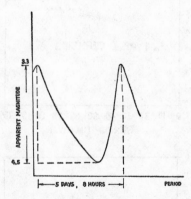

FIG. 149. Light Variation Curve typical of a Cepheid I. Note the rapid increase in brightness vs. the slow rate of decrease in same.

The numbers given here are for the first Cepheid I star discovered, Delta-Cephei.

Recent research indicates that there really are three kinds of cepheids. These are identified as Cepheids I, Cepheids II and RR-Lyrae Variables.

Cepheid I stars are on the average 1.5 magnitudes brighter than Cepheids II. They brighten rapidly, dim rather gradually. See Fig. 149. Their periods range from 1.5 to 40 days.

Cepheid II have characteristic leveling off intervals both in the brightening and in the dimming parts of the curve. See Fig. 150. Their periods are from 10 to 25 days.

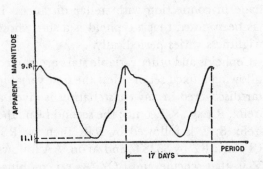

Fig. 150. Light Curve typical of a Cepheid II star. Neither the brightening part of the curve nor the dimming part is smooth. There are characteristic leveling off intervals in both parts of the curve.

The numbers given are for the star W-Virginis.

The two cepheid groups result in two distinct curves on a graph of Absolute Magnitude vs. Period. See Figs. 151, 152.

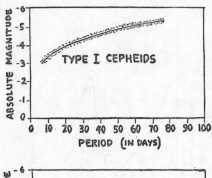

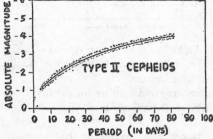

Figs. 151 & 152. Two Curves of Absolute Magnitude vs. Period.

The curve relating the absolute magnitude of a Cepheid I with its period is similar to the curve for a Cepheid II; the difference between the two curves is in brightness. For the same period a Cepheid I star is 4 times as bright as a Cepheid II. This can also be stated by saying that Cepheid I stars have values of absolute magnitudes smaller by 1.5 than Cepheid II stars having the same period of variation.

It will be recalled that stellar distances were computed on the basis of an Absolute Magnitude vs. Period curve. The discovery of two such curves has greatly upset the previous results, making it necessary to recompute many stellar distances. The new values differ by as much as 100% from previously accepted values.

RR-LYRAE VARIABLES

These are cepheids of very short period, the longest known being 29 hours, the shortest, a little less than an hour and a half. The first star of this type to be discovered was a 7th magnitude star in the constellation of Lyra; hence, the name. These cepheids were formerly known as "cluster type cepheids" because they were first discovered in globular star clusters. This name is obsolete now as they are known to be present in all parts of the sky.

LONG PERIOD VARIABLES

These variables are usually giant red stars with periods longer than 100 days. Their light variation is not quite as regular as in the case of other variable stars. The most famous of the long period variables is certainly Omicron-Ceti. Discovered in 1596, the star was soon thereafter called Mira, the "Wonderful." At maximum, Mira has been known to reach an apparent magnitude of 1.5; at that stage, it is the most brilliant star in that part of the heavens. At minimum brightness its magnitude is about +9, totally invisible to the naked eye. Its average period is 330. Individual periods may be less than 300 or more than 350.

NOVAE

Occasionally a star rises from relative obscurity to great brightness and then gradually returns to obscurity. Such a star is called a Nova (a New Star). The adjective "new" is inaccurate—the star is not new; its apparent increase in brightness **is**.

A close spectroscopic study of novae reveals that the star literally "blew its top." The star quite suddenly sheds its whole surface, which forms an ever expanding shell surrounding the star. The major part of the increase in brightness is due to the large surface exposed by that shell. Later the ejected material, still expanding, becomes too rarified and ceases to shine.

Little is known of the pre-nova stage of these exploding stars. The first nova of which a fairly complete history is available is Nova-Aquilae. The spectrum of this nova was known before it exploded in 1918. It is a main sequence star. Both in its luminosity and its spectral characteristics, it is fairly similar to our sun. No irregularities could be detected in these spectra, thus indicating that an apparently perfectly normal star, such as our sun, can burst into a terrific explosion unpredictably.

The probability that this will happen is extremely small. Computations show that the chance of such a solar cataclysm (that of course would in a matter of days bring life on earth to an end) is extremely small—one in several billion.

This probability is further decreased by *a.* the possibility that the sun has *already* been a nova, and hence is not likely ever to be again; and *b.* recent research into novae shows that such explosions are much more likely to happen in very hot white stars (having stellar spectra of type O and B) than in fairly cool yellow stars (type G) like our sun.

In all recorded history, only about 100 novae have been observed. Currently, with improved observational technique, one or two novae are discovered every year.

A schematic light curve for a nova would indicate (a) an almost abrupt increase in luminosity by as much as 10,000 times its value in the pre-nova stage; (b) a brief pause followed by a further increase in brightness by a factor of ten; (c) a decline in brightness to pre-nova stage. The decline varies in shape with the individual nova. See Fig. 153.

The initial rise may be concluded in several days. The final decline may continue for several years. In terms of apparent magnitude, some of these novae are bright enough to be seen in broad daylight; others are visible only through a telescope.

When the nova reaches the post-nova stage, it resumes its former luminosity. Apparently

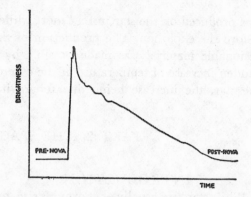

FIG. 153. Schematic Light Curve for a Nova. An increase in brightness by a factor of as much as 10,000 may take place in several days. This increase is usually followed by a day or so of no change in brightness, and another increase in brightness by a factor of ten. The decline is less regular and usually lasts several years.

no permanent damage has been done. The loss in mass has been estimated to be a small and rather unimportant fraction of the star.

SUPERNOVAE

Records show several cases of exceptionally bright stellar explosions. The increase in luminosity in these cases is more than 10,000 times greater than that of ordinary novae. These are grouped separately and are known as Supernovae. The brilliant star that suddenly manifested itself in the constellation of Cassiopeia in 1572 and led Tycho Brahe to devote his life to Astronomy is of that classification. The last recorded supernova in Our Galaxy was observed in 1604, and closely studied by another great scientist, Johannes Kepler.

The data on supernovae seem to indicate that there are about three supernovae in every 1000 years; this applies merely to Our Galaxy. Supernovae have also been recorded in other galaxies. One of these, in the Andromeda galaxy, was recorded in 1885. That exploding star increased in brightness to a tenth the brightness of the whole galaxy.

Many astronomers now believe that the increase in brightness of the supernovae is caused by a chain reaction, releasing enormous amounts of nuclear energy. The chemical element that is undergoing the fission process was produced on the star just a "short while" before the explosion. The production of the fissionable material was made possible by a sudden increase of temperature at the core of the star, the increase being due to gravita-tional contraction. This series of events is highly feasible in the case of a star that is in an advanced stage of its history, about the time that it is beginning to run out of its supply of hydrogen.

PART 2: THE SPACE BETWEEN THE STARS

INTRODUCTION

While stars are usually of enormous size, the spaces among them are vastly larger. A very tenuous gas pervades most of this space. In this space, there are also several types of large clouds. Some of these are made up of gases; others are primarily composed of minute dust particles. This gas and these clouds are of great interest, as they may very well be the material of which stars are made.

INTERSTELLAR GAS

Interstellar gas was discovered in 1904 during a study of a stellar spectrum. In the spectrum of Delta-Orionis, a line was noticed (K line of ionized calcium) that "should not have been there." It was also the only line in that spectrum that did not show the Doppler Effect. The reasonable explanation was that this line was not part of the star's spectrum. Most likely it originated in a gas through which the star's light passed. It was designated as an "interstellar line." From the years of study that have uncovered many such interstellar lines, it was concluded that the gas pervading the space between stars consists of a number of elements and compounds: interstellar lines due to sodium, potassium, iron, CN and CH are now on record. Hydrogen, as in the combination of CH, is overwhelmingly the most abundant element.

Interstellar gas is not evenly distributed, though it seems to pervade most of observable space. It is now used in determinations of stellar distances; the more remote the star, the stronger will be the spectral lines due to interstellar gas.

It is, of course, extremely tenuous, affecting almost not-at-all the dimming of distant stars. Its density is much less than that of the most perfect laboratory vacuum. However, its total mass is quite considerable. It is estimated that the mass of all interstellar gas is of the same order of magnitude as the total mass of all the existing stars.

INTERSTELLAR DUST

These are tenuous clouds of extremely small solid particles, greatly affecting the light going through them, and materially obscuring the stars beyond them. A great deal of our knowledge about these clouds is based on this obscuration effect. The fact that they dim the light indicates that they are composed of dust; small solid dust particles are able to absorb or scatter light of all wave lengths, thus causing dimming.

The thickness of these clouds is estimated from star counts, which are usually made for one square degree of angle of the sky. The procedure is to count the stars within that area to successive limiting magnitudes. That is:
First, count all the stars brighter than first magnitude.
Then, count all stars brighter than the second magnitude. (This number, of course, would include all the first magnitude stars.)
And then, count all the stars brighter than third magnitude. (This number will include both the previous numbers.) And so on.
Finally, plot the number of stars in each count (vertical axis) vs. the apparent magnitude (horizontal axis). The graph is a straight line for every unobscured region in the sky. Deviations from such a linearity indicate the presence of a dust cloud. Careful measurements of these deviations indicate the thickness of the cloud, which range in the tens of parsecs. See Fig. 154.

The other dimensions of these dust clouds have also been measured: Average lengths and widths of a 100 parsec are not uncommon.

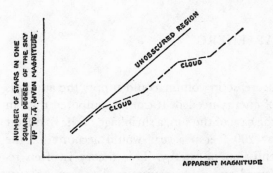

FIG. 154. Graph of Star Counts. The scale along the horizontal axis is in terms of apparent magnitude of stars. The scale on the vertical axis is in terms of the total number of stars up to a given magnitude within one square degree of the celestial sphere (e.g., the total number of stars in that square that are brighter than apparent magnitude five). In an obscured region of the sky the graph is a straight line. Deviation in slope indicates clouds. The thickness of the clouds can be estimated from the lengths of the deviating portions of the line.

A detailed description of the dust itself is not yet available. The dimming that they cause is typical of particles having a diameter of about 10^{-4} cm, and this value is confirmed by the reddening effect on light going through them, which may be thus explained: light going through a layer of dust will undergo a partial scattering. As blue light is scattered more effectively than red, the light that does get through contains an excess of red.

NOTE: Colors of the sky are explained in the same manner: the blue in the solar rays is scattered by atmospheric dust to give the sky its typical hue; the red of the sunset is a by-product of this scattering. Light at sunset has had removed all its blueness in passing through the thick atmospheric layers close to the earth's surface. The part of the light that gets through is the typical sunset-red.

It is also known that the dust is probably non-metallic; but its constitutent chemicals cannot even be guessed at the present stage of research.

Estimates of the mass of one dust cloud in Our Galaxy yield a figure about 10 to 100 times the mass of the sun. Their densities are of the order of 10^{-25} grams per cubic centimeter. It is not likely that this figure is too small, as higher densities would affect the motion of the neighboring stars; and there is no evidence of such an effect.

NEBULAE

In many parts of interstellar space, there can be found rather "heavy" concentrations of either gas or dust or both; such a "dense" cloud is called a nebula. (Nebula is the Latin word for "cloud.") **If the nebula happens to be near a star, it is called a bright nebula.** The light given off by a bright nebula has its source in the involved star. **If the nebula has no neighboring star to supply it with light, it is called a Dark Nebula.** One of the most striking examples of the latter is the famous Horsehead Nebula in Orion.

An analysis of light reaching us from a bright nebula reveals that part of it is merely reflected starlight; the rest has been greatly changed in quality by the cloud. The reflected portion of light has, of course, the same kind of spectrum as the star, the reflecting having probably been done by the dust particles in the cloud. The remainder of light underwent a change in wave length; quite likely, the light was first absorbed by the nebula and then re-emitted. The re-emitted light differs from the absorbed wave length.

The absorbed light is probably in the short ultra-violet. The light after emission by the nebula was in the visible part of the spectrum. This portion of the light is, of course, characteristic of the gases that compose the particular nebula.

(This process of changing wave lengths is known as fluorescence, the process responsible for the light in fluorescent lamps.)

The density of the gas-dust mixture has been estimated at 5×10^{-22} grams per cc. The dimensions of these diffuse nebulae can be calculated with reasonable precision.

On the basis of density and volume calculations, it is possible to derive estimates for the mass. The mass of the Nebula in Orion is usually stated as equal to the mass of about 500 suns.

PART 3: STELLAR ENERGY

INTRODUCTION

It is estimated that the stars have been emitting light energy and heat energy for several billion years. Where did all that energy come from?

Many theories have attempted an answer; but, before theories are considered, it is well to get an idea of the magnitude of the energies involved. A fairly exact value for the total amount of energy produced in one minute by one of the stars (our sun) can easily be computed.

I. Every minute, each cm² of the earth's surface perpendicular to the sun's rays receives a total amount of heat and light energy equal to 1.94 calories. (This number is known as the Solar Constant of Radiation.) Solar energy reaches the surface of the earth at the rate of nearly 5 million horsepower per square mile. The total amount of energy received yearly by the entire surface of the earth is fantastic. It exceeds by nearly 5 million times the annual production of energy obtained from coal, gas, waterfalls, fuel oil, and all other artificial sources of energy.

II. Knowing the distance of the earth's surface from the sun, it is possible to compute the total energy radiated by the sun per minute: 472,300 billion billions of horsepower! (The earth intercepts only one two-billionths of the energy radiated by the sun.) 472,300 billion billions of horsepower of energy for several billion years!

Ordinary combustion such as coal could not account for it. If the sun were made of the best coal, it would have turned to ashes a long time ago.

THE GRAVITATIONAL THEORY

Until the beginning of this century, there was only one rational explanation, the one formulated by the German physicist Helmholtz. According to Helmholtz's theory, stars were gradually shrinking in diameter. A small decrease in volume could supply the amounts of energy needed. It can be computed that, in the case of the sun, a shrinkage of the diameter by 200 feet per year would account for the emission of energy. This theory is often referred to as the gravitational theory, because the primary cause of shrinkage is the gravitational pull on the outer layers in the direction of the center of the sun.

ENERGY FROM NUCLEAR SOURCES: MAIN SEQUENCE STARS

In recent years, explanations based on nuclear reactions have come under consideration. That energy can be derived on earth from annihilation of part of the mass of atomic nuclei is a pretty well established fact. It is very likely that stellar energy is produced in a similar way. Such processes could easily explain the data we possess.

The conversion of mass to energy is, of course, governed by the famous Einstein equation:

$$E = mc^2$$

m, measured in grams, is the amount of mass annihilated; c, measured in cm/sec., is the velocity of light; and E, measured in units of erg, is the energy obtained in return.

Let us test the assumption that stellar energy may be derived from stellar matter.

a. Do the stars have the elements that usually react to produce nuclear energy?

b. Are the temperatures of the right order of magnitude for such a reaction?

c. Are these reactions and temperatures able to produce the observed stellar luminosities?

In the case of a typical star (our sun), the theory accounts for the known data:

a. It is now fairly well established that the sun derives its energy from fusion of hydrogen, which is present in the sun, and in all other stars. In this process of fusion, four hydrogen atoms are joined together to form an atom of helium, accompanied by a surplus of mass, as one helium atom weighs less than the sum of the four hydrogen atoms. This excess mass is converted into energy at the formula rate: $E = mc^2$.

The conversion of four hydrogen atoms into one helium atom is, of course, more complicated than it sounds. The transmutation of elements will not take place except under very high temperatures and in the presence of two other elements. Both carbon and nitrogen must be present for the reaction to take place; both are present in the sun.

The carbon and nitrogen help change the hydrogen into helium. At the end of the reaction, both the carbon and the nitrogen reappear, seemingly unchanged.

b. Twenty million degrees are necessary for the reaction to take place, and that temperature is probably available in the interior of the sun.

c. Finally, a computed luminosity must be checked with the actual luminosity of the sun. The computed value of luminosity is obtained on the basis of the above theories, as well as fundamental physical laws; the computed value is reasonably close to the observed one.

While most of the research has been in connection with our sun, the conclusions probably apply generally. It is very likely that all the stars in the "main sequence" derive their energies in a similar manner.

ENERGY FROM NUCLEAR SOURCES: RED GIANT STARS

The hydrogen into helium source of nuclear energy cannot be utilized by red giants, nor by any other cool stars. The central cores of these stars have much too low temperatures (a million degrees, or even less) for that nuclear reaction to proceed satisfactorily.

Other nuclear reactions are probably taking place in the interior of these stars. Three distinct types are possible at these "low" temperatures, depending on how low the "low" temperature is.

Type I. Temperatures of about 1,000,000 degrees. Hydrogen combines with deuterium (heavy hydrogen) to form an isotope of helium. The reaction proceeds quite freely even at these temperatures and liberates large quantities of heat energy.

Type II. Temperatures in the range of several million degrees. Several distinct reactions may be taking place in this temperature range. One involves the interaction of beryllium with hydrogen. The reaction produces lithium and helium, as well as some excess mass, which is transformed into energy.

Type III. Temperatures in the range of ten to twenty millions of degrees. A likely reaction in this case is the combination of boron with hydrogen. The final product is an isotope of carbon, with some excess mass. The energy released in this reaction is due to this excess of mass.

The specific isotope of carbon is $_6C^{11}$. It has the same electric charges as ordinary carbon, $_6C^{12}$, but different nuclear masses. **Atoms with identical electric charges, but different in mass, are called "isotopes."**

THE PRODUCTION OF ENERGY BY WHITE DWARFS

The production of light in the case of white dwarfs is again a special case, involving Helmholtz's gravitational theory. Potential energy of the atoms, and its components, is converted into heat and light. In the early stages of contraction, the individual atoms of the star come closer and closer. At the late stages of contraction, the atoms themselves are crushed into their constituent protons, neutrons, and electrons. The process resembles somewhat the industrial process of dehydration. This "dehydrated" matter explains the high value of density usually associated with the White Dwarf stars.

PART 4: LIFE HISTORY OF A STAR

INTRODUCTION

It is now possible to sketch, in some detail, the life of a star. Future astronomers may, of course, find fault with the underlying theories; but at present, the portrait seems reasonable and complete.

The life of a typical star can be divided into six distinct periods:

Birth (large non-radiating mass of gas)
Infancy (Red Giant stage)
Three Stages of Youth (variable stars)
Maturity (main sequence)
Later Years (White Dwarf)
Death (cool solid fragment of mass)

Present estimates of the life span of a star are as high as eighty billion years. The stars we see are all in stages of development: some, astronomically speaking, have just been born; others have passed their "childhood diseases" and are in their prime; still others are declining. Synthesizing these stages, it is possible to obtain the complete picture.

As with all theories of development, an assumption must be made about the starting point—thus for the pre-Star Period the assumption is that matter in a very diluted state occupied all space. Approximate calculations indicate that the density of that matter was 0.000 000 000 000 000 000 000 1 times the density of water, with prevailing temperature of several hundred degrees Absolute.

THE BIRTH

Slight motions within the gas created local concentrations. Forces of gravity aided greatly the build-up of matter in these concentrated regions, causing the gas to break up into spheres. Sir James Jeans, the noted British astronomer, suggests that the diameter of the sphere of gas was about two or three light years, or about one parsec, in size. The mass of one such unit was 10^{30} kilograms.

Smaller masses than that would not possess enough gravitational pull to become a unit;

masses much larger would be in unstable equilibrium, splitting into a number of smaller stars.

Thus, then, the stars were born. Probable date of the primary division is about several billion years ago. It is quite possible that the process continues, that at this moment new stars are being born. Either the interstellar gas or gaseous nebulae supply the material for these new stars.

Births of new stars should not be confused with novae: by definition a nova is a well-established star that has a sudden increase in brightness. A new star is really new, created from primordial gas.

As its surface is much too cold to emit visible light, a new star cannot be seen. In several million years, however, the surface temperature will increase sufficiently to allow it to become a "red giant"—at the surface it will exceed a 1000 degrees Absolute; at the core it will be close to a million degrees. The increase in temperature results from gravitational energy: the process of contraction involves a transformation of potential energy into heat energy.

THE INFANCY

The star is now a red giant or a red supergiant. Its volume is still enormous; but it differs from the previous type in one important respect: it now emits and is made visible by red light.

THE THREE STAGES OF YOUTH

Whereas gravity had been the sole source of energy, the end of infancy is marked by the appearance of a new source: nuclear energy. The star uses both sources, alternately, which perhaps causes the pulsation that in turn produces the variability of brightness of stars.

There seems to be three distinct stages in "youth," each stage characterized by its particular nuclear reaction, and by a particular mode of variability.

Stage I. Temperature at the core of the star is approximately a million degrees. The nuclear reaction is between deuterons and hydrogen atoms; and the conflict between the gravitational production energy and the nuclear production somehow causes instability. In this stage, the star is a Long Period Variable.

For some time, the star continues to use up its deuterons, the extra supply of energy increasing its central temperature. When the temperature reaches 3 or 4 million degrees, a new source of energy becomes available.

Stage II. The beryllium-hydrogen reaction characterizes this stage; alternation between sources of energy again causes periodic variation in brightness. This variation in brightness may explain the behavior of the cepheids.

Stage III. Towards the end of its youth, it is quite possible that both the deuterons and the beryllium have been all used up. But the temperature of the star is now high enough to tap the nuclear energy of the boron-hydrogen reaction. The conflict between energies in this case may very well explain the behavior of the RR-Lyrae Variables.

All through its youth, several elements were being exhausted. These elements, like beryllium and boron, were probably present only in limited quantities, and may very well have been totally exhausted by the end of the period. Their presence, though, was of great importance, serving as fuel to increase the central temperature. At the end of the period, it is believed that the star has reached a temperature in excess of 20 million degrees, at which point it can use the main supply of energy, starting the conversion of hydrogen into helium. The youth has become an adult.

ADULTHOOD

Now, tapping its main source of energy, all other sources are of minor importance. The star is a "main sequence" star. The thermonuclear reaction proceeds rather smoothly.

Carbon and nitrogen are assisting in the transformation of hydrogen into helium. A new disturbing factor appears, however. Calculations show that main sequence stars move along that line, upward and towards the left.

Our own sun is a case in point. The supply of energy inside the sun is such that it becomes increasingly luminous and hot. In ten billion years, the sun will be 100 times as luminous as it is now. Life, as we know it on earth, will disappear. Average temperatures on mountaintops will be in the hundreds of degrees Fahrenheit. The oceans will "boil away" a long time before the temperatures reach their maximum.

Then a time comes when all hydrogen will have been exhausted, making it necessary for the star to depend again on gravitation for its source of energy. Luminosity, having reached a maximum at the time that the last bit of hydrogen reacted, starts on a decline, the star becoming fainter and fainter.

THE LATER YEARS

The star obtains energy at the expense of its decreasing volume (gravitational or potential energy). The atoms of matter come closer and closer, and yet compression continues. This is now followed by the crushing of the very atoms of which matter is composed, creating the last supply of energy. The star is now a "white dwarf," its supply of energy almost exhausted.

THE DEATH

A highly concentrated mass is now moving in space. It is cooling rather rapidly, having no source to replenish its energy. Soon the last rays of light will have been emitted. Contact with the earth will be severed. Only by its gravitational pull does it make known its existence; only by its disturbance of the path of another star are we made aware of an object that shone for billions of years.

CHAPTER IX

THE GALAXIES

PART 1: OUR GALAXY

INTRODUCTION

The sun and some 100 billion other stars form the community known as Our Galaxy.

The study of distribution of stars in Our Galaxy has demonstrated that this vast collection resembles a somewhat flattened disk; in fact, it is often represented as a gigantic grindstone.

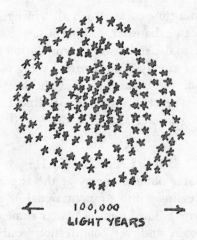

← 100,000 LIGHT YEARS →

FIG. 155. Top View of Our Galaxy reveals its circular outline. The stars are not evenly distributed over that area. There is a concentration of stars in the center of the galaxy as well as along two arms that start at opposite sides of the center and spiral about it.

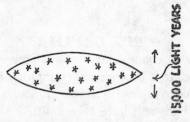

15,000 LIGHT YEARS

FIG. 156. A Side View of Our Galaxy. A side view of Our Galaxy points up its relative thinness.

Viewed from above, it would appear circular in outline, the stars forming a spiral or pinwheel design; a side view would reveal its thinness. See Figs. 155, 156.

The most reliable figure for the diameter of the galaxy is 100,000 light years. The maximum thickness is estimated at 10,000 to 15,000 light years.

Our sun with its system of planets occupies an unspectacular position. The Solar System is located about 30,000 light years from the center, and fairly close to the equatorial plane.

Looking at this multitude of stars from our own small planet, one gets two distinct views. See Fig. 157. In the direction parallel to the

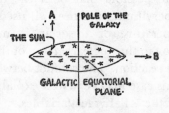

FIG. 157. Two Views of the Galaxy. Looking from the Solar System along the smaller dimension (direction A) stars are seen against a black background.

The nearby stars along direction B are seen against the background of the Milky Way. The luminosity of the latter is due to the merging points of light produced by tens of billions of stars. The Galactic Equatorial Plane slices the galaxy horizontally in two equal parts. The pole of the galaxy is perpendicular to the Galactic Equatorial Plane at its center.

pole of the galaxy, due to thinness of the latter, individual stars are seen against a dark background. The view along the equatorial plane is different—the closer stars are seen against a background of a faint luminous band (Milky Way), the band being due to the merging light of the billions of stars present in the thick part of Our Galaxy.

This band of light thus indicates the direction of the equatorial plane of Our Galaxy.

STUDIES OF THE GALAXY WITH THE AID OF STAR COUNTS

The shape and dimensions of Our Galaxy are in principle derived from a study of star counts.

These are made in all directions of the sky. The faintest star (largest value of apparent magnitude) in each direction indicates the dis-

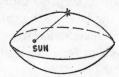

FIG. 158. Distance to Boundary of Our Galaxy. The faintest (highest number for apparent magnitude) star in the direction of the line is an indication of the *length* of the line from the sun to the boundary of the galaxy.

tance between the solar system and the boundary of the galaxy in that particular direction. See Figs. 158 and 159.

Several assumptions are involved in this method of computing the shape of the galaxy. The most important, and probably crudest, of these is that: Apparent magnitude is dependent primarily on distance. This assumption implies that the *average* stars are quite similar in their intrinsic brightness, the difference in their apparent magnitudes being primarily due to differences in distance.

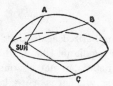

FIG. 159. Shape of Boundary of Our Galaxy. By computing the distance from the sun to many points on the boundary (e.g., points A, B, and C) the shape of the galaxy can be visualized.

STUDIES OF THE GALAXY WITH THE AID OF GLOBULAR CLUSTERS

Another method of estimating the size of Our Galaxy is based on globular star clusters, which, as the name implies, are **swarms of stars crowded together in the shape of a globe.** See Fig. 160.

One of the most beautiful globular clusters —barely visible to the naked eye—is M13, in the constellation of Hercules. Telescopic studies reveal that it consists of more than

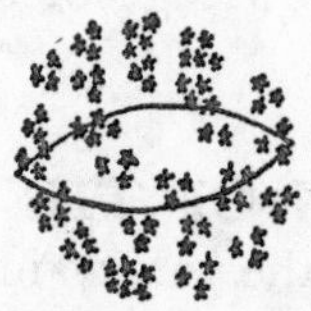

FIG. 160. Distribution of Globular Star Clusters. A symbolic representation of these star clusters would show them to be distributed in the form of a sphere about Our Galaxy. The diameter of the sphere is equal to the diameter of the Milky Way.

50,000 stars. Although each is only of apparent magnitude 13 or fainter, together they are extremely luminous, visible at great distance.

The distance of a globular cluster can easily be computed if:

a. the cluster contains one or more cepheid stars, or

b. the cluster contains a red giant type of star. (All globular clusters do.)

In the first case, the distance is obtained by: I. observing the period of the cepheid; II. finding its absolute magnitude from an Absolute Magnitude vs. Period curve; III. observing the average apparent magnitude of the star; and IV. using the formula for distance in terms of apparent and absolute magnitudes.

In the second case, the distance to the globular star cluster is computed on the assumption that the brightest red giants that are in these clusters have an absolute magnitude of —3.0, and then using the formula that relates distance with absolute and apparent magnitudes.

The assumption that the brightest red giants in these clusters have an absolute magnitude of —3.0 is reasonable. Globular clusters are remarkably similar to one another in size and in many other respects.

A study of the distance of the hundred or so known globular clusters brings out the fact that they are distributed to form a sphere about Our Galaxy, the Milky Way cutting this sphere in two equal halves. The diameter of the sphere agrees quite well with the value of the diameter of the Milky Way (100,000 light years), which serves as an additional check on our knowledge of the size of Our Galaxy.

ROTATION OF THE GALAXY

The shape of the galaxy implies that it is rotating; in fact, it could not exist as a flat disk without rotation. The axis of rotation is perpendicular to the equatorial plane of the galaxy. This motion of the galaxy as a whole is superimposed on the movement of its individual stars. In this respect it is similar to the rotation of the earth about its axis, while all kinds of movements proceed on the surface of the earth. However, there is a great difference between these two rotations. The galaxy does not rotate as a solid body. The stars rotate around the center of the galaxy in much the same way as the planets move around the sun; the stars close to the center of the galaxy move at great orbital velocities; stars far from the center, at small velocities. Our sun has an orbital velocity of 160 miles per second. Stars close to the center seem to outrun the sun. Stars closer to the edge of the galaxy seem to move at slower speeds. Relative to the sun, these latter seem to be going in the opposite direction.

The period of revolutions, of course, will depend on the distance of the star from the center. It takes the sun 224,000,000 years to complete one revolution.

PART 2: OTHER GALAXIES

INTRODUCTION

Our Galaxy is not alone in this world. The universe is populated by more than two billion galaxies. Several terms are used interchangeably for these galaxies. Sometimes they are referred to as "Island Universes" (implying that the universe is interspersed with islands that are similar to our own Milky Way Galaxy). Sometimes they are referred to as "Extragalactic Nebulae" (in spite of the fact that they are galaxies of stars and not nebulae).

Some of the galaxies are fairly close to us; others, remote.

THE LARGE MAGELLANIC CLOUD

The galaxy nearest our own is the Large Magellanic Cloud—less than 150,000 light years away, visible to the unaided eye in the constellation Dorado. It is of irregular elliptic shape; visually, the dimensions are about 12° by 4°. It is not improbable that the angle subtended by that is larger than the unaided eye would indicate.

The Large Cloud contains many objects of great interest. Of particular interest are the almost 1500 cepheid variables as well as the great Looped Nebula, designated as 30 Doradus. 30 Doradus is the largest known gaseous nebula, much larger than the diffuse nebula in Orion. That it is also extremely bright would be much more apparent if it had been in Our Galaxy. In fact, if 30 Doradus were placed at the distance of Orion, it would appear 200 times brighter than Sirius.

It should be emphasized again that:

a. The Large Magellanic Cloud, which is the nearest extragalactic nebula, is **not** a cloud, and is **not** a nebula. It is a galaxy. That is, it is a large island consisting of light emitting stars, globular star clusters, diffuse nebulae, and all other entities that can be found in our own galaxy.

b. A diffuse nebula is a cloud, consisting of a mixture of dust and gases. The light by which it is seen is due to a star in its center or in its immediate neighborhood.

The star, S-Doradus, in the Large Magellanic Cloud, is by far the most luminous star known, one of a group known as "irregular variables." At its maximum brightness, it is

600,000 times (some computations indicate 2,000,000 times) as bright as our sun.

The Large Cloud recedes from us at a velocity estimated to be more than 160 miles per second.

THE SMALL MAGELLANIC CLOUD

Its estimated distance of 164,000 light years places it only slightly farther than the Large Cloud; it is visible to the unaided eye in the constellation Tucana. However, it has only about ½ the diameter of the Large Magellanic Cloud. A study of its cepheids, it should be remembered, led to the discovery of the Period-Absolute Magnitude curve. This "cloud" contains a great number of faint stars, ranging from magnitude 11 to the faintest known stars.

The recessional velocity of the Small Cloud is appreciably less than that of the Large Cloud, approximately 100 miles per second. Both the Large and Small Magellanic Clouds are often regarded as satellites of Our Galaxy.

THE LOCAL GROUP OF GALAXIES

These include the galaxies that are closer than 2 million light-years, of which there are thirteen, in addition to Our Galaxy and the Magellanic Clouds. See Fig. 161.

THE ANDROMEDA GALAXY

Of particular interest in the local group of galaxies is the Great Galaxy in Andromeda (also known either as M31 or NGC 224)—an interest due primarily to its great resemblance to Our Galaxy, about which it provides information.

Although slightly larger than ours, from a distance of 1,500,000 light years it appears to the naked eye as a fairly hazy 5th magnitude star. It requires long exposure photographs to reveal its real beauty. On such photographs the galaxy appears as a flat disk, making an angle of 15° with the line of sight. The center of the ellipse is extremely bright, surrounded by two spiraling arms that seem to have their origin in the very center.

Fig. 161. Several Members of the Local Group of Galaxies.

Name	Type	Distance (in Light Years)
Our Galaxy	Spiral	0
Large Magellanic Cloud	Irregular	145,000
Small Magellanic Cloud	Irregular	164,000
M31, Andromeda	Spiral	1,500,000
M32 (Satellite of Andromeda)	Elliptical	1,500,000
NGC 205 (Satellite of Andromeda)	Elliptical	1,500,000
M33, Triangulum	Spiral	1,560,000

The spiral arms had been resolved into individual stars as early as 1923, but efforts to distinguish individual stars in the center were unsuccessful for nearly twenty years. The center of the galaxy appeared on all photographs as uniform bright mass without any detail.

The bright mass in the center was successfully resolved in 1943 when pictures were made on a new type of red-sensitive plates, instead of the regular blue-sensitive plates used up to that date. The individual stars were clearly resolved into distinct units on the new type of plates.

This discovery led to new conclusions, chief among which is that the stars can be divided into two general classes, known as Population I and Population II stars.

Population I stars are usually to be found in the arms of spiral galaxies, as well as in irregular galaxies, such as the Magellanic Clouds. This class of stars is characterized by the fact that the brightest stars in it are blue in color and have high surface temperatures.

Population II stars are usually found in globular clusters, elliptical galaxies, as well as at the centers of spiral galaxies. The brightest stars of this class are not blue and hot, but red and cool.

In the past twenty years, more than a hundred novae have been discovered in the Galaxy of Andromeda, most of them close to the center of the galaxy. Of particular interest, however, was the supernova dating back to 1885.

The galaxy is moving with a speed of close to 180 miles per second towards the sun; most of its velocity, however, is due to the rotation of our own galaxy, which brings the solar system closer to the galaxy in Andromeda by nearly two hundred miles each second.

REMOTE GALAXIES

The sixteen galaxies that form the local group are only a minute fraction of all existing island universes, the total number being estimated in the billions.

The 200″ telescope at Mount Palomar can detect galaxies as far as two billion light years away. There are more than two billion galaxies within that distance from earth.

CLASSIFICATION OF GALAXIES

A. **Irregular.** Typical of these are the Magellanic Clouds. These galaxies have no simple geometric form or clear design.

B. **Elliptical.** These take on the shapes of more or less flattened disks. No spiral arms are discernible. About 25 per cent of all galaxies are in this group.

C. **Spirals.** Typical of these are the Andromeda galaxy as well as our own galaxy. Spiral galaxies are usually divided into two subgroups: (a) **Normal Spirals** and (b) **Barred Spirals.** In the case of normal spirals, the two arms begin their spiraling immediately upon coming out of the core of the galaxy. In the case of barred spirals, the two arms extend straight out at first, and begin to spiral at the end of the extension.

THE "RED SHIFT"

A remarkable feature known as the "red shift" is exhibited by all galaxies. Red shift, it will be recalled, means that all the lines of the spectrum are shifted from their normal positions **toward new positions that are closer to the red end of the spectrum.** This shift is interpreted as a Doppler displacement, indicating a recession of the galaxies from the earth.

Further studies of the red shift brought out the fact that there is a close relationship between the velocity of recession and the distance of the galaxy. The farther the galaxy is from the earth, the faster it recedes. Specifically, galaxies recede at a speed of 60 miles per second for every 1,000,000 light-years of distance; thus, a galaxy 2,000,000 light-years away recedes at a rate of 120 miles/sec.; 5,000,000 light-years away, at 300 miles/sec., and so on. The 200″ telescope has already discovered galaxies that recede at velocities as high as 40,000 miles per second.

It has been difficult to explain reasonably why our insignificant earth or Our Galaxy should be the point from which all galaxies recede. The explanation now widely accepted is included in the concept of the expanding universe.

THE EXPANDING UNIVERSE

This concept implies that not only do all the galaxies move away from Our Galaxy, but every galaxy is moving away from every other galaxy. This increase in distance is due to the fact that the whole universe is expanding and the distance between any two galaxies is increasing at a constant rate.

A one-dimensional analogy may help to clarify this concept. Suppose one marks a 10″ rubber string at three points: A, B, and C. A and C are at the ends, B is in the middle, 5 inches away from A and C. That is, AB = BC = 5 inches. Now suppose that the string is stretched to 16 inches. AB = BC has increased to 8 inches. Now suppose the stretching was done at a constant rate, and it took 2 seconds to complete. B would, in such a case, seem to move away from A at a rate of 1.5 inches per second and C would be increasing its distance from A at a rate of 3 inches per second.

The theory of the expanding universe makes it possible to compute its age. Assuming that the expansion has always proceeded at the present rate, it is possible to determine the date the expansion began—about five billion years ago.

PART 3: THE BIRTH OF THE UNIVERSE

THE PRELIMINARY STAGE

The theory of the development of the universe from its beginnings assumes that "once upon a time" there was a vast ball of extremely hot and dense gas. Both the temperature and the density of that gas had fantastically high values: the density is assumed to have been several billion times that of water; the temperature, billions of degrees. As evidence, the physical theory demonstrates that many of the heavy elements can be formed only at such fantastic pressure. For example, the building of an atom of uranium or thorium from protons and neutrons is only possible when the density and temperature are of that extent.

THE EXPANSION

Then, about five billion years ago, the ball began to expand, and has been expanding ever since, bringing about a decrease both in temperature and in density but an enormous increase in volume. The universe, at this stage of evolution, can be pictured as an enormously large flattened sphere of gas.

THE FORMATION OF THE GALAXIES

As time went on, "concentrations of matter" developed in many places of this flattened sphere. These concentrations grew in size by attracting more and more material from its surroundings, thus breaking up the universe into large masses of gas—each mass destined to become a galaxy. These masses continue to take part in the ever-expanding universe.

Eventually each large mass of gas fragmented again to form stars, thus becoming an island universe or a galaxy.

THE SIZE OF THE UNIVERSE

There are two schools of thought concerning the size of the universe: one theory holds that the original ball of matter was finite in size, say, the size of the Solar System, and that the universe is still finite. Larger and better telescopes will eventually reach to the outer surface of this universe. Beyond this surface, presumably, there is no more matter. The Einsteinian theory of "curved space" suggests that there is no "beyond."

The other theory holds that the ball was infinite to begin with and that this radius is becoming ever larger. At present this theory is generally favored.

According to the infinity school of thought this is the complete picture: Several billion years ago, an "infinite" ball of extremely hot and dense gas began to expand. At a certain stage of the expansion, the gas fragmented to form galaxies, one of which is Our Galaxy. As expansion continued, the stars were formed, Our Galaxy containing 100 billion stars. When the stars in our galaxy were fairly close together, collisions were not uncommon. In one of these, several masses were ripped off to form planets, one of which is our earth. Later, when the earth became cool enough life appeared on the globe. Eventually, man made his appearance.

LOOKING INTO THE STARS

Theory also looks into the future. The sun, our main benefactor, is growing hotter, and will eventually destroy life on this planet—billions of years from now. The sun will subsequently enter a period of cooling off, followed by its "death." Death in one place is followed by birth elsewhere in the sky. Out of the interstellar gas, new stars are born to take their place in our marvelous universe.

CHAPTER X

THE SOLAR SYSTEM

PART 1: THE SUN

SOLAR DATA

Diameter: 865,400 miles; 110 times that of the earth.

Distance from earth:

      mean 93,000,000 miles

      max. 94,500,000 miles

      min. 91,500,000 miles

Apparent Angular Diameter:

      mean 31 minutes, 59 seconds

      max. 32 minutes, 30 seconds

      min. 31 minutes, 28 seconds

Mass: 2.2×10^{27} tons; 333,400 times that of the earth.

Density mean: 0.4 times that of the earth.

Surface gravity: 900 ft. per sec.^{2}; 27.9 times that of the earth.

Effective temperature: 5750° A, 9900° F.

Magnitude: −26.7 apparent.

                + 4.8 absolute.

Spectral class: G-O

Inclination of Solar Axis to Ecliptic: 7° 10′

Period of Spinning, at Equator: 24 days, 16 hours

Solar Constant (energy received at earth's surface): 1.94 calories per cm^2 per minute.

Energy Output (of whole sun): 5×10^{23} horsepower.

INTRODUCTION

Compared to many of the billions of stars in Our Galaxy, the sun is rather small and faint. Its apparent brightness is due entirely to its closeness to the earth, as is its apparent size. The next nearest star, Alpha Centauri, is 270,000 times farther than the sun. Alpha Centauri is the third brightest star in the sky; by sheer coincidence, Alpha Centauri and our sun are similar in their characteristics, almost identical.

Of the vast amount of data concerning the sun, two seem particularly startling:

a. The sun, unlike the earth, is completely gaseous.

A boundary exists, though, between the sun and its atmosphere which is called the photosphere (Sphere of Light) and from which sunlight originates. The photosphere is quite opaque, making it impossible to see anything beneath it. **The solar atmosphere consists of three distinct layers: The Reversing Layer, The Chromosphere, and The Corona,** all fairly transparent to the light emitted by the photosphere. See Fig. 162.

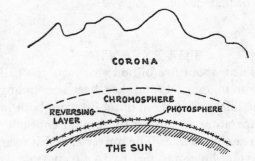

FIG. 162. The Solar Atmosphere. Three layers are recognized in the solar atmosphere; no sharp and definite boundaries exist between them.

The layer immediately above the Photosphere (the surface of the sun) is known as the Reversing Layer. It is only 1000 miles thick, but materially affects the quality of light given off by the Photosphere, by removing some components from it.

The intermediate layer about 6000 miles thick is known as the Chromosphere. It is here that prominences and chromospheric flares, which cause radio fadeouts, have their origin.

The outer layer is known as the Corona. It forms a pearly gray layer, half a million or so miles thick about the sun.

b. The other "startling" fact is that the sun does not spin about its axis at constant angular speed. A point on its equator completes a full revolution in 25 days, while a point at 60° North or South of the equator completes a revolution in 31 days.

DISTANCE

The average distance of the earth from the sun (derived by triangulation) is 93 million miles, less in January than in July by as much as 3 million miles.

DIAMETER

Given the distance to the sun and its angular diameter, it is easy to compute its real diameter.

The average distance is 93,000,000—more precisely 92,870,000 miles.

The apparent diameter at that distance is slightly over a half degree of angle—precisely 31 minutes, 59½ seconds, or 1919.5 seconds of angle.

The linear diameter is obtained from the formula:

Linear Diameter = Distance × Angular Diameter.

Angular Diameter must be stated in a special unit, known as a radian, equivalent in size to 206,265 seconds of angle.

Substituting the known values in the formula, Linear Diameter = 93,000,000 × $\frac{1919.5}{206265}$, the result is that the diameter of the sun is 865,400 miles.

The solar diameter is more than a hundred times larger than that of the earth—the earth, together with the moon revolving about it in its orbit, could easily be contained by the sun.

Compared to other stars the sun is of average size: the smallest star has a diameter of only 4,000 miles; the largest, a diameter estimated to be nearly 3,000 times greater than that of the sun.

VOLUME

Given the diameter, the volume can be determined: it is a million and a quarter (1,250,000) times greater than that of the earth.

MASS

The mass is calculated by a simple formula:

$$\text{Mass} = \frac{2 \times (\text{distance to sun})^2 \cdot d}{\text{gravitational constant}}$$

This formula is derived from three basic equations in elementary mechanics:

a. Newton's Second Law, $F = ma$;

b. The Universal Law of Gravitation, $F = $ gravitational constant $\cdot \frac{Mm}{r^2}$; and, *c.* $d = \frac{1}{2} at^2$, for which if $t = 1$ sec, $d = \frac{1}{2} a$.

As applied here,

m is the mass of the earth;

M, the mass of the sun;

r, the distance between the sun and earth;

a, the acceleration of the earth toward the sun;

d, the distance the earth would fall toward the sun in the absence of centrifugal force—1/9th of an inch for each second. That is, if the earth for some reason stopped revolving about the sun, it would fall toward the sun 1/9th of an inch per second.

Eliminating F from the first two equations, the following is obtained:

$$ma = \text{gravitational constant} \cdot \frac{Mm}{r^2}$$

or,

$$a = \text{gravitational constant} \frac{M}{r^2}$$

substituting from the third equation

$$2d = \text{gravitational constant} \frac{M}{r^2}$$

or,

$$\text{Mass} = \frac{2r^2 d}{\text{gravitational constant}}$$

In this formula, if r is in cms,

d is in cms,

the gravitational constant is 6.7×10^{-8}.

The mass of the sun thus computed is 2×10^{33} grams, or $= 2 \times 10^{30}$ kilograms, or approximately 4.5×10^{30} pounds, or 2.2×10^{27} tons, or more than two billion billion billions of tons.

That is ⅓ of a million times more massive than the earth. The sun placed on one side of a balance would equal in weight 333,400 earths placed on the other.

Compared to other stars, the sun's mass is

rather average. There are stars a hundred times as massive; others have a mass 1/7th or less that of the sun.

DENSITY

Knowing the mass of the sun and its volume, it is easy to compute its density.

$$\text{Density} = \frac{\text{Mass}}{\text{Volume}}$$

The result of such a computation can be stated in two ways.

a. The density of the sun is 1.4 times that of water. A cubic foot of its matter would weigh $62.4 \times 1.4 = 87.4$ pounds.

b. The density of the sun is about .4 that of the earth.

The density, of course, is not constant. The density close to the center is much greater than it is near the surface, due in part to the sheer weight of matter. The weight of the material of which the sun is made would cause a pressure exceeding a billion atmospheres at the center of the sun. This value is probably an understatement. It is very likely that the pressure near the core of the sun greatly exceeds that number; and the density of the gas at the center is correspondingly large.

NOTE: Despite this pressure and density, it is believed that the sun is gaseous throughout. This belief is based upon the accepted value for temperature at its center—20 to 30 million degrees Absolute. No known substance could possibly remain in liquid form at that temperature.

SURFACE GRAVITY

Surface gravity on the face of the sun is 28 times that on the face of the earth: a ten-pound baby would register 280 lbs. on a spring balance there.

This surface gravity is due primarily to the mass of the sun, which exerts a strong gravitational pull. This strong gravitational attraction is somewhat diminished by the sun's large radius.

So much for the sun "as a whole"; now we shall consider its individual parts.

THE PHOTOSPHERE

Through dark glasses, the sun appears as a bright disk—the part of the photosphere facing the observer, in which sunlight has its origin. Its temperature has been computed by several different methods; the average is about 6,300° C or about 11,000 degrees on the Fahrenheit scale.

The uniform brightness of the disk is only approximately correct. Careful study of the photosphere reveals that the photosphere is not uniformly bright, but rather speckled or marked by granulations, with diameters hundreds of miles long. These granules, probably covering the whole area of the photosphere, are not fixed on the surface; they change constantly in size and in structure.

Also appearing from time to time are (a) Sunspots, and (b) Faculae.

a. **Sunspots** are gigantic areas on the solar disk that appear dark by comparison to surrounding regions, and have diameters of hundreds of thousands of miles.

b. **Faculae** are areas on the surface of the sun that appear brighter by comparison to surrounding regions.

It is likely that the granulations, sunspots, and faculae are caused by swirling chaotic currents of gas. The surface of the sun is not static; motions in the photosphere most likely resemble waves in an ocean during a hurricane. The granules are believed to be crests of waves moving about continuously in the photosphere. **Sunspots resemble tornadoes, which very likely start out as internal disturbances just under the sun's surface and at a later stage in their development succeed in causing a break through the photosphere. Faculae, it is believed, are clouds of solar matter that are thrown off by the sun and stay above the surface for brief periods of time.**

SUNSPOTS

Since Galileo first discovered them, sunspots have been under study for the last 350 years. The result of this research may be summarized as follows:

a. **Structure.** Most spots consist of two portions that differ greatly in "darkness."

The inside portion—the technical name of which is Umbra (L. for shadow)—is the darker of the two. Surrounding the umbra is the semi-dark portion, the Penumbra.

NOTE: The terms "dark" and "semi-dark" as applied to sunspots need clarification. Actually, the dark umbra emits brighter light than the most efficient electric arc. The area *appears* dark against the background of the still brighter solar disk. The umbra is 3000° F cooler than the rest of the photosphere. But its temperature is still tremendous: 8000° F.

b. **Size.** Sunspots vary greatly in size—from 20,000 miles across to more than ten times that figure. The largest known spot, seen in April 1947, covered an area larger than 30 times the surface of the earth.

c. **Latitude.** Spots occur in two belts of the solar surface: one, between 5° N and 40° N solar latitudes; the other belt has numbers similar to those for the hemisphere below the solar equator. There are, of course, a few exceptions to this rule.

d. **Duration.** About 50% of sunspots have a life span of less than four days; occasionally, however, spots last for more than 100 days.

e. **Magnetic Field.** Each spot is a center of a magnetic field, the strength of the field varying with the size of the spot. Some spots have a "north-seeking" polarity; others, the opposite polarity.

Studies of magnetic fields are based on the Zeeman Effect. (Pieter Zeeman, of Holland, discovered in 1896 the effect of a magnetic field on spectral lines.) **Spectral lines either split into several components or widen materially under the influence of a powerful magnet.** See Fig. 163.

The mode of splitting or the amount of widening is dependent upon the magnetic field. Information about the magnetism of sunspots is based on the widening of the spectral lines in the light coming from the spots.

f. **Variation in Spottedness.** The area of the sun covered by spots varies greatly. Weeks may pass without a single spot; again, scores of sunspots can be seen on the solar disk.

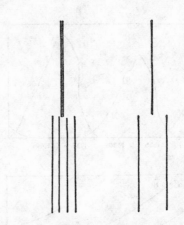

FIG. 163. Effect of Magnetic Field on Spectral Lines (Zeeman Effect). The upper half of the picture shows two lines in a spectrum of the element Vanadium as they appear without a magnetic field. The lower part of the picture shows the effect of inserting a large magnetic field (about 15,000 Gauss) parallel to the light producing the spectrum. One of the lines "splits" into four components; the other into two.

The Royal Observatory at Greenwich and the Cape of Good Hope Observatory keep a close watch on these areas. Every day, precise determinations are made. The results are stated in terms of 1/1,000,000 of the visible area of the sun, and are averaged over the year. The mean daily spot area in 1933 was 88; and 2019 for 1937. The latter means that on the average 2,019/1,000,000 of the visible area of the sun was covered by spots.

g. **Cycles.** A definite cycle in sunspottedness was suggested as early as 1843, and has since been verified. The period of a complete cycle is 22 years; each complete cycle is divided into two halves, 11 years each. The half cycles are alike in their variations in spot area, as shown in Figure 164. They differ in the magnetic polarity. The details of one such hypothetical cycle follows:

I. The beginning of the cycle is at a minimum of spottedness, marked by the appearance of two spots in latitude 35° N, and two spots in latitude 35° S. Each pair of spots lies along an east-west axis—one is called a "leader"; the other, a "follower." The two are about 3 or 4 degrees apart.

The magnetic properties of the two pairs are different. If the leader of the 35° N pair has the property of a north-seeking pole, the

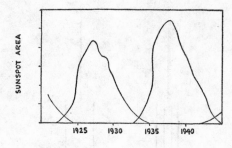

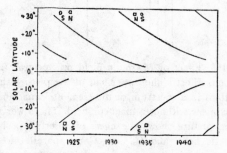

FIGS. 164 & 165. Sunspot Cycles. The upper diagram shows the variation in area of the sun covered by spots during one complete cycle (1922–1946). The complete cycle consists of two half cycles, with maxima in the years 1928 and 1937.

The lower diagram points out the variations in latitude, and in magnetic polarity.

At the beginning of the cycle one pair of spots appears in latitude 35° N; the western spot has a south-seeking magnetic polarity, the other a north-seeking; another pair appears at 35° S with reverse polarities. About 1928 the area covered was at a maximum (1390 parts in a million of the visible area of the sun were covered on the average). The spots moved closer to the equator: their mean latitude was only about 18°. In the early 1930's the sunspottedness was at a minimum, and the location was within a few degrees of the solar equator: a new half cycle is in the making, though at higher latitudes. The only difference between the second half cycle and the first is in the reversed magnetic polarity.

follower will act as a south-seeking pole. The polarities of the pair at 35° S will be reversed. The leader of the group below the equator will be a south-seeking pole, and the follower, north-seeking. The arrangement of spots at the beginning of the cycle is shown in Figure 165.

II. The original spots last several days; others then make their appearance. Three changes should be noticed:

(a) The number of spots is increasing.

(b) The size of the individual spots becomes larger.

(c) The spots move closer to the equator.

This continues for about four years, after which the maximum area is reached. Then, the area covered by spots may be 300 times larger than at the beginning of the cycle.

III. During the next seven years, the travel toward the equator continues; but the area covered by the spots gradually diminishes. The area reaches a minimum at the end of this period. This is the end of half the cycle. Minimum to Minimum.

IV. While the final spots are on their way out at latitudes 5° N and 5° S, the pioneering spots for the second half of the cycle make their appearance at latitudes 35° N and 35° S. One pair appears in the northern latitudes, the other in the southern. The second half of the cycle is similar to the first, with one major difference: the magnetic polarity of each spot is now reversed. Thus, if the leader at 35° N, 11 years ago, was a north-seeking pole, it will now show the properties typical of a south-seeking pole.

At the end of 22 years, a new cycle begins. Recent minima took place in the years 1889, 1913, and 1933.

NOTE: 1. The characteristics of sunspot cycle become evident only in an averaging process. During a period of maximum sunspot activity, the sun may be perfectly clear; during a period of minimum activity, a large proportion of the sun may be covered with spots. The two half-cycles, therefore, become apparent only in averaging a large amount of data.

2. The figure of 11 years for a half-cycle is also an average; observed periods may differ materially. Half-cycles of only 8 years are known; as are half-cycles of 14 years.

ROTATION OF THE SUN

Sunspots also yield information about the spinning of the sun on its axis. That the sun spins on its axis is suggested by two facts:

a. All sunspots move across the sun in the same direction.

b. Sunspots are behind the solar disk for as much time as they are in front of it.

Chief among other proofs is the one based on the Doppler Effect. The spectra of light from opposite sides of the sun show marked differences: that from the edge of the sun "going away" from the observer indicates a red shift; that from the limb of the sun approaching the observer indicates a shift of its lines toward the blue end of the spectrum.

The direction of the sun's spinning is the same as that of the earth. For an observer on the sun, the stars would rise on the eastern horizon and set in the west. Or, an observer outside the sun, looking down at its North Pole, would see it spinning in a counterclockwise direction.

The period of one complete revolution about its axis is *not* a constant, but varies with the latitude. At the equator, it is 24.6 days. The period for other latitudes is given in the table.

Solar Latitudes	Period of One Revolution
Equator 0°	24.6 days
30°	26.0 "
45°	28.4 "
60°	31.2 "
80°	35.3 "

The study of Astronomy would be far more complicated if this were true of the earth—if, say, a day at the equator were 24 hours, and a revolution about the axis of the earth at latitude 60° took 30 hours.

INCLINATION OF THE SUN'S AXIS

Further, sunspots yield information about the inclination of the sun's axis, based on the slight curvature in the route followed by the spots: the solar axis is inclined by 7° 10′ of angle to a line making 90° with the earth's orbit. In March, the sun's north pole is tilted away from the earth; in September, toward the earth.

THE EFFECT OF SUNSPOTS ON THE EARTH'S MAGNETIC FIELD

There seems to be a close correlation between sunspot activity and the earth's magnetic field, as the presence of large spots on the sun often greatly disturbs the earth's normal magnetic field. **Such disturbances last several days and are called Magnetic Storms.** A magnetic storm usually starts when the spots are close to the central meridian of the sun. The storm on the earth may commence any time between 2 days before to 4 days after meridian passage; the most likely time for the start is one day after central meridian passage. Magnetic storms are not detectible by the five senses. They play havoc, though, with equipment that is affected by the earth's magnetic field. The ordinary navigational compass is of little use, as its needle does not point to a fixed direction, but may change directions from minute to minute. Due to the storm, electrical currents are set up in the earth, which materially disrupt telegraphic communications.

There are major exceptions in the sunspot-earthmagnetic field relationship. An important magnetic storm occurred on November 13-14, 1894, when there were almost no spots on the solar disk. Conversely two large, active spots crossed the solar meridian on December 17 and December 20, 1946, without causing any severe magnetic disturbances.

THE EFFECT OF SUNSPOTS ON AURORAS

There seems to be a close relationship between sunspots and auroras, since the latter are most frequent and most brilliant during sunspot maxima. The auroras seen in the northern hemisphere of the earth are known by one of two names: Aurora Borealis and Northern Lights. It is one of the most dramatic of terrestrial phenomena, resembling a gigantic curtain of multicolored light, most often green, but also rose, lavender and violet.

On rare occasion the aurora covers the whole visible sky, from horizon to zenith.

To the best of our knowledge auroras result from charged particles (electrons, protons) that are ejected from the sun. The interaction of these particles with the outlying gases of the earth's atmosphere produces the beautiful light of the aurora. It is believed that the shape of the aurora is greatly influenced by the earth's own magnetic field. The incoming solar particles are routed the last thousand miles by the magnetic field of the earth.

THE EFFECT OF SUNSPOTS ON TERRESTRIAL AFFAIRS

Ever since the period for the sunspot cycle was determined, astronomers have been looking for corresponding cycles on earth. Astronomers and statisticians have tried to find a correlation between sunspots and birth rate, sunspots and business activity, sunspots and liquor consumption, etc. Few clearcut correlations have been found: one concerns the thickness of annual rings of growth in trees; another, still debated, is the average temperature of the earth. It is claimed by some weather experts that the earth's average temperature is lower by as much as 2° F in the year of sunspot maximum.

Turning from the surface of the sun let us regard its atmosphere.

THE REVERSING LAYER

This is the name given to **the lowest of the three layers in the sun's atmosphere.** The base of the layer is the surface of the sun; the top extends to about 1000 miles above the surface. This thickness is obtained from studies of solar eclipses. The time it takes the moon to cross that layer and the known value of the moon's speed are used in that computation.

The reversing layer is responsible for the many (thousands) dark lines in the otherwise continuous spectrum of sunlight; the gases in the reversing layer absorb these particular wave lengths. The resultant spectrum appears dark in the places usually occupied by these wave lengths. A curve showing the energy distribution of the sun's energy indicates that absorption. At certain wave lengths the energy normally present was "ripped out." See Fig. 166.

The wave lengths of the dark lines identify clearly the chemical composition of the reversing layer.

The identification is obtained by comparing the wave lengths of the dark lines with those in spectra produced by chemical elements in the laboratory, thus identifying the presence of 61 out of the 92 elements present on the earth. Among the 61 elements present in that layer are hydrogen, carbon, nitrogen, oxygen, aluminum, iron, cobalt, cadmium, lead and platinum. It is very likely that more than 61 elements will eventually be identified.

Very likely the ratio of the several elements in the reversing layer holds for the sun as a whole: due to the violent turbulence in the atmosphere there is a continuous interchange of material between the sun and the reversing layer. In the several billions of years that this interchange has taken place a fairly homo-

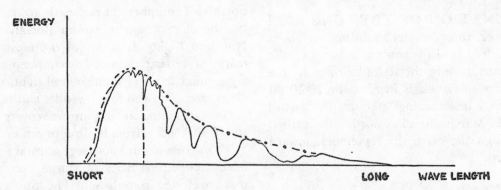

FIG. 166. Distribution of Solar Energy. The smooth dot-dash curve indicates the distribution of energy with wave length of the light leaving the photosphere of the sun. The vertical distance to the curve indicates the amount of energy present at any particular wave length.

The solid line curve indicates the distribution of solar energy reaching the terrestrial observer. The dips in the curve imply that energy has been removed ("ripped out") at these particular wave lengths.

Some of the dips in the solid curve are due to the gases in the reversing layer; others are due to absorption by water vapor and carbon dioxide in the earth's atmosphere.

geneous mixture was created, and the reversing layer is a good sample of it.

By weight hydrogen accounts for 46 per cent of the gases in the layer; oxygen for 24 per cent; helium for 6 per cent. The metals comprise most of the weight in the remaining 24 per cent.

During a solar eclipse a flash spectrum of the reversing layer—which has the same number of lines and the same wave lengths as the dark lines in the solar spectrum—can be obtained. The difference between them is that the flash spectrum consists of bright lines on a dark background, while the normal solar spectrum consists of dark lines on a rainbow background.

The existence of the flash spectrum was forecast theoretically. If the "cooler" gases of the reversing layer absorb certain wave lengths from a continuous spectrum, they must emit the same wave lengths when the continuous spectrum is not present. A spectrum taken of the reversing layer during an eclipse verified this forecast. To the moment of totality the regular solar spectrum was observed; at totality a dramatic change occurred, and the flash spectrum appeared. The "flash" spectrum lasts only two or three seconds.

THE CHROMOSPHERE

This is the name for **the middle layer in the sun's atmosphere,** the average thickness of which is about 6000 miles. In some zones of the sun the thickness may be as much as 8000 miles; in others, as little as 5000.

The chromosphere (i.e., Color Sphere) owes its name to its very bright color (orange), due largely to a line in the spectrum of hydrogen, denoted by "H-alpha," of wave length 6563 Angstrom.

Much of the research on the chromosphere can be conducted during daylight. The slit of the spectroscope is set tangent to the solar disk, so that the sunlight entering the slit is dispersed by the prism and hence greatly weakened. The orange color is all of one single wave length and is not dispersed. Hence the light from the chromosphere stands out brightly by comparison with the rest of the light.

Studies of the chromosphere indicate that the top layer is in a continuous state of great turbulence in which large masses of gas are thrown upward in all directions, often to great heights.

PROMINENCES

When the height of a disturbance exceeds 15,000 miles above the surface of the chromosphere, it is called a Prominence. These often occur in the region of sunspots, and may persist from several days to several months.

Prominences can best be described as thin sheets of orange colored flame standing on edge—at times resembling a feathery structure; at other times, gigantic trees. Their dimensions are formidable: an average height of 40,000 miles, and a cross-section of 10,000 × 100,000 miles. Many exceptions occur: prominences can reach heights of half a million miles, and more; and they have exceeded the diameter of the sun, which is close to a million miles.

For two reasons, an outstanding characteristic of a prominence is its speed:

    a. Its value, and
    b. The way it changes.

a. Speeds of 200 or 300 miles per *second* are common. In September, 1937, a great eruptive prominence was timed at a maximum speed of 450 miles per second, and ascended to a height of ¾ of a million miles in less than half an hour.

b. The change in speed is abrupt; the new velocity is a single multiple of the former. Thus a prominence may be rising at a speed of 80 miles per second, then rather suddenly change speeds to 160 miles per second; continue for a while at that speed, and then again suddenly start moving at 240 miles per second.

This phenomenon is known as the First Law of Prominences. There is no available explanation for that law.

CHROMOSPHERIC FLARES

Extremely bright clouds—known as "Flares" —appear from time to time above the chromosphere, differing from prominences in brilliance, size, and duration. Flares, at their maximum intensity, are easily the brightest spots on the sun, although much smaller than prominences. They develop and disappear extremely rapidly, reaching an intense brightness in 10 or 15 minutes, fading within several hours.

Flares are usually found in conjunction with active sunspot groups.

The scientific interest in chromospheric flares is due to their effect on radio communication, which is greatly disturbed during a "flare period." Normal communications may be impossible for hours and at times even for days.

Radio fadeouts are caused by strong ultraviolet light emitted by flares, starting a series of three events:

I. The Ionosphere is disturbed.

[Radio reception over long distances is made possible by the presence in the earth's atmosphere of electrified layers, which, like mirrors, reflect electromagnetic waves back to the earth. Several such concentric shells are present at various heights from about 40 to 200 miles above sea level. **The group of shells collectively is known as the Ionosphere.**

Low frequency radio waves are reflected by the lower shells; intermediate frequency by the shells at 150 miles; and so on. See Fig. 167.

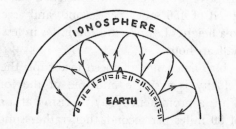

Fig. 167. The Ionosphere. The ionosphere acts as a mirror for radio waves.

Waves emitted from a transmitting antenna at point A on the earth's surface are reflected back and forth between the earth's surface and the ionosphere, and thus manage to reach all the way around the globe.

Fadeouts are due primarily to an excess of ions in these layers; such an excess absorbs the radio waves and does not reflect them back to the earth.

In the absence of such reflection radio transmission is only possible in line of sight. No signal could be received around the curved surface of the earth.]

The maintenance of electrified shells is attributed to the action of ultraviolet rays from the sun, the function of which is to maintain the right number of **electrified particles, known as ions,** in these layers. When some of these particles lose their electric charge, the ultraviolet rays provide replacements, which are produced by interaction between the radiation and normal oxygen and nitrogen atoms at those levels. In these interactions the atoms lose electrons (negative charged particles), and the remaining atoms become positively charged ions.

The production of the particles by ultraviolet radiation is a very delicate process. Too much production, or too little production, will upset the reflecting powers of the shells.

The disturbance in the ionosphere is most likely produced by flares, which cause the lower layers of the atmosphere to become ionized.

II. The lower layers being the denser, they produce an abnormally large number of electrons and positive ions.

III. The waves coming from the radio transmitter are exhausted in interaction with the large number of electrically charged particles. The result of these three events is that the radio waves are not reflected back to the earth, but are wholly absorbed by the ionosphere.

On July 31, 1937, high frequency radio communication over the entire Pacific Ocean was blotted out for nearly an hour as a result of a solar flare.

Interruptions in radio performance are, of course, of great interest to the military. Attempts have been made at various times to forecast these disturbances, but the forecasts, based materially on sunspot activity, are reliable only about 70 per cent of the time.

THE CORONA

The corona is the uppermost layer of the solar atmosphere, visible to the naked eye during a total eclipse of the sun. It resembles a pearly gray halo of intricate design surrounding the body of the sun, vastly larger than the two layers beneath it, being roughly half a million miles in thickness.

The shape of the corona is closely connected with the 11-year period: at sunspot maximum, it is circular and few pronounced rays protrude; at minimum, it is elongated and enormous streamers radiate. See Fig. 168.

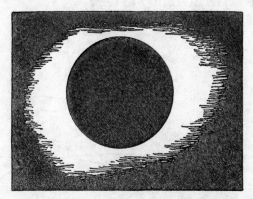

FIG. 168. The Corona. A drawing of the corona during the eclipse of the sun in the year 1900. Sunspottedness at the time was at a minimum; the corona is fairly elongated. The thickness is largest in the equatorial regions of the sun.

THE SPECTROHELIOGRAPH

Much of the knowledge about the sun and its atmosphere was obtained with the aid of an instrument known as a Spectroheliograph. Introduced by Professor Hale in 1890, it has been invaluable, enabling the astronomer easily to obtain the distribution of any element on the disk of the sun. In a few moments an astronomer can determine the distribution of hydrogen, oxygen, calcium, or any other element on the part of the solar surface facing the earth.

The spectroheliograph determines not only the location of the element on the sun's surface, but also the nature of its motion. Spectroheliograms taken of sunspot areas indicate, for example, the whirling motion of the hydrogen gas there present.

The instrument consists of an ordinary spectograph, to which an additional slit has been added, called the Spectrum Slit; the slit on the spectrograph proper is called the Source Slit. The function of the spectrum slit is to exclude all but the desired single wave length of light, characteristic of the element (say hydrogen) under study. If hydrogen is not present in the source, no light will enter the spectrum slit.

A photographic plate is placed next to the spectrum slit, connected to the source slit. Both move synchronously. As the source slit is made to move across the image of the solar disk, the plate will follow that motion across the spectrum slit. The developed photographic plate will show the areas on the sun where hydrogen, say, is present. See Fig. 169.

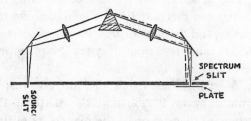

FIG. 169. The Spectroheliograph. The source slit and the spectrum slit are rigidly connected. As the first one is moved across the solar disk, the second moves in step across a photographic plate.

The source slit admits light from a very narrow strip of the solar disk. The light admitted is resolved into a multitude of wave lengths by the prism. The spectrum slit is adjusted for one particular wave length characteristic of one of the elements, say hydrogen.

As the two slits are moved in unison, each time hydrogen is present on the surface of the disk, its characteristic wave lengths will go through the spectrum slit and react with the chemicals on the photographic plate. Wherever the element is absent on the surface of the solar disk, no light will go through the spectrum slit and this particular part of the negative will remain unexposed.

Thus the locations of hydrogen, for instance on the surface of the sun, can be found by moving the source slit clear across the solar image.

The working of the spectroheliograph can also be explained as follows:

I. The source slit admits light from a small area of the solar disk.

II. The prism disperses that light into a spectrum.

III. The spectrum slit allows only one

narrow line of the spectrum, due to one element, to enter into the plate and affect its chemicals. If this area of the solar disk does not contain that element, no light enters. The chemicals on the plate are not exposed.

IV. The source slit, in unison with the plate, is then moved to another area on the solar disk, and then still another, until the whole disk of the sun is covered.

NOTE: This instrument is used primarily with an image of the solar disk. It cannot be used with stars, as they appear only as points of light, even at great magnification. It is of little use with planets, as theirs is merely reflected sunlight.

PART 2: THE MECHANICS OF THE SOLAR SYSTEM

INTRODUCTION

The Solar System consists of the sun; the planets and their satellites; the planetoids, the comets, and the meteorites. Both the adjective "solar" and the noun "system" are appropriate.

"Solar" indicates that the sun governs: it contains nearly 99.9% of all the matter in the system. (The mass of all the planets, satellites, etc. comprises the other .1 of 1%.) As a result of this division of mass, the "massive" sun is nearly stationary while all the "lighter" bodies revolve around it.

The word "system" implies that all the bodies observe great regularity in their motions. The laws governing these motions have been known for several centuries. Of great importance among the several laws are the three that are known by the name of their discoverer (Johannes Kepler), and the Universal Law of Gravitation (first stated by Isaac Newton).

KEPLER'S FIRST LAW OF PLANETARY MOTION

The orbit of every planet is an ellipse which has the sun as one of its foci.

DEMONSTRATION:

Object: To draw an ellipse.

Equipment: Pencil, piece of string, two thumbtacks, paper.

Procedure:

I. Place string to form an angle, ABC.

II. Fix the ends A and C with the thumbtacks, and place the pencil at B.

III. Keeping the string taut, move the pencil around to form the oval curve. See Fig. 170.

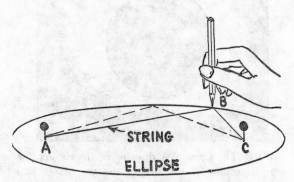

Fig. 170. Drawing of an Ellipse. Fix the end of the string at points A and C. Stretch the string to form the angle at B. Keeping the string taut at all times move the pencil about to form the oval curve.

A is one focus of this ellipse, C is the other.

Result: The curve described by the pencil is an ellipse. The two points that were kept fixed by the thumbtacks are called the foci of the ellipse (sing. focus).

PROBLEM 23:

Given an ellipse. Its major axis is 5 inches long, its minor axis is 3 inches long.

Find: 1. The distance between the foci; 2. the eccentricity of the ellipse.

Solution: 1. The major axis, the minor axis, and the distance between the foci are related by a simple formula. If the length of the major axis is denoted by a; if the length of the minor axis is denoted by b; and the distance between foci is denoted by c; the formula is:

$$b^2 + c^2 = a^2 \text{ or } c = \sqrt{a^2 - b^2}.$$

In this case, $c = \sqrt{5^2 - 3^2} = 4$ inches. The distance between the foci is 4 inches. See Fig. 171.

2. "Eccentricity" of an ellipse is defined as the ratio of distance between foci to length of major axis. It is denoted by "e."

$$e = \frac{c}{a}$$

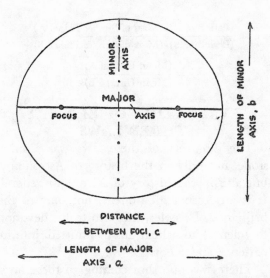

FIG. 171. In an ellipse the length of the major axis, a, the length of the minor axis, b, and the distance between the foci, c, are related by the formula—

$$b^2 + c^2 = a^2$$

This ratio, in the case of an ellipse, is always larger than 0 and less than 1. It indicates how "eccentric," compared with a circle, the ellipse is. When the ratio is small, say 0.1, the ellipse is very little eccentric. It is almost circular. When the eccentricity is large, say 0.8, the ellipse is highly elongated. In this problem the eccentricity is given by:

$$e = \frac{4}{5} = \cdot 8$$

Planets move in nearly circular orbits. The eccentricities of Venus and of the Earth are 0.01 and 0.02, respectively.

Comets move in elongated orbits. The orbit of Halley's Comet is an ellipse, with an eccentricity of 0.97.

KEPLER'S SECOND LAW OF PLANETARY MOTION

This law deals with the speed of the planets in their respective orbits. The speed is not constant, the planets moving faster the closer they are to the sun. The maximum speed of any planet is attained when it is closest to the sun, the minimum when it is farthest. The point on the orbit closest to the sun is known as Perihelion; the farthest, Aphelion.

Though the speeds of the planets in their orbits are not constant, another feature closely connected with speed *is* constant—namely, the speed with which the line connecting the sun and any particular planet passes over areas.

This is expressed in the formal version of Kepler's Second Law: **The radius vector of each planet passes over equal areas in equal intervals of time.**

The radius vector is an imaginary line that connects the sun with a planet—short at the perihelion and long at the aphelion.

The Second Law indicates that at aphelion, the planet moves slower than at perihelion in order to pass over equal areas of the ellipse. See Fig. 172.

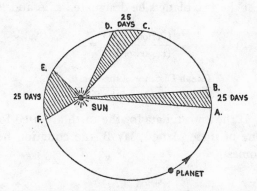

FIG. 172. Kepler's Second Law of Planetary Motion.

The radius vector would cover equal areas (three such areas are shown here shaded) in equal times (25 days).

At aphelion the planet moved relatively slowly to get from A to B.

At perihelion the planet had to move at a relatively high speed to cover the distance from E to F.

The term radius vector used in the formal version of the law is an imaginary line joining the sun with the planet. The line connecting the sun to A, or the sun to B, or the sun to D, etc., is a radius vector.

The earth's average velocity along its orbit about the sun is 18.5 miles per second. Since the orbit is almost a circle, its speed does not vary materially along the path. At aphelion, the earth moves only by ½ a mile per second slower than at perihelion.

In the case of highly eccentric orbits, such as those pursued by comets, the orbital speed varies greatly. Halley's Comet, when at perihelion, has a speed of 100 miles per second; and at aphelion, of less than 1 mile per second.

KEPLER'S THIRD LAW OF PLANETARY MOTION

The Third Law deals with the relationship between the period of a planet and its mean distance from the sun.

The "period" is the time that it takes a planet to complete one revolution about the sun. For the earth, this is 365.26 days; for the planet Mercury, only 88 days; for Pluto, the farthest planet, 248 *years*.

Kepler's Third Law states that: **The squares of the periods of any two planets are proportional to the cubes of their mean distances to the sun.**

This can be stated as an algebraic equation: Let the two planets be designated as A and B.

$$\frac{(\text{Period of A})^2}{(\text{Period of B})^2} =$$

$$\frac{(\text{Mean Distance of the Sun to A})^3}{(\text{Mean Distance of the Sun to B})^3}$$

If the known data for the earth are used for one of these planets, say B, the equation becomes:

$$\frac{(\text{Period of A})^2}{(365.26)^2} =$$

$$\frac{(\text{Mean Distance of the Sun to A})^3}{(93,000,000)^3}$$

This equation has two variables: the period of a planet and its mean distance. If one of these is obtained by observation, the other can be computed algebraically.

PROBLEM 24:

The period of the planet Mars is 687 days. Compute the mean distance of Mars from the sun.

Solution: Inserting the given data in the equation:

$$\frac{(\text{Mean Distance of Mars from Sun})^3}{(93,000,000)^3} = \frac{(365)^2}{(687)^2}$$

Answer: The distance of Mars from the sun is 142,000,000 miles.

NOTE: Kepler's Third Law is not quite complete. The complete form was evolved by Newton. In the complete form, "the squares of the periods" have to be multiplied by the combined mass of the sun and the planet. The corrected equation reads:

$$\frac{(\text{Period of A})^2 (\text{Mass of Sun \& Planet A})}{(\text{Period of B})^2 (\text{Mass of Sun \& Planet B})}$$

$$= \frac{(\text{Mean Dist. of A})^3}{(\text{Mean Dist. of B})^3}$$

EVALUATION OF KEPLER'S THREE LAWS

The discovery of these laws was a milestone, not only in the history of Astronomy, but also in the history of science in general. It is an eternal monument, not only to the brilliance of Kepler, but also to his devotion to science, to which he committed infinite patience and labor.

There was one shortcoming to these laws, however—a very important shortcoming. Kepler's Laws did not explain the behavior of the planets, why they move in elliptical orbits, or why their speeds change as they do.

The answers were soon forthcoming in Sir Isaac Newton's epoch-making book, *Mathematical Principles of Physics*. There, Newton showed that the planets behave as they do because of a most fundamental universal law —the Law of Gravitation; and that Kepler's Three Laws are merely consequences of that universal law.

NEWTON'S UNIVERSAL LAW OF GRAVITATION

The law, dealing with forces between material objects, states that every particle of matter attracts every other particle of matter with a force, depending on three factors:

a. Mass of one object.
b. Mass of the other object.
c. The distance between the objects.

These factors are often denoted as M, m and r, respectively.

The formal statement of the law is: **Every particle of matter in the universe attracts every other particle with a force that is proportional to the product of their masses, and inversely proportional to the square of the distance between them.**

The law can also be expressed as an algebraic equation:

$$F = \text{gravitational constant} \cdot \frac{Mm}{r^2}$$

The gravitational constant depends on the units used for the masses, for the distance, and for the force. If M and m are expressed in grams,

r in centimeters, and
F in dynes,

then the value for the gravitational constant is 6.7×10^{-8}. The formula for the Universal Law of Gravitation will then be:

$$F = 6.7 \cdot 10^{-8} \frac{Mm}{r^2}$$

PROBLEM 25:

A mass of 2000 grams, about 4.4 pounds, is at a distance of 2.54 centimeters (about 1 inch) from another mass of 5000 grams. Find the force of attraction between these two bodies.

$$F = 6.7 \cdot 10^{-8} \frac{2000 \times 5000}{(2.54)^2} = .1 \text{ dyne}.$$

Answer: The force with which each mass attracts the other is .1 dyne.

A dyne is an extremely small force, much smaller than a pound of force. Approximately 500,000 dynes are equal in value to one pound of force.

APPLICATION OF THE LAW OF GRAVITATION

The law was of enormous aid in solving a host of problems. Chief among these are:

I. Freely falling bodies. Any body not properly supported, will fall toward the center of the earth.

II. Ocean tides and tides in the atmosphere.

III. Motion of comets.

IV. Precession of equinoxes.

V. Motion of planets. If the gravitational force between the earth and the sun ceased to operate, the earth would go off on a tangent. It is the direct result of this law that planets revolve about the sun as they do.

This result is shown in Figure 173.

The nine planets move in elliptical orbits at various distances from the sun, counter-clockwise.

Although gravitation applies, of course, to the stars and galaxies as well, its effect is easier to see in the case of planets because of the

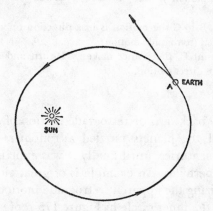

FIG. 173. Effect of Gravitational Attraction. It is due to the gravitational attraction of the sun that the earth continues to move in its orbit.

In the absence of this attraction the earth would leave its elliptical orbit and go off on a tangent, such as at point A, farther and farther away from the sun.

presence of *one* large mass (the sun) acting on several close, smaller masses (the planets). The perturbation on these motions by distant stars is extremely small.

APPARENT MOTION OF PLANETS AS SEEN FROM THE EARTH

The true motion of the planets cannot be observed from the earth, because the earth itself is constantly in motion. Observations indicate only the motion of the planets relative to that of the earth. At times a planet's relative velocity, with respect to the earth, is greater than its true velocity, as when the earth and the planet move in opposite directions; at other times the planet's relative velocity is less than its true velocity, as when a planet and the earth move in the same direction.

Of particular interest in the apparent motion of planets is the Retrograde Phase. Then, planets seem to move in a direction opposite to their normal one. See Fig. 174.

FIG. 174. Retrograde Motion. As seen against the background of the celestial sphere the planet was moving at A in the normal direction (this is called "direct motion"), and continued to do so until point B.

From B to C the motion is in a direction opposite to normal (retrograde motion).

At point C, the planet makes a U-turn and continues in direct motion.

The backward or retrograde motion of several of the planets puzzled astronomers for many centuries, until finally it was explained by Copernicus. An example is of great aid in visualizing the apparent retrograde motion.

Let the inner circle in Figure 175 represent the orbit of the earth around the sun. Let the large circle represent the orbit of Mars. The earth, being closer to the sun, moves faster than Mars. Let the top of the figure represent

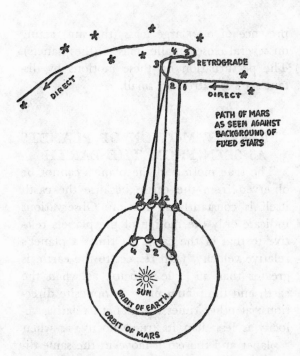

FIG. 175. Explanation of Retrograde Motion. The earth, being closer to the sun than Mars, moves faster than Mars (the earth completes its circle in 365 days; Mars in 687). At point 1, Mars is "ahead" of the earth; its motion is direct. At point 5 the earth is "ahead" of Mars, and the latter seems to retrograde.

part of the celestial sphere. The sphere serves as a background upon which the movements of Mars are observed.

When the earth is in position 1, Mars will be seen in place 1 on the celestial sphere. Several weeks later, both the earth and Mars will have moved in their orbits. Mars is now at point 2. As the earth moves through positions 3, 4, and 5, the trace described by Mars on the celestial sphere will be of a body in retrograde motion.

SIDEREAL AND SYNODIC PERIOD OF A PLANET

In connection with planets, there are two definitions of period: (a) Sidereal period; and (b) Synodic period. These differ in length due to the motion of the earth.

a. Sidereal Period is the time it takes the planet to complete one revolution in its orbit. Another way of saying the same thing is: It is the time required by a planet to complete a circle on the celestial sphere, **as seen from the sun.**

b. The Synodic Period of a planet involves the motion of the earth. A formal definition is: **It is the interval between one time that the sun, the earth, and planet are aligned and the next time.** Since both the earth and the planet are in motion, the synodic period differs materially from the sidereal.

Thus, the sidereal period of Mars is 687 days; its synodic period is 780 days.

In the case of Saturn, the sidereal and synodic periods are 29.5 years and 378 days, respectively. The former signifies that it takes Saturn nearly 30 years to complete its orbit about the sun; the latter that every 378 days, the sun, the earth, and Saturn are situated along a straight line. This is shown in Figure 176.

The 378 days are composed of (a) 1 revolution of the earth about the sun (365 days); and (b) 13 days to catch up with Saturn which, in the meanwhile, has moved to a new position in its orbit.

There are two simple formulas to compute the synodic periods of planets. One formula

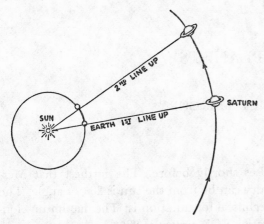

FIG. 176. The Synodic Period of Saturn. This period is the interval of time between one lineup of sun-earth-Saturn to the next time these planets form a straight line.

The synodic period of Saturn is 378. It consists of 365 days for a complete revolution of the earth plus 13 days needed for the earth to catch up with Saturn, which in the meanwhile moves on to a new position.

is to be used for interior planets, the other for exterior.

Mercury and Venus are Interior Planets. They are closer to the sun than the earth.

The orbits of the other planets are outside the earth's orbit. See Fig. 177.

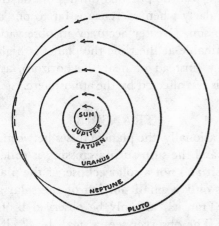

FIG. 177. Orbits of Five Outer Planets. The orbits are ellipses of small eccentricity, hence closely resemble circles. All the planets move in a counterclockwise direction, as shown by the arrows.

The length of the arrow indicates the distance the planet travels in one year.

The four innermost planets (not shown) move along orbits inside the orbit of Jupiter.

These are Exterior Planets.

The formula for interior planets is:

$$\text{Synodic Period of Planet} = \frac{360}{P - E}$$

P is the number of degrees of arc that a planet moves in its orbit in one day.

E is the number of degrees that the earth moves in its orbit in one day.

For Mercury and the earth,

$$P = \frac{360}{88} \text{ ; and}$$

$$E = \frac{360}{365\frac{1}{4}}$$

Substituting these numbers in the formula, we then get:

$$\text{The Synodic Period of Mercury} = \frac{360}{\dfrac{360}{88} - \dfrac{360}{365\frac{1}{4}}}$$

$$= 116 \text{ days}$$

For exterior planets, the formula is:

$$\text{Synodic Period of Exterior Planets} = \frac{360}{E - P}$$

where E and P have the same meaning as in the previous formula.

The proof of this formula is fairly simple. The denominator E — P stands for the number of degrees that the earth gains on a planet in *one* day. But in a synodic period, the earth gains a complete revolution (360°) on the planet; hence, that period is equal to the number of times (E — P) is contained in 360.

PROBLEM 26:

Compute the Synodic Period of Mars.

Given: The Sidereal Period of the earth is 365¼ days, or $E = \dfrac{360}{365\frac{1}{4}}$;

and the Sidereal Period of Mars is 687 days, or

$$P = \frac{360}{687}$$

Answer: 780 days.

CHAPTER XI

THE INNER PLANETS

PART 1: THE PLANET MERCURY

BASIC DATA

Diameter: 3,000 miles
Volume: 0.06 that of earth
Mass: 0.05 that of earth
Density: 0.8 that of earth
Distance to sun: mean 36,000,000 miles
                max. 43,400,000 miles
                min. 28,600,000 miles

Orbital velocity: mean 30 miles per sec.
               max. 36 miles per sec.
               min. 23 miles per sec.

Period of one revolution, sidereal: 88 days
Period of one revolution, synodic: 116 days
Eccentricity of orbit: 0.206
Inclination of orbit to orbit of earth: 7°
Period of rotation about axis: 88 days
Albedo: 0.07
Surface gravity: 0.35 that of earth
Velocity of escape: 2.7 miles per second

INTRODUCTION

The nine planets can be divided into two distinct groups: **Terrestrial Planets and Major Planets. Mercury, Venus, Earth, Mars, and Pluto are terrestrial planets, the name implying that these planets are similar to the earth in size.**

Jupiter, Saturn, Uranus, and Neptune are the "major planets," and are much more massive than the terrestrial ones.

Mercury is the planet nearest to the sun; at its brightest, it is more brilliant than a first-magnitude star.

TIMES FOR OBSERVATIONS

Mercury—due to its nearness to the sun—can be observed only during evening or morning twilight. The planet, when east of the sun, sets soon after the latter; when west, it rises shortly before. The farthest that Mercury can be from the sun is 28° of angle. The technical formulation is: The maximum elongation of Mercury is 28°.

(Elongation is the angle subtended at the earth by the sun and one of the planets.)

The length of time that Mercury can be observed is further reduced by the slant of this elongation.

The elongation is never perpendicular to the horizon, but somewhat inclined toward it. March, April, August, and September are the best months in which to observe Mercury, when the elongation is closest to being vertical.

Astronomers do not limit their observations to the twilight hours. By eliminating diffuse sunlight from the telescope, observation of Mercury can be pursued during the daytime, particularly when Mercury is far to one side of the sun. Greater accuracy in observations is attainable at the time the planet is high in the sky (instead of near the horizon), as its light is less affected by the atmosphere.

TRANSITS

Occasionally, the planet crosses between the earth and the sun; **such a crossing is called a Transit and not a solar eclipse, as the planet covers only a small portion of the solar surface. Transits can only be observed by telescope.** The observer sees a small black circle, less than 1% the diameter of the sun, slowly crossing the solar disk.

Transits only occur either in May or November. (The next transits of Mercury will occur on May 8, 1970, November 10, 1973, and November 12, 1986.) Transits occur so rarely because the large (7°) inclination of its orbit to the orbit of the earth results in the planet usually passing either north or south of the sun.

Accurate measurements of transits are used not only in exact determination of the orbit of Mercury, but also in computing the earth's period of rotation—which latter indicates that the earth is slowing down. (The period of one revolution about its axis will increase by one second in the next 100,000 years.)

PHASES

Mercury goes through a series of phases, from full to new, similar to those of the moon. When it is beyond the sun, most or all of its illuminated face can be seen by telescope; but when it is on the same side of the sun as is the earth, only a small crescent is visible.

The brightness of the planet varies with changes in phase, although when "full" it is far from the earth and the "fullness" is offset by the distance.

A DAY EQUALS A YEAR

It takes Mercury 88 days to complete a trip around the sun. A year on Mercury, therefore, lasts 88 terrestrial days.

It takes Mercury 88 days to complete a rotation about its own axis. Thus a mercurial day is equal to 88 terrestrial days.

The fact that these two periods are equal is responsible for the phenomenon that Mercury always exposes the same face to the sun. And if it were not for libration (see below), 50 per cent of Mercury's surface would always be exposed to the sun, while the other 50 per cent would be in eternal darkness.

LIBRATIONS

Libration is a to-and-fro motion of a planet, similar to the oscillating motion of a balance before coming to rest (or similar to the motion of shaking the head, when saying "no"). Due to this motion, large areas of Mercury are alternately exposed to sunshine and to darkness. Computations show that one

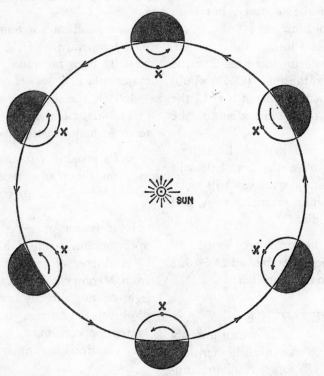

FIG. 178. If orbit of Mercury were a circle, there would be no librations. One half of the planet would always receive sunshine, the other would always be dark.

Note that an observer, represented by point X, completes one rotation, while the planet makes one revolution about the sun.

zone, 134° wide, continuously receives light from the sun. The sunshine zone is bordered on each side by 47° wide zones alternately exposed to sunlight and to darkness. The rest of Mercury's surface is a zone about 132° wide, over which the sun never shines.

The librations of Mercury are caused by the fact that the planet rotates about its axis at constant rotational speed, completing one rotation in 88 days, while it moves along its orbit at speeds varying from 36 miles per second (at perihelion) to 24 miles per second (at aphelion), also completing one revolution in 88 days. Thus at certain times, Mercury is ahead in rotation relative to revolution, and, at other times, it is farther along its orbit than it made progress in rotation.

Figure 179 shows in detail the chronology of one such libration.

a. At point A, the planet is at perihelion. The black dot represents an observer on Mercury, who would see the sun on the meridian.

b. During the 20 days between A and B, the orbital velocity was greater (near perihelion) than the spin velocity. The sun is no longer on the meridian of the observer, but is at point B, 23.5° east of him.

c. As Mercury speeds toward the aphelion, point C, the spin velocity increases. For the hypothetical observer, the angle (23.5°) would become smaller. When the planet is at C, the sun will again be in the meridian of the observer.

d. During the second half of the ellipse, through points D to A, the first half will repeat itself; however, now the sun will move to the west 23.5° and on returning to A, will be back at the meridian.

To recapitulate: the sun moved first 23.5° eastward and returned; then moved 23.5° due west and returned to the meridian.

TEMPERATURE

The temperature of the side continuously facing the sun is, of course, much higher than the other; the two 47° zones, receiving sunshine alternately, have an intermediate temperature. Direct measurement of the sunshine facing Mercury, when the planet is closest to

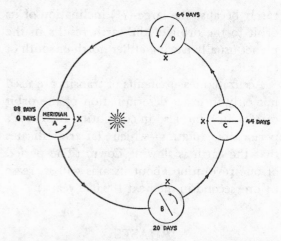

Fig. 179. Libration of Mercury. At point A the planet is at perihelion. An observer at point X would see the sun on his meridian.

During the next 20 days (from A to B) the sun revolves faster than it spins; the sun will now be 23.5° east of the observer at X.

During the next 24 days, Mercury spins faster than it revolves about the sun, so that at aphelion the sun is again at the meridian.

In the upper half of the circle the same phenomena will be repeated in reverse order.

An observer at X will see the sun move 23.5° east, then 23.5° west, repeatedly, similar to the oscillating motion of a balance before it comes to rest.

the sun, indicates a temperature of 779° F. The temperature of the dark side has never actually been measured, but reasonable estimates place it at close to absolute zero, —460° F, the lowest temperature possible.

The high temperature on Mercury is due to three major factors:

a. Its proximity to the sun. Every unit of area on the planet receives seven times as much radiation as an equal unit of area on the earth.

b. It is not protected by an atmosphere. Spectrograms taken of Mercury show a complete absence of gases. The spectrum of light from Mercury is identical to the spectrum of light coming directly from the sun. No trace of absorption by any gas can be found in the Mercury spectrum.

c. Continuous sunshine on the same area.

ALBEDO

Albedo pertains to the ability of an object to reflect light. Some objects—e.g., tops of clouds—reflect most of the light falling upon them; others absorb most of the light, reflecting little. Stones, rocks and soil are poor reflectors of light.

Albedo is usually defined as the ratio of the quantity of light reflected to the light received by the object.

Mercury's albedo is found to be .07—i.e., 7 per cent of the light received by Mercury from the sun is reflected back into space, and 93 per cent of the light is absorbed by the planet.

SURFACE GRAVITY AND VELOCITY OF ESCAPE

The surface gravity of Mercury is about 0.35 times that of the earth—i.e., the gravitational force is only about $\frac{1}{3}$. A 9-pound object would indicate 3 pounds on a spring balance there.

Its surface gravity explains the absence of a gaseous envelope (atmosphere) around Mercury.

Because of the low value of surface gravity, the velocity of escape from the surface of the planet is only 2.7 miles per second: any object leaving Mercury with a velocity of 2.7 miles per second would leave forever. (On earth, the velocity of escape is 7 miles per second.)

Gases have the property of expansiveness— every gas spreads in all directions and occupies ever larger volume. The surface gravity of earth is strong enough to counteract the expansive tendency of the atmosphere. On Mercury, however, the gravitational force is too weak to prevent the escape of gases. Gas molecules that usually have a speed in excess of 2.7 miles per second can thus escape from the planet. If there had been any atmosphere on Mercury, it must have escaped a long time ago, materially aided by the intense temperature on part of the planet.

PART 2: THE PLANET VENUS

BASIC DATA

Diameter: 7700 miles

Angular diameter: max. 67 seconds of angle
min. 11 seconds of angle

Mass: 0.81 that of earth

Density: 4.8 times that of water; 0.89 that of earth

Distance to sun: mean 67,270,000 miles; 0.72 that of earth

Maximum elongation: 47 degrees

Orbital velocity: 22 miles per second

Period of one revolution about sun: 225 days, sidereal
584 days, synodic
mean

Eccentricity of orbit: 0.007

Inclination of orbit to earth's orbit: 3°

Period of rotation about axis: Unknown; possibly 30 days

Albedo: 0.6

Surface Gravity: 0.87 that of earth

Velocity of escape: 6.5 miles per second

Distance from earth: max. 160,000,000 miles
min. 26,000,000 miles

INTRODUCTION

The planet is outstanding in many respects:

a. It is the brightest of the heavenly objects, with the exception of the sun, the moon and extremely rare comets. At its brightest, it is visible during daytime and is strong enough to cast shadows of objects at night.

b. It comes closest to earth, approaching to a distance of 26,000,000 miles.

c. It has the most nearly circular orbit: the eccentricity of its ellipse is a mere 0.007.

d. Its diameter is 400 miles smaller than earth's.

And yet, very little is revealed about Venus, either by telescopic observations or by photographic methods—for both the view is a uniformly illuminated, intensely white disk. Photographs of Venus in ultraviolet light indicate the presence of dark belts which change from day to day.

The surface of the planet has probably never been seen: the image is almost certainly due to dense clouds high above the surface, which obstruct view and prevent penetration of sunlight.

TELESCOPIC OBSERVATIONS

These observations are often made during the daytime, because Venus, when visible in the evening, is too close to the horizon. Two closely related features are of interest to the observer: (a) the phases; and (b) the changes in the apparent diameter.

PHASES AND
APPARENT DIAMETER

As the planet approaches the line joining the earth and the sun, it reveals a crescent, which grows narrower as it approaches—the length increasing as the width decreases. Just before the light is entirely cut off from Venus (as with a new moon), its crescent is six times larger than when it is full. **When the planet is directly between the sun and the earth, it is said to be at Inferior Conjunction.** Venus is full (as with a full moon) when it is on the opposite side of the sun from the earth. **That point on the orbit of an interior planet is called Superior Conjunction.** See Fig. 180.

BRIGHTNESS

Its remarkable brightness results from several favorable factors:

    a. its closeness to the sun;

    b. its closeness to the terrestrial observer; and

    c. the high value of its albedo. Nearly 60% of the light received by Venus from the sun is reflected back into space.

Venus does not appear at maximum brightness in its full phase, because of its remoteness from earth at that time. It appears brightest just before and just after it passes inferior conjunction. (Specifically, it is brightest 36 days before and 36 days after it crosses the line joining the earth with the sun.) Then, it is close enough to the earth to appear large, and the crescent is wide enough to supply a sizable reflecting surface.

TRANSITS

On rare occasions, Venus passes directly in front of the sun; such a transit may be observed through a smoked glass without the aid of a telescope. The complete face of the sun is not eclipsed because the shadow of Venus covers only a small portion of it. If the transit is central, the crossing may last as long as eight hours.

Such a transit was first accurately observed in 1639; four later transit visits have been closely studied, the last in 1882. The next one is due in 2004.

Transits of the sun do not occur at every inferior conjunction because of the inclination (3°) of the orbit in which Venus travels to the orbit of the earth. As a result, Venus is sometimes on one side and, sometimes, on the other side of the earth's orbit, i.e., half the time it is slightly above the ecliptic and the other half slightly below the ecliptic. During the time of inferior conjunction when Venus is either above or below the ecliptic, no transit will occur. It is only when Venus is (a) just crossing the ecliptic, and (b) at inferior conjunction, that transit is possible—the two oc-

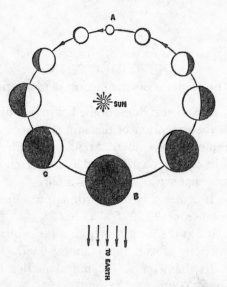

FIG. 180. Phases of Venus. Venus appears as a circular disk of light (full) when it is at Superior Conjunction (A on diagram).

As it moves toward position B (inferior conjunction), less and less of the illuminated surface of Venus can be seen by a terrestrial observer.

However, because its diameter increases, Venus will appear at its brightest 36 days before (position C) or 36 days after inferior conjunction.

curring simultaneously on the average of once every 50 years.

The two points of intersection between the orbit of a planet and the plane in which earth revolves (the ecliptic) are called nodes—one point is called an "ascending node"; the other, a "descending node." The line joining the two points is called the nodal line.

The conditions for the occurrence of a transit of Venus can also be stated as follows: A transit will occur if the line joining the earth and the sun coincides with the nodal line.

THE CLOUDS

There is no direct proof that the visible surface of Venus consists of a dense layer of clouds; but the indirect evidence is manifold.

a. The brightness of Venus is attributed to reflection from clouds. Dull rock is a poor reflector.

b. No fixed surface marks have ever been photographed. The usual photograph of Venus reveals a smooth, uniform, white disk.

c. Accurate measurements show that the radiation emitted by the planet itself (not reflected sunlight) is nearly the same from the bright as from the dark hemisphere of the planet. This equality of radiation can only be explained on the assumption that the radiation was emitted by the clouds. Clouds above the dark hemisphere could emit almost as much radiation as clouds above the hemisphere exposed to the sunshine. An estimate of the temperature of these clouds would be $-30°$ F.

d. Definite cloudlike markings, such as billows, can be detected on photographs.

One theory holds that the clouds consist of droplets of formaldehyde, for which the chemical formula is CH_2O. The formaldehyde is supposedly produced on Venus by the combination of H_2O and CO_2 to form $CH_2O + O_2$.

The lack of H_2O on Venus is explained as having been exhausted in the formation of the formaldehyde clouds; the lack of oxygen, as having been exhausted in chemical combinations (oxidation) with the surface material of the planet. Such oxidation could easily take place at the high temperatures prevailing on the surface of the planet.

THE ATMOSPHERE

Atop the clouds on Venus is a heavy concentration of CO_2, which very likely also fills the space between the surface of the planet and the base of the clouds. There seems to be no oxygen nor is there any suggestion of water vapor in the atmosphere. If oxygen or water vapor is present, it must exist under the cloud layer.

The height of the atmosphere is estimated to be from 1 to 5 miles, based upon studies made during inferior conjunction. When the planet is about 2 degrees of angle from conjunction, the crescent extends greatly and forms an envelope around the entire planet. Sunlight comes through this atmospheric shell from behind. When the planet is almost in line with the sun, the atmospheric refraction may produce a luminous ring around the entire planet.

SURFACE TEMPERATURE

No direct measurements have been made of the surface temperature of Venus, but it is thought to be quite high, probably far above the boiling point of water.

This conjecture derives primarily from a phenomenon known as the "Greenhouse Effect."

GREENHOUSE EFFECT

This effect, best demonstrated in greenhouses, can be observed on the earth, as well. The glass roof acts as an energy trap very readily admitting sunlight, mainly of wave lengths between 4000 and 7000 Angstrom, at which wave lengths it is perfectly transparent. It does not permit the radiation coming from the warmed earth inside the house to leave, being opaque to that "dark heat" which has wave lengths of, say, 100,000 Angstroms. The result is that energy in the form of heat is accumulated in the greenhouse.

Air behaves in much the same way, perfectly transparent to sunlight, opaque to radiation emitted at the surface. It is believed that for Venus, the "greenhouse effect" produces a surface temperature of several hundred degrees Fahrenheit.

ROTATION

That the dark side of Venus is almost at the same temperature as the illuminated side seems to indicate that the planet is spinning on its axis. The rate of such spin must be fairly large. But measurements of the Doppler Effect proved negative: no Doppler shift of lines due to fast rotation could be detected. If there is any rotation of Venus about its axis, it must be fairly slow.

As a compromise between the two extremes, it is now suggested that the period is approximately 30 days.

LIFE ON VENUS

It is unlikely that life of the terrestrial kind is present on Venus.

The total lack of oxygen on Venus suggests the absence of both animals and plants: animals cannot live without inhaling oxygen; plants cannot exist without exhaling oxygen.

A temperature of several hundred degrees Fahrenheit is not conducive to the welfare either of animals or plants.

Quite possibly an eternal darkness prevails at the surface, as sunlight probably cannot penetrate the layer of clouds, and only the heat portion of solar radiation penetrates.

This is conjecture; there is a *slight* possibility that there is an earthlike atmosphere beneath the thick cloud layer on Venus.

Very little is known about the surface conditions on Venus. Some astronomers think that Venus has a mountainous surface; others believe that its surface is a homogeneous dust bowl; and still others theorize that the surface is completely covered with water. Those who believe that Venus has a mountainous surface base their view on the observation of irregularities in the terminator or in the boundary between the planet's day and night hemispheres. These observations, however, are not conclusive. It is possible that the irregularities are caused by atmospheric conditions.

All of the above theories are highly tentative. More exploration will be required before definite answers can be given. Data obtained from high altitude balloons revealed the presence of water vapor in the planet's atmosphere. The combination of water vapor, carbon dioxide, and solar radiation increases the probability that some form of life exists on Venus. This probability would be even greater if the surface of the planet is covered with water.

Definitive answers to questions concerning the planet's surface, the composition of its atmosphere, and the possibility of life on Venus will be obtained by a manned space probe, without landing on the planet, or by an actual landing on Venus.

THE TRIP TO VENUS

The average distance from the earth to the sun, 93,000,000 miles, remains constant because the centrifugal force caused by the earth's orbital velocity about the sun, 18.5 miles per second, is just equal to and opposite the gravitational pull of the sun. To bring the space ship that is traveling with the earth's orbital velocity closer to the sun, the space ship's velocity must be decreased to about 17 miles per second or a relative velocity of *minus* 1.5 miles per second with respect to the earth. The negative sign implies that the space ship must be launched in a direction opposite to that in which the earth is moving.

In addition to the velocity of 1.5 miles per second, the space ship would require enough speed to escape from the earth's gravitational field, an additional 7 miles per second.

From the standpoint of gas economy, the best route to follow is an ellipse, with the launching point on earth being the aphelion and the contact point with Venus being the perihelion. See Fig. 180A.

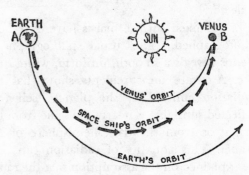

Fig. 180A. The orbit that the space ship would follow for minimum fuel consumption is indicated by the heavy arrows.

Giving the space ship the proper speed and direction are only two of the tasks involved in getting a space ship from earth to Venus. Other factors that must be considered are:

1. Getting the space ship through the earth's atmosphere by a route that would minimize mechanical drag caused by friction.

2. Regulating the ship's velocity so that it is low when the air is dense and so that the velocity is increased when the density of the air decreases.

3. Decreasing the speed of the space ship as it approaches the planet's surface.

4. Planning for landing on a surface, the consistency of which is unknown. It may turn out to be as solid as rock or as fluid as water.

5. Determining the biological reactions to which the human body will be exposed during the various phases of the trip.

CHAPTER XII

THE EARTH AND ITS MOON

PART 1: THE EARTH

BASIC DATA

Diameter: Equatorial—7,927 miles
          Polar—7,900 miles
Surface area: 195 million square miles
Volume: 260 billion cubic miles
Mass: 6.6×10^{21} tons
Density: 5.5 times that of water
Distance to sun: 93,000,000 miles
Orbital velocity: mean 18.5 miles per second
Period of one revolution about the sun: sidereal—
    1 year, or 365.24 mean solar days
Eccentricity of orbit: 0.17
Period of rotation about axis: 23 hrs., 56 min., 4 sec.
Inclination of equator to orbit: 23.5 degrees
Incoming solar radiation: 1.94 calories per cm² per
    minute
Albedo: 0.4
Acceleration at sea level: 32.2 feet per second per
    second
Velocity of escape: 7.0 miles per second

INTRODUCTION

The earth is one of the smallest of the nine planets revolving about the sun, ranking fifth in diameter, fifth in mass, and third in distance from the sun. Otherwise, it is very like several other planets.

So far as is observed, it is the only place in the universe on which "life" exists.

As a base for astronomic observation, it is far from excellent, its major drawback being that it is not stationary, so that all observations must be corrected for its motion. Nor is its motion simple; it is, rather, a highly complex combination of at least *six* elementary motions:

a. It rotates about its axis (once a day).

b. The axis revolves about the sun (once a year).

c. The axis precesses.

d. The axis nutates.

e. The sun, with the earth and the other planets, speeds through the local cluster of stars at a speed of 12 miles per second.

f. The local cluster of stars takes part in the rotation about the center of Our Galaxy at a speed of hundreds of miles per second.

The senses do not make one aware of these motions, much as passengers in a smoothly running train are hardly aware of its speed.

Only when measurements are made of the movements of other heavenly bodies does the effect of the motion of the earth have to be carefully considered.

ROTATION

The earth spins counterclockwise about its axis, completing one revolution in a sidereal day, the duration of which is 23 hours, 56 minutes, and 4 seconds (The sidereal day is shorter than the "clock" day, which is known as the "mean solar day")

Many experiments prove that the earth spins about its axis; one of the most decisive is that devised by the French physicist, J. B. L. Foucault, in 1851, in which the rotation of the earth becomes directly visible.

The only necessary equipment is a pendulum, which may consist of a sphere of lead, and a suspension wire. To obtain accurate results:

a. the suspension wire should be long;

b. the lead sphere should be heavy; and

c. the pendulum suspended on good bearings.

According to the theory on which the experiment is based, a freely swinging pendulum maintains its plane of oscillation—that is, if a pendulum is started in a North-South direction, it will continue to swing in that direction until air resistance or friction brings it to rest. See Fig. 181.

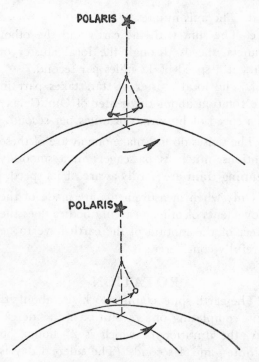

FIG. 181. (a) The Foucault Pendulum (above). Experiment as performed above the North Pole. Note the line traced at the start of the experiment.

(b) The pendulum (below) continues to swing in the same plane. The line has moved on in a counter-clockwise direction. At the end of six hours the trace makes an angle of 90° with the plane in which the pendulum swings.

(The best place, scientifically, to conduct the experiment is at the earth's North Pole.)

The procedure follows:

a. Start the pendulum swinging.

b. Mark a line on the ground indicating the trace of the pendulum's bob.

c. Observe that an hour later, this line has turned 15° in a counterclockwise direction, relative to the plane in which the pendulum swings.

d. Observe that in one sidereal day, the line completes one revolution, counterclockwise.

The original experiment was performed in the Pantheon in Paris, with a 200 ft. length of suspension wire. At the Paris latitude, the experiment is slightly more complicated; the consequence, though, that the earth spins about its axis is inescapable.

NOTE: We are not aware of the true motion of the earth. What is observed is an **apparent one**, consisting of an apparent rotation of the celestial sphere—that is, the stars and the sun rise on the eastern horizon and set on the western horizon. This relationship between true and apparent motion has its counterpart in a moving train. Looking from a window of a north-bound train, one sees the apparent due south motion of the neighoring terrain.

Several effects are directly due to the spinning of the earth:

a. The procession of day and night. Every place on earth alternately faces the sun (day) or is on the opposite side of the sun (night).

b. The rigidity of the axis. The earth's axis maintains its inclination to its orbit, pointing at all times to the North Star; in this respect, the spinning earth resembles greatly a spinning gyroscope. Also, like a gyroscope, the earth's axis precesses.

c. A centrifugal force—larger at the equator and zero at the poles—acts on every object on earth, accounting in part for the fact that objects weigh more at the poles than they do at the equator. (The difference in weight is minute and is primarily of scientific interest.)

d. The flattening of the earth at the poles was probably caused by its spinning at the time when its surface was still in liquid or plastic form.

THE SHAPE OF THE EARTH

The earth is very nearly spherical in shape, only slightly modified by its mountains and valleys; in fact, if it were scaled to the size of a billiard ball, it would be a more perfect ball.

The sphere is slightly flattened at the poles: the polar diameter is 27 miles less than that of the earth, at the equator. This flattening is the "oblate spheroid" which describes the shape of the earth.

The oblateness of the earth is also responsible in part for the variation of weight with latitude; since an object at the pole is closer to the center of the earth, it is greater in weight. The change in weight from equator to pole is about ½ of 1%.

REVOLUTION ABOUT SUN

The earth also revolves about the sun, counterclockwise. (The orbit of the earth is shaped like an ellipse, with the sun as one of its foci.) See Fig. 182.

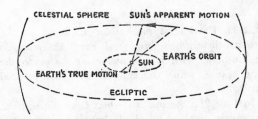

FIG. 182. The true motion is that of the earth about the sun. This results in an apparent motion of the sun about the earth. The path of the sun as projected against the celestial sphere is known as the Ecliptic.

The latter term (the Ecliptic) can also be defined in two other ways:

The Ecliptic is the path of the earth as seen from the sun against the background of the celestial sphere, or

The Ecliptic is the intersection of an infinite plane containing the earth's orbit with the celestial sphere.

Again, we see not the **true** motion, but rather the **apparent** motion of the sun, which appears, in the course of a year, to make one revolution about the earth. **This apparent orbit of the sun is called the Ecliptic; a belt 8° wide on each side of the Ecliptic is called the Zodiac.** There are twelve prominent constellations within the belt (Zodiacal Constellations), through which the sun, in its apparent motion, passes once every year. These are: Aries, Taurus, Gemini, Cancer, Leo, Virgo, Libra, Scorpio, Sagittarius, Capricorn, Aquarius, and Pisces. The sun is in the constellation Pisces towards the end of March.

If the bright sunlight could be eliminated, the sun could actually be seen within that constellation in March. Aries and Taurus serve next as temporary hosts. During the summer months, the sun passes through Gemini, Cancer and Leo, and so on, to complete the twelve zodiacal constellations.

This apparent motion of the sun about the earth is used to define "year." **"Year" is the time it takes the sun to complete the circuit of the stars.** This is a "Sidereal Year," **not** the year we normally think of, which is known as "Tropical Year," and is twenty minutes shorter.

INCLINATION OF EQUATOR TO ECLIPTIC

The path in which the sun follows its apparent motion on the celestial sphere is inclined to the celestial equator, the angle between the two circles being 23 degrees and 27 minutes.

One of the points at which the circles intersect is designated by the symbol ♈ and is known as the First Point of Aries; here, the sun crosses the celestial equator on its way from the southern to the northern portion of the Ecliptic.

The other point is designated by the symbol ♎ and is known as the First Point of Libra. When the sun is at either point, day is equal in length to night, everywhere on earth.

The sun is at ♈ on or about March 21st; this point is also known as the Vernal Equinox (translation: Spring equal night). It is at ♎ on or about September 23rd; the First Point of Libra is also known as the Autumnal Equinox. See Figs. 183, 184.

The inclination between the two paths is the primary cause of terrestrial seasons. When the sun is north of the equatorial plane, it is warm in the northern hemisphere, and cold in the southern for two major reasons:

a. The sun's rays are more concentrated. This is illustrated in Figure 185. In the northern hemisphere, the rays supply the heat for the small arc AB; in the southern, they are distributed over a much larger arc, CD. The southern hemisphere receives less heat per unit area.

b. The sun is above the horizon longer in the northern hemisphere. At 40° N, say, in June, daylight is nearly 15 out of every 24 hours. See Fig. 186.

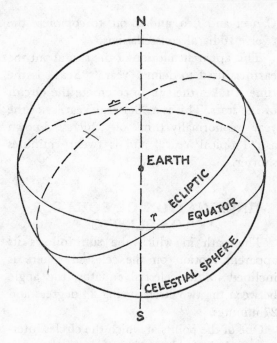

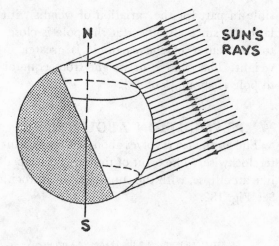

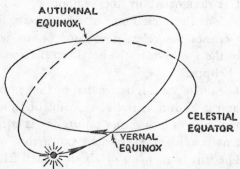

FIGS. 183 & 184. The apparent path traced out by the sun on the celestial sphere is known as the Ecliptic. It is inclined 23° 27′ with the earth's (or celestial) equator. The points of intersection of the two orbits are called equinoxes.

FIG. 186. Daytime is more than 12 hours in the northern hemisphere, and less than 12 hours in the southern. This is a contributing factor to the warm season, while the sun is above the celestial equator.

On June 21st the sun is farthest from the equator. The hottest weather in middle latitudes occurs later: average temperatures in the United States, say, do not reach their height until late July or early August. This lag results from the balance of radiation.

The earth not only receives radiation (light and heat) but also emits it. (This latter is in the invisible infrared range.) During July, the incoming radiation exceeds the outgoing, so that the average temperature continues to rise during that time.

The earth, moving in its true elliptical orbit, is closest to the sun during the southern summer. Due to the difference in distance, the southern hemisphere receives about 6% more solar energy than does the northern.

This increment of heat will not continue forever. In about 10,500 years, the northern hemisphere will receive that additional 6% of heat. This alternation is continuous, and results from a phenomenon known as Precession of Equinoxes.

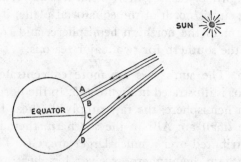

FIG. 185. The rays in the northern hemisphere are concentrated in the small arc AB.

The same group of rays falling on the southern hemisphere are spread out over the large arc CD. This is the primary reason for the warm season in the northern hemisphere.

PRECESSION OF EQUINOXES

The equinoxes are not permanent. Each point moves very slowly along the equator, completing one round in about 25,800 years. **The movement of the points is known as Precession of Equinoxes.**

The precession moves clockwise, while the apparent motion of the sun is counterclockwise. Thus, when the sun is approaching the vernal equinox, say, the latter moves forward to meet the sun.

The vernal equinox is used to define the Tropical Year (from the Greek word "trope," which means "turning") or the Season Year— what we normally mean by "year." Technically, Tropical Year is: **The period of time elapsed between two successive passages of the sun through the vernal equinox.**

Because of the motion of the equinox to "meet the sun," this year is shorter than the sidereal year, based on the fixed stars. The comparison is:

	Tropical Year	Sidereal Year
Days	365	365
Hours	5	6
Minutes	48	9
Seconds	46.0	9.5
	365.24220 days	365.25636 days

To understand the cause of the precession, it is best to use the true, not the apparent, motions of the bodies. The true picture is that the **sun is stationary, while the earth rotates about it in an elliptical orbit.** The earth's axis is not perpendicular to that orbit, but makes an angle of 23 degrees and 27 minutes with that perpendicular. See Fig. 187. As it

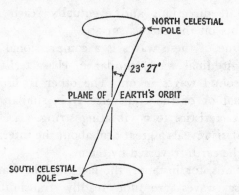

Fig. 187. The celestial poles trace out two circles each of 23° 27' radius.

revolves about the sun and spins about its axis, the axis traces a small circle in the sky. At present the axis pierces the sky within 1° from Polaris. See Fig. 188. The piercing point is, of course, the North Celestial Pole. In 1500 A.D., the North Celestial Pole was 3½°

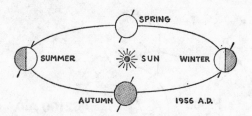

Fig. 188. The axis of the earth at present points toward the North Star. On this picture the axis is "up to the right."

from Polaris. About the year 2100 A.D., the celestial pole will be directed to a point on the celestial sphere only half a degree from Polaris. That is the closest the pole can be to Polaris.

About the year 14,000 A.D., the pole will be directed to a point 5° away from the star Vega.

Note that at that time, the axis of the earth will point "to the left," still making an angle of 23 degrees, 27 minutes with the perpendicular. See Fig. 189.

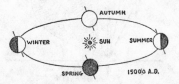

Fig. 189. In the years about 14,000 A.D., the earth's axis will point "up to the left."
Compare this to the present "up to the right" inclination.
Note that the magnitude of the angle 23° 27' did not change.

Following that, the pole will continue to trace the small circle of 23 degrees, 27 minutes radius in the sky, completing one revolution each 25,800 years.

The path of the celestial pole among the stars is indicated in Figure 190.

The cause of the motion of the earth's axis is the same as that of a spinning top.

The pull of gravity causes the leaning axis of the top to precess, describing the surface of a cone. See Fig. 191. The force that causes the earth's axis to precess is exerted by the sun and the moon on the slight equatorial bulge.

The effect of this force is to change the

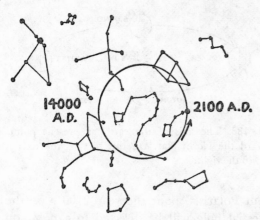

FIG. 190. In the year 2100 A.D. the North Celestial Pole will be within half a degree of Polaris.

In the year 14000 A.D. the pole will be within 5° of Vega. Vega will be the North Star at that time.

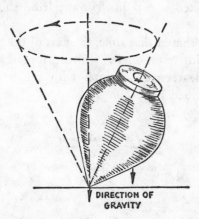

FIG. 191. In the case of a spinning top it is the force of gravity that causes the axis to "precess," that is, to describe a cone.

direction of the axis, not its inclination; the axis remains at 23° 27′ while it describes a complete surface of a cone once every 25,800 years.

The equinoxes move with the rotation of the axis, also making one revolution in 25,800 years.

NUTATION

The curve traced by the earth's axis is not a smooth circle. It has small waves, due to the "nodding" of the earth's axis about the mean position of 23° 27′. The true motion of the axis is a combination of precession and the nodding motion—the latter motion is known as Nutation (from the Latin word for "nod-

ding"). The period of one such complete wave is 19 years; the nod at its maximum is 9 seconds of angle. See Fig. 192. The gravitational pull of the moon is the primary cause of nutation.

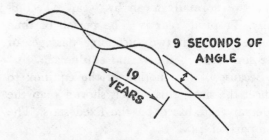

FIG. 192. The curve traced out by the North Celestial Pole is not a smooth circle. The waves in that curve are called Nutations. These waves have a wave length of 19 years, and an amplitude of 9 seconds of angle.

THE INTERIOR OF THE EARTH

Direct observations of the interior of the earth are possible only for the top several miles. The crust of the earth is about 30 miles thick and consists mostly of granite. Our knowledge of the layers beneath this crust is based on analysis of earthquake waves.

Earthquakes are caused by the slipping of one part of the earth's crust relative to the neighboring crust. The point of slippage is the origin of two sets of waves, which travel in all directions and eventually reach all points on the earth's surface.

One of these waves is a compressional or longitudinal wave, similar in characteristics to sound waves in air. The other is distortional or of the transverse type, similar in characteristics to a vibrating string. Careful analysis reveals a great deal about the interior of the earth traversed by them.

Thus, for instance, the fact that the transverse waves are not readily transmitted through the inner core of the earth seems to indicate that it is still in liquid form. (Liquids and gases are poor transmitters of such waves.) This core extends to about 2,000 miles from the center of the earth and is surrounded by the Intermediate Zone, 2,000 miles thick, extending to the crust of the earth. See Fig. 193. There is apparently a clear-cut boundary between the core and the intermediate zone,

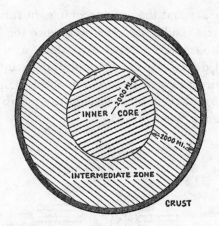

FIG. 193. Below the crust of the earth lies the Intermediate Zone. This is about 2,000 miles thick.

The inner core has a radius of 2,000 miles. It probably consists of iron-nickel in liquid form.

indicated by a sudden increase in the speed of earthquake waves about 2,000 miles from the earth's center.

Density-analysis indicates that the inner core is composed of some combinations of nickel and iron. The core must be rather dense to account for the earth's overall density, 5.5 that of water.

MAGNETISM OF THE EARTH

The earth is a great magnetized sphere. The magnetic axis is inclined 12° to the earth's geographic axis. (One of the poles of the magnet is near Hudson Bay; the other is in the Antarctic continent.) Magnetic poles are not fixed, but seem to shift, indicating that terrestrial magnetism is more likely due to a liquid than to a solid magnetic body.

While we have no conclusive explanation, it seems reasonable that the magnetic field is due to electric currents circulating within the earth's core.

THE ATMOSPHERE

Surrounding the earth's surface is an envelope of air.

The air is a mixture, not a chemical combination, of several gases. The composition, by volume, is 78 per cent nitrogen, 21 per cent oxygen, less than one per cent of argon, and minute parts of carbon dioxide and water vapor. It is quite possible that these percentages are different in the upper air, probable that hydrogen and helium play an important part in the composition of the air at heights of about 30 or 40 miles.

The average pressure exerted by this atmosphere is 14.7 pounds per square inch; 1013.2 in units of millibars, used in Meteorology. This is an average value—the actual value varies with time. Usually, high pressures, say 1030 millibars, are associated with good weather; low pressures, say 980 millibars, with precipitation.

The pressure at sea level is caused by the weight of the overlying air: at elevations above sea level, the pressure is less; at 3½ miles, the pressure is half of 14.7 pounds per square inch; at 7 miles, the pressure is ¼ of 14.7; and so on. Every 3½ miles, the pressure decreases to 50% of its previous value.

The density of the air follows the same rule as does pressure: at 3½ miles above sea level it is 50% that of sea-level value. At 100 miles, the density of the air is less than that obtainable in the best laboratory vacuum.

The earth's atmosphere has no sharply defined upper level. A study of meteors indicates the presence of air at levels up to 100 miles; a study of auroras, indicates the presence of air at least 400 miles above sea level.

The shell of air lying next to the earth's surface is called the Troposphere; the air above that, the Stratosphere: the boundary between the two layers is the Tropopause. The height of the tropopause varies with latitude, decreasing from a height of 10 miles above sea level at the equator to a height of 5 miles at the poles.

One of the functions of the troposphere is to adjust the temperatures at the earth's surface. Solar energy is usually supplied excessively at the lower latitudes, and rather sparsely in the northern latitudes. The exchange of air between latitudes moves part of the excess heat to the cooler parts, and vice versa, with the aid of large masses of air. Warm masses of air bring large quantities of heat with them to the north; cold air masses move south, to cool off the southern latitudes. **The boundaries between these large masses of air are known as Fronts.**

It is at the boundaries between air masses, at the fronts, that most of the inclement weather takes place—clouds, fog, and all forms of precipitation.

THE ATMOSPHERE IN ASTRONOMY

The earth's atmosphere affects in several ways incoming radiation: (a) reflection, (b) absorption, (c) diffusion, and (d) refraction.

a. **Reflection.** The phenomenon of twilight is a direct result of reflection by very small particles of dust and smoke which reflect the rays from the sun after it sets, or before it rises, back to the earth, thus providing additional daytime. See Fig. 194. Astronomical

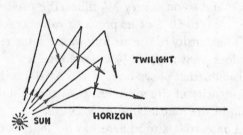

FIG. 194. Twilight is due to the reflection of light by particles in the upper air. Because of this reflection, daytime continues for long after the sun has set, or considerably before the sun rises.

twilight lasts until the sun's center is 18° below the horizon: then, even the faintest stars may be seen.

b. **Absorption.** The earth's atmosphere is a selective absorber, absorbing nearly 100% of some wave lengths of light; but only partially absorbing other wave lengths. Short ultraviolet rays are wholly absorbed in the atmosphere; light waves are only partially absorbed.

Selective absorption complicates the work of the astronomer: The light reaching the eye is materially different from the light leaving the star. This difference must be considered in the study of stellar spectra.

c. **Diffusion. This effect results from the scattering of light by individual molecules of air,** the amount depending on the color of the light. Blue light is scattered or diffused much more readily than red light. This selective scattering accounts for both the blueness

of the sky and the red and orange of sunsets: blueness results from the preference for it by the molecules of upper air, which scatter it in all directions; the red and orange, in that the direct rays of light at sunset are stripped of most of their blue, leaving the red to predominate. See Fig. 195.

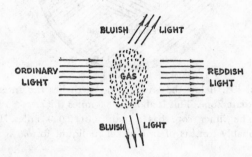

FIG. 195. Ordinary light on going through a gas is partly diffused and partly transmitted. The diffused light is richer in the bluish wave length; the transmitted part appears reddish because of its deficiency in the blue wave lengths.

d. **Refraction.** Light on passing from interstellar space through the atmosphere is refracted, the amount increasing as the light approaches the denser layer close to the earth.

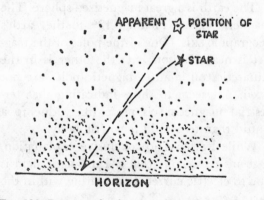

FIG. 196. Because of refraction the real rays of a star are bent. The human eye sees the star higher in the sky than it really is. For stars close to the horizon the error may amount to half a degree.

As a result, all celestial bodies appear higher than they really are. The amount of elevation is greatest near the horizon and diminishes rapidly as it approaches the overhead. Close to the horizon, it is slightly over half a degree. See Fig. 196. At altitudes of 10° above the horizon, the amount diminishes to 1/10th of a degree; at zenith, of course, the amount is zero.

Refraction permits the stars and the sun to be seen shortly before they rise and for a short while after they have set.

Refraction also produces the twinkling of the stars. The density of the air at various levels changes fairly rapidly due to the winds prevailing at those levels. Starlight on its way through is refracted in amounts that vary from second to second. This accounts for the "high speed jumping," the "twinkling," of stars.

PART 2: THE MOON

BASIC DATA

Diameter: 2160 miles

Mass: $\frac{1}{81.3}$ that of earth

Density: 3.39 that of water

Surface gravity: $\frac{1}{6}$ that of earth

Distance from earth:

      mean 239,000 miles; 60 times earth's radius
      max. 253,000 "
      min. 222,000 "

Period of revolution: sidereal 27.32 days
                    synodic 29.53 days
Orbital velocity about earth: 0.64/miles/sec.
Eccentricity of orbit: 0.05
Inclination of orbit to orbit of earth: 5° 9′
Period of rotation about own axis: 27.32 days
Inclination of moon's equator to moon's orbit: 1.5°
Albedo: 0.07
Surface temperature: max. 215° F
                      min. −300° F

INTRODUCTION

The earth has one satellite revolving continuously about it, while it is pursuing its own journey about the sun. Although its volume is only $\frac{1}{50}$ and its mass $\frac{1}{81}$ that of the earth, it affects the latter in a rather striking way. The periodic rise and fall of the ocean—the tides—is one instance of the moon's effect on the earth.

The extreme closeness of the moon has made possible its study since the early days of astronomy. The average distance is a mere 30 times the earth's diameter.

Some data had been obtained by telescope; but much of what is known is from naked eye observations—much of this is, in fact, common knowledge—for example, the fact that the moon goes through a complete set of phases every month, from new to crescent, to quarter, and so on; and also that the moon moves in almost the same path as the sun.

That the moon rises each day an average of 51 minutes later than on the previous day is well known, as is the fact that part of the moon always faces the earth, while another part is always hidden.

THE MOON IN ITS ORBIT

The moon moves about the earth in an elliptical orbit, with the earth as one of its foci. **The point on the ellipse nearest the earth is called Perigee**—the distance between the moon at perigee and the earth is 221,463 miles. **The point on the ellipse farthest from the earth is known as Apogee,** and that distance is 252,710 miles. The moon traverses this path counterclockwise. See Fig. 197.

The plane of the moon's orbit lies very close to the plane of the Ecliptic, the apparent path of the sun on the celestial sphere and is inclined about 5° with the Ecliptic. See Fig. 198. **The two points at which the moon's path intersects the plane of the Ecliptic are known as nodes.** These are not constant in space, but move clockwise along the Ecliptic, completing one revolution in 19 years.

The moon seems to move along its orbit much faster than the sun: it takes the latter a full year to complete the circuit; the moon, only one month. Half of this time, the moon is above the celestial equator; the other half, below that equator.

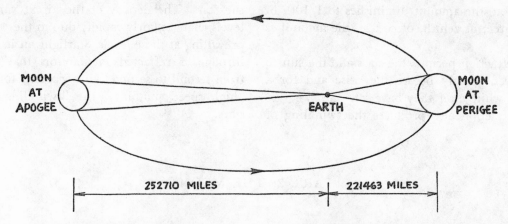

FIG. 197. The Moon in its Orbit. An observer above the North Pole of the earth would see the moon describe an ellipse in a counterclockwise direction.

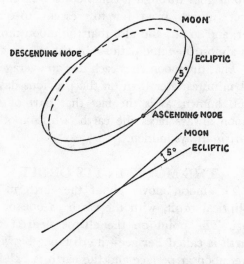

FIG. 198. The orbit of the moon is inclined by 5° to the apparent orbit of the sun (the Ecliptic). This can be seen both in perspective (above) and in the side view (below).

This seemingly faster motion causes the moon to rise and set a little later each day, the average delay being about 51 minutes.

OCEAN TIDES ON EARTH

The surface of the ocean rises and falls at any given place at more or less regular intervals. On an average, the period between two successive high tides is 12 hours and 25.5 minutes—exactly one-half the time it takes the moon to complete the circuit about the earth, i.e., one-half of 24 hours and 51 minutes. This is not a coincidence: the ocean tides are caused primarily by the moon's gravitational pull, an effect to which the sun contributes.

The formation of the tides is illustrated in a slightly exaggerated form in Figure 199.

A represents the center of the solid earth; B is a body of water facing the moon; and C is a body of water on the opposite side of the earth.

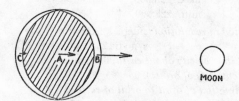

FIG. 199. The Formation of Tides. The force at A pulling on the solid earth is larger than at C and hence the earth pulls away (toward the right) from C, causing the high tide there. The force at B is larger than at A and hence the body of water at B pulls away from the solid earth causing the high tide on the face of the earth facing the moon.

The gravitational force of the moon is, of course, exerted on B and C as well as on A. The intensity of the force is largest at B, because of B's closeness to the moon and is least at C, because of its remoteness. The arrows on C, A, and B indicate the different sizes of lunar "pull." This difference in "pull" causes:

a. high tide at B, because it is pulled with greater force to the moon than at A;

b. high tide at C, because the earth is pulled away from it, thus leaving the water level high, relative to the earth; and,

c. low tide at the other two sides of the

earth, D and E, as the water flows from there to supply the high tide sides. See Fig. 200.

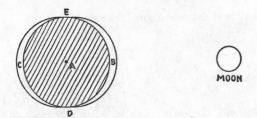

FIG. 200. The water at B is "escaping" from the earth causing high tide there.

The water at C is being left behind by the "escaping" earth causing high tide there.

The bodies of water at E and D will be at low tide at that time.

The tides travel with the apparent motion of the moon, from the eastern horizon toward the western horizon of the observer. Except for lags due to secondary effects, high tide at any place on the earth occurs when the moon is at the local meridian or at the antimeridian.

The effect of the sun on tides is secondary to that of the moon—the ratio of the tide-raising force of the sun is only about 7% that of the moon—due to its much greater distance.

When the tide-raising forces of the moon and the sun coordinate, the resulting tides are at a maximum—i.e., at new moon, when the two are at the same side of the earth. **Maximum tides are known as Spring Tides.** The other extreme is reached when the sun is at 90° to the moon—**the tides are then at a minimum, and are known as Neap Tides.**

The moon's closeness also has an influence on the magnitude of the tide. When the moon is at perigee, the tide-raising force is greater than normal by some 20%.

PHASES OF THE MOON

The moon's apparent change in shape from a narrow crescent to a full circle and then again to a narrow crescent, is due to the fact that:

It revolves **around the earth;** see Fig. 201, but it receives its illumination **from the sun.** At new moon, the configuration is:

The lighted side of the moon is turned away from the earth; the side facing the earth is dark. See Fig. 202.

Several days later, the configuration of earth, sun and moon are as shown in Figure 203. A crescent of light at point A will be seen by terrestrial observers.

In the course of half a month, the moon can be seen in the new, crescent, quarter, gibbous, and full phases.

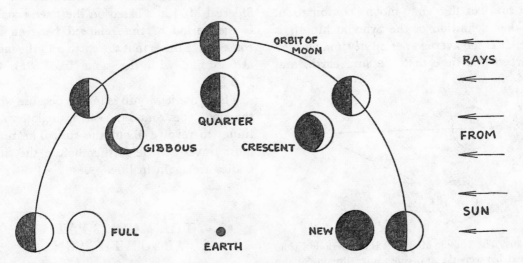

FIG. 201. The Moon in its Various Phases. The five circles along the orbit of the moon indicate the lighted hemisphere on the moon. The inner five circles indicate the corresponding illumination of the moon as seen from the earth.

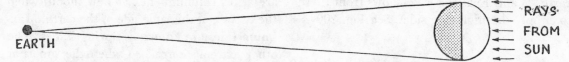

FIG. 202. The sun, the earth, and the moon at the time of the new moon. The side facing the earth is dark.

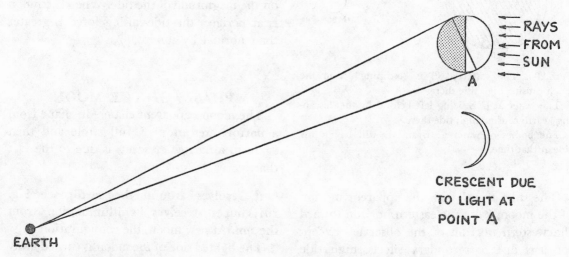

CRESCENT DUE
TO LIGHT AT
POINT A

FIG. 203. The Young Moon. Part "A" of the moon's sunlit surface is now seen by terrestrial observers, in the form of a thin crescent.

TWO KINDS OF MONTH

a. The Synodic Month is the interval of time elapsed between two consecutive new moons, or two consecutive full moons: its duration is 29.53 days—or more exactly, 29 days, 12 hours, 44 minutes, and 2.78 seconds. The definition of Synodic Month is based on the sun, earth, and moon combination. Another definition of the Synodic Month is that: **It is the average period of time elapsed between one time that the sun, earth, and moon form a line to the next time they do.** The Synodic Month is also known as the Lunar Month. See Fig. 204.

b. The Sidereal Month, or the Star Month, is shorter than the synodic, its duration being only 27.32 days, or 27 days, 7 hours, 43 minutes, 11.47 seconds. The definition of the Sidereal Month is based on the fixed stars. **It is the period of time elapsed between two consecutive times that the earth and the moon are in line with the same fixed star.** See Fig. 205.

The Synodic Month is longer because while the moon goes round the earth, the latter continues to revolve about the sun. The moon must travel a little farther before the three bodies are again in line.

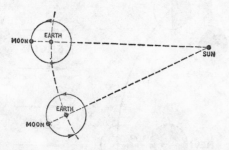

FIG. 204. The Synodic Month. It is the period of time elapsed between the two consecutive lineups of the sun, earth, and moon. In the upper part of this picture the three bodies are on a straight line; a Synodic Month later, the three are again aligned.

THE MOON'S PATH ABOUT THE SUN

With respect to the earth, the moon moves in a smooth ellipse with a speed that varies only slightly from an average value of .64

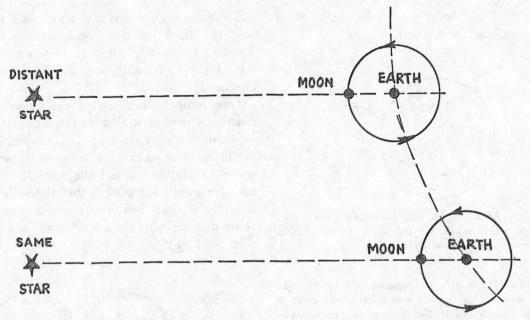

FIG. 205. The Sidereal Month. This is the period of one complete revolution of the moon about the earth, as seen from a distant star.

miles per second. With respect to the sun, both the path and the velocity of the moon are materially different—the path of the moon is wavy; the velocity, variable.

Half the time, approximately, the moon is outside the earth's orbit. The speed of the moon with respect to the sun is the sum of the two velocities—about 19 miles per second.

The rest of the time, the moon moves inside the earth's orbit. See Fig. 206. The speed of the moon with respect to the sun is the difference of these two velocities—about 18 miles per second.

Thus, it seems that the moon alternately moves in and out of the earth's orbit; and changes its velocity from a maximum of 19 miles per second to a minimum of 18 miles per second.

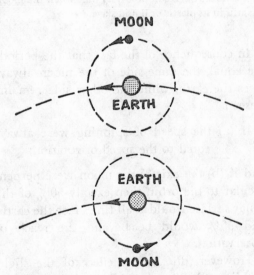

FIG. 206. The path of the moon about the sun. Half the time the moon is outside the earth's orbit, and moves in the same direction as the earth; the rest of the time the moon is inside the earth's orbit and moves in a direction opposite to that of the earth.

NOTE: In reality, the path of the earth about the sun is also wavy in character, and variable in speed. Precisely: the **center of gravity of the earth-moon combination** goes around the sun in a smooth ellipse, the earth and the moon describing circles about this center of gravity. As a result, the earth is at times inside the ellipse described by the common center of gravity; at other times, it is outside, following a wavy path with variable speed.

THE MOON'S ROTATION ABOUT ITS AXIS

The moon, while revolving about the earth, is also rotating about its axis. Its period of rotation is exactly equal to the period of revolution about the earth. With respect to the fixed stars, the moon completes one rotation in 27.32 days. The direction of the rotation, like the direction of the revolution, is counterclockwise. See Fig. 207.

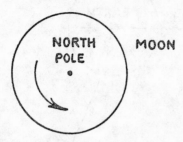

FIG. 207. An observer looking *down* at the north pole of the moon would see the moon spinning in a counterclockwise direction about its axis.

NOTE: The earth's gravitational pull on a slight bulge on the side of the moon facing the earth is probably responsible for the equality of the two periods, causing the period of spin to be equal to the period of revolution. It is also possible that this deformation of the lunar surface was originally formed by the earth; the result of a tidal pull when the moon was still in its plastic or liquid stage.

In consequence of the fact that the periods are equal, the same side of the moon always faces the earth, while the other side remains unseen.

If (a) the speed of spinning were always equal to the speed of rotation;

and if (b) the axis of the moon were perpendicular to the orbit, then exactly 50% of the lunar surface would at all times face the earth, and 50% would be beyond the reach of observation.

However, due to the effect of the slight noddings (the librations), the ratios are slightly different. 41% of the moon always faces the earth; another 41% is never visible; 18% is sometimes visible and sometimes not. The last is similar to the first, and it seems probable that the hidden surface is similar in character to the visible one.

LIBRATIONS

These are **apparent to-and-fro motions of the part of the moon facing the earth.** There are two distinct kinds of librations: (a) longitudinal, and (b) latitudinal. Due to longitudinal librations, an observer is able to see not only the "face" of the moon but also the "cheeks." Due to the latitudinal librations, the top of the "forehead" and the "chin" are alternately exposed.

Longitudinal librations of the moon are caused by reasons similar to those described in connection with Mercury—i.e., the spinning of the moon on its axis is at a **constant speed,** while its motion around the earth is at a **variable speed.** Spinning is sometimes ahead of and sometimes behind the revolving, thus alternately exposing the left side and the right side. See Fig. 208.

FIG. 208. Librations in Longitude. Due to these oscillatory motions, we are able to see not only the "face" of the moon, but also the right and left cheeks alternately.

Librations in latitude are due to the inclination of the lunar axis to the lunar orbit. The moon's axis is tilted by 6½° to a perpendicular line to that orbit. Terrestrial observers can see 6½° past the northern pole of the moon when that pole is tilted toward the earth; two weeks later, 6½° past the south pole of the moon is exposed. See Fig. 209.

FIG. 209. Librations in Latitude. Due to the tilt of the moon's axis to its orbit, observations can be made a little beyond the north pole as well as a little beyond the south pole of the moon. This is indicated in these figures by showing that during a period of two weeks the "forehead" of the "man in the moon" is in view, while during the other two weeks the "chin" is to be seen.

THE MOON'S SURFACE

Even the unaided eye notices "marks" on the "face" of the moon, the meaning of which is revealed by the telescope. The surface of the moon is covered with (a) craters, (b) seas, (c) mountains, (d) rills, and (e) rays.

a. **Craters.** The outstanding feature of the moon's surface is mountain rings, resembling somewhat craters of terrestrial volcanoes, of which, on the side of the moon facing the earth, there are more than 30,000. The mountain rings vary greatly in size; the largest has a base of 140 miles diameter, the smallest, a few hundred feet. The rims of these craters vary considerably in height. Some of them are bounded by high walls rising 3 or 4 miles above the surrounding terrain; others have heights of only a few hundred feet.

There is no general rule about the height of the floor in the hollow part of the crater. Some of these floors are at the same level; some are lower; and others are higher than the surrounding terrain. Nor is there any rule about the character of the inside floor. The floors of some craters are perfectly smooth; others are rough. See Fig. 210.

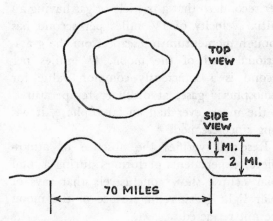

FIG. 210. A Crater on the Moon. Dimensions typical of a lunar crater are shown on the side view.

The prominent craters have been named after noted scientists and philosophers. In May, 1955 a twenty eight mile wide crater (near the Isaac Newton one) was proposed in honor of Professor Albert Einstein. Note on the map (Figure 211) the location of the craters named after Aristotle, Plato, Archime-

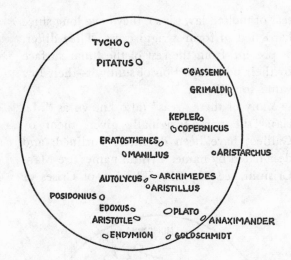

FIG. 211. Craters of the Moon. These were named after noted men of science.

des and Kepler. The origin of the lunar craters is still a matter of speculation.

There are two schools of thought; neither is absolutely convincing. One assumes the craters to be of volcanic origin; the other suggests that they were caused by the fall of giant meteorites.

I. Volcanic Origin.

For: (1) The similarity of the lunar craters to terrestrial volcanoes,

(2) their steep interior walls.

Against: (1) The enormous size of the lunar craters as compared with terrestrial volcanoes: a lunar crater covers an area thousands of times larger than the area occupied by a volcano:

(2) the presence of mountains inside the crater;

(3) the absence of any ejected volcanic material in the area close to the craters.

II. Meteoric Origin.

For: (1) The resemblance of these craters to deformation that would follow the impact of a meteorite.

Against: (1) The enormous size of the walled-in indentation, with a diameter in the dozens of miles. Large meteorites reaching the earth may be several feet in size. It is surmised that the earth was hit twice during its recorded history by "colossal" meteorites—probably of diameters of one or two miles. No meteorites having a diameter of dozens of miles are known.

b. **Seas.** This name was mistakenly given to the darker and smoother areas on the surface of the moon. They may have been at one time seas of molten lava; if so, they have long since hardened to form a rigid crust. They differ, at present, from the rest of the lunar surface by their poor reflection of sunlight—their low value for albedo.

Many of these "seas" (also known as "Marias," the name originally given them by Galileo) have been definitely outlined, and designated by name. Typical names are Mare Crisium, see Fig. 212 (The Sea of Crises or

FIG. 212.

Conflicts), Mare Fecunditatis (The Sea of Fruitfulness), and Mare Serenitatis (The Sea of Serenity).

The seas are approximately circular in shape and all but a few are connected. The diameter of the seas is in the hundreds of miles.

c. **Mountains.** There are ten mountain ranges on the part of the lunar surface exposed toward the earth, as well as many isolated mountain peaks. Several of the ranges have been named after terrestrial mountain ranges (e.g., Alps, Apennines); others, after eminent mathematicians and astronomers (e.g., Leibnitz). The lunar mountains rise to greater heights than the earthly ones. Many peaks of the Leibnitz and Doerfel ranges, which lie near the south pole of the moon, rise to heights exceeding 26,000 feet.

d. **Rills.** These are long, narrow crevices in the surface of the moon. These crevices, a mile or so wide, stretch in irregular shapes, passing

across other surface features, over distances in the hundreds of miles. The depth of these crevices is yet to be determined.

e. **Rays.** These are light-colored streaks on the surface of the moon, radiating in all directions from several of the more prominent craters.

These are best observed, because most conspicuous, near the period of full moon. They are 10 to 15 miles wide and at times stretch over other surface features for 500 to 2,000 miles.

SURFACE GRAVITY OF THE MOON

The surface gravity of the moon is only 1/6 that of the earth. This can easily be computed from the known figures of the radius of the moon and from its mass. The number 1/6 implies that the weight of every object on the surface of the moon is only 1/6 its weight on earth; and also that a body thrown upward would rise six times higher on the moon than on earth.

A direct result of the low value of the surface gravity is a low value of escape velocity, which in turn accounts for an absence of atmosphere. The escape velocity is 1½ miles per second, so that a particle of gas having an initial velocity of 1½ miles per second has enough momentum to escape from the gravitational pull of the moon. 1½ miles per second is a sufficiently common value for atmospheric gases at ordinary temperatures. If the moon ever had an atmosphere, it has long since escaped.

Research verifies the absence of atmosphere: experiments performed during a total solar eclipse show conclusively that rays of solar light grazing the surface of the moon are not refracted.

TEMPERATURE OF THE MOON

The temperature range on the surface is very large. The surface is exposed to the rays of the sun continuously for a period of two weeks, and then deprived of sunlight for an equal period of time. The difference in temperature between the light and the dark side is increased by the absence of an atmosphere and by the low value of 0.07 for the albedo.

Measurements of radiation that reach the earth from the sunlit side of the moon register temperatures well above the boiling point of water (212° F); measurements taken of the dark side of the moon indicate extreme cold there. The temperature of the dark side is probably close to −300° F.

The sun's heat does not penetrate very deeply below the moon's surface. This is evident from studies of lunar eclipses. The temperature at the moon's surface drops rapidly as soon as the supply of sunlight ceases. A change of 100° F in one hour is the rule. The temperature rises with even greater speed soon after the surface emerges from the darkness.

LIFE ON THE MOON

To the best of our knowledge, the moon is an arid, barren waste—neither animal nor vegetable life is possible.

The major reason for this supposition is, of course, the absence of atmosphere, which implies also the absence of water, for water evaporates and the vapor would escape into space just as do the other gases. The absence of water also implies an absence of clouds in the sky, as well as an absence of dust produced by water erosion and winds.

Without atmosphere, there is no transmission of sound, hence no possibility of speech. There is no twilight period; sunrise and sunset are abrupt. Without atmosphere there is no blue sky; the sky appears black. The sun is just a circle of light and the stars are visible during the day time.

A TRIP TO THE MOON

The moon is an average distance of 239,000 miles from the earth. Since rockets now exist that can give space ships a velocity of tens of thousands of miles per hour, a trip to the moon is feasible. In planning such a trip the following factors must be considered:

1. Getting the space ship through the earth's atmosphere by the shortest possible route. This must be done to minimize the mechanical drag caused by the friction of the air. It is advisable to make a vertical ascent for the first several scores of miles.

2. Planning the space ship's velocities so that they are relatively low where the air is dense and then gradually increased as the air becomes thinner. The idea is to minimize the heat produced by friction.

3. Navigating the proper course to reach the moon.

4. Giving the space ship a velocity of about 7 miles per second so that it may escape the earth's gravitational pull and enter into the gravitational pull of the moon. The neutral point at which the gravitational pull of the earth and moon balance each other is 24,000 miles from the moon.

5. Decreasing the speed of the space ship as it approaches the moon's surface. The gravitational pull of the moon would accelerate the speed of the space ship to a velocity of more than 5000 miles per hour by the time it approaches the moon's surface. Brakes of some sort (such as rockets firing against the direction of motion) would be required to reduce the velocity to a landing speed.

6. Providing facilities (fuels, etc.) for a return take-off from the moon. The take-off would be facilitated by two factors. The escape velocity would have to be about 1.5 miles per second (about 5000 miles per hour) and there would be no atmosphere to contend with.

7. The reactions of the human body to such changes as weightlessness and traveling at high speeds.

CHAPTER XIII

ECLIPSES OF THE SUN AND THE MOON

INTRODUCTION

a. **Eclipse of the Moon.** The earth, in its orbital motion around the sun, is accompanied by its shadow, which extends into space in a direction opposite to that of the sun.

A Lunar Eclipse occurs when the moon enters the shadow-cone. Figure 213 shows that such an eclipse must occur at full moon, that is, when the lighted face of the moon is toward the earth. Also notice that a lunar eclipse may

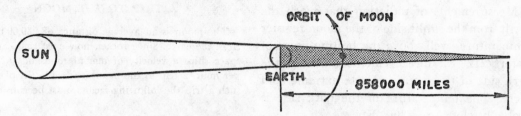

FIG. 213. The Lunar Eclipse. This kind of eclipse occurs when the moon is inside the shadow-cone of the earth. A lunar eclipse can be observed from any point on the night side of the earth. Such an eclipse can occur only if the usually lighted side of the moon is toward the earth, i.e., if the moon is full.

be observed anywhere on the night side of the earth.

The mean earth-moon distance being only 239,000 miles, a lunar eclipse "could" occur once every month. The frequency of these eclipses is much less than 12 times a year. In fact, there are many years in which there are no lunar eclipses; during other years, there is only one such eclipse in that period.

The shadow has the shape of a cone, the base of which is the cross-section of the earth, the average length of which is 858,000 miles.

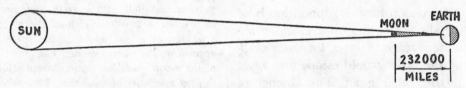

FIG. 214. Eclipse of the Sun. A total eclipse of the sun can be seen by terrestrial observers at all places on the earth touched by the moon's shadow-cone.

When the shadow-cone does not quite reach the earth an Annular (or Ring) Eclipse of the sun takes place.

Due to the variation in distance between the earth and the sun, the length of the shadow may differ from the average by about 25,000 miles.

The moon, due to the inclination of its orbit to the earth's orbit, usually bypasses the shadow-cone, the diameter of its base being a mere 2,160 going into eclipse.

b. **Eclipse of the Sun.** The moon, following its path about the earth, carries its shadow along with it.

This shadow, too, has the shape of a cone, though much slimmer than the earth's shadow-cone, the diameter of its base being a mere 2,160 miles. The length of the moon-shadow is on the average equal to 232,000 miles, varying by about 4,000 miles either way. See Figs. 214, 215.

Often it is not quite long enough to reach the earth. The moon-earth distance varies

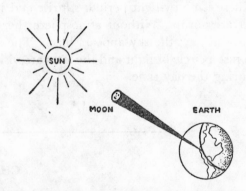

FIG. 215. A Total Solar Eclipse can be seen by terrestrial observers anywhere along the arc described by shadow-cone of the moon.

from 222,000 miles at perigee, to 253,000 miles at apogee; the mean distance being 239,000 miles.

A solar eclipse occurs when the path of the earth's surface is in the lunar shadow-cone;

when the shadow-cone does not quite reach the surface, a phenomenon known as "Annular Eclipse" or "Ring Eclipse" occurs. Under those circumstances, the cross-section of the moon is too small to cover the apparent diameter of the sun, and the "outskirts" of the sun, in the form of a bright ring, are visible to the observer.

CONDITIONS FOR A LUNAR ECLIPSE

A top view of the ecliptic would mislead one to think that there should be one lunar eclipse a month. This top view is shown in Figure 216. The apparent orbit of the sun

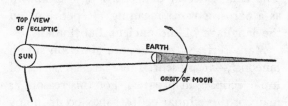

FIG. 216. Top View of Ecliptic. Looking down at the apparent orbit of the sun and the orbit of the moon, one gets the mistaken impression that lunar eclipses should occur once every month.

about the earth, the ecliptic, is shown in this figure as a heavy line.

The orbit of the moon about the earth is the thin broken line. The fallacy is revealed in the side view, which shows that the three bodies are, in reality, not in the same line.

FIG. 217. Side View of the Ecliptic. This view points up the fact that the moon is actually not in a straight line with the sun and the earth. The moon in its inclined orbit may pass by as much as 20,000 miles above the shadow-cone.

Due to the inclination of the lunar orbit to the ecliptic, the moon, may pass as much as 20,000 miles above or below the shadow-cone. See Fig. 217. The number of times it passes through the shadow is a small fraction of those it crosses above and below it.

For a lunar eclipse to occur, two important conditions must be fulfilled simultaneously:

Condition 1: The sun, the earth, and the moon must lie on a straight line, as in a top view—that is, the moon must be in its full phase as seen from the earth. This occurs once every month.

Condition 2: The moon, moving in its orbit, should just be piercing the plane of the ecliptic, that is, it should be at one of the nodes.

It has already been observed that the moon, half a month, is below the plane of the ecliptic and above the other half. **The points at which the moon pierces the ecliptic plane are known as Nodes: one, the Ascending Node; the other, the Descending Node. The line joining the two is called the Nodal line.**

Figure 218 shows two positions of the moon in which Condition 1 is fulfilled. Both at A and B the moon is full.

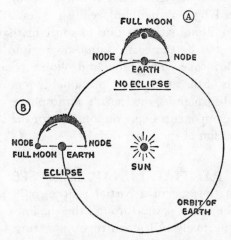

FIG. 218. Conditions for Lunar Eclipses. Both at A and at B the moon is full. There is no eclipse at A because the moon is well above the ecliptic; it will pass above the shadow-cone of the earth. There is an eclipse at B because the moon is in the plane of the ecliptic, and will have to go through the earth's shadow-cone.

There is no lunar eclipse at A the moon in its orbit is far above the ecliptic There will be a lunar eclipse at B because the full moon occurs at the time when the moon is at a node.

DURATION OF A LUNAR ECLIPSE

A lunar eclipse is of relatively long duration, as the thickness of the earth's shadow-cone where the moon passes through it is nearly 5,700 miles. If the moon passes centrally, it would be totally eclipsed for a period of close to two hours, since the moon's diameter is 2,160 miles and its average speed is 2,000 miles an hour. See Fig. 219.

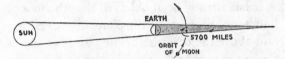

FIG. 219. Duration of a Lunar Eclipse. It takes the moon nearly an hour to enter the shadow. If the moon passes centrally through the cone the total eclipse time will be nearly two hours. The emerging lasts an hour.

The earth's shadow does not hide the moon altogether. Even when totally eclipsed, it is quite visible, its normal brilliance being replaced by a rather dull reddish color. This slight illumination is due to sunlight that is refracted by the earth's atmosphere into the shadow-cone. The blue and violet components of the sunlight are presumably removed by diffusion in the earth's atmosphere, the red components being responsible for the illumination of the lunar disk.

PARTIAL LUNAR ECLIPSES

In the case of a partial eclipse, only part of the moon passes through the shadow-cone, the normally full moon then appearing with a darkened notch either at its north or south side.

Partial eclipses, of course, precede as well as follow every total lunar eclipse. It takes about an hour for the full face of the moon to enter the shadow, and a similar period to emerge completely from the shadow.

SERIES OF LUNAR ECLIPSES

Eclipses come in series, a complete series consisting of either 48 or 49 individual eclipses, extending over a period of 865 years. The interval between two successive eclipses in a series is 6,585⅓ days. Successive eclipses show close resemblance to one another, demonstrating series-membership.

The process of deriving the figure 6,585⅓ follows:

In order to have a repetition of an eclipse:

I. The moon must again be full. This condition occurs every 29.53059 days.

II. The sun must again be in the same position with respect to the nodes. This occurs at intervals of 346.6201 days.

The least common multiple of these numbers is 6,585, that is, that every 6,585 days (or, exactly, 6585⅓ days) the moon, earth and sun will configure to repeat a previous eclipse. The time interval of 6,585⅓ days is known as a Saros, a word meaning "Repetition" in the language of the ancient Babylonians.

Many series of eclipses are going on simultaneously—at present, there are 28 series of lunar eclipses in progress. For this reason, as many as three lunar eclipses may occur in any one calendar year. Three eclipses is the possible maximum; the minimum is, of course, zero.

ECLIPSES OF THE SUN

Eclipses of the sun differ in several important ways from those of the moon:

a. Solar eclipse can occur only at new moon; lunar eclipse, only during full moon.

b. All lunar eclipses, both total or partial, can be observed simultaneously from every point on the terrestrial hemisphere that is turned toward the moon. Only the thinnest part of the shadow-cone produced by the moon ever touches the earth. The maximum diameter of the circle intercepted by the earth's surface is less than 170 miles. A much larger diameter is intercepted in the case of penumbra—that diameter is close to 4,000 miles.

The shadow-cone itself is often called the Umbra (Latin for shadow); the half-tone region in Figure 220 is called the Penumbra. Observers in that region will see only a partial eclipse of the sun, the percentage of the sun's surface eclipsed depending on the distance

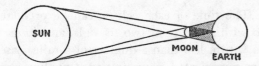

FIG. 220. The Umbra and Penumbra. The dark cone is the Umbra. Observers located at that place on the earth will see a total eclipse of the sun. The half-dark region next to the shadow-cone is the Penumbra. Terrestrial observers located there will see a partial eclipse of the sun.

to the umbra—the closer it is, the greater the percentage.

As the moon and its shadow-cone move in their assigned orbits, the small circle and the circle due to the penumbra follow. A typical route pursued by an eclipse is shown in Figure 221, taken from the 1947 edition of a

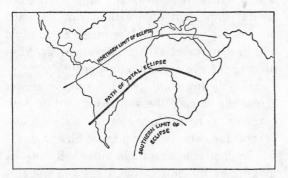

FIG. 221. Path of the Total Solar Eclipse in 1947. The width of the totality path was less than 100 miles. The Northern and Southern limits indicate the regions on the earth from which a partial solar eclipse could be observed.

publication by the Nautical Almanac office of the U.S. Naval Observatory in Washington, D.C. known as *The American Ephemeris and Nautical Almanac.* The moon's shadow-cone first touched the earth near the west coast of South America, and moving eastward, left the earth 3¼ hours later near the east coast of Africa. The total eclipse band in that case was less than 100 miles wide.

The speed of the shadow on the earth depends greatly on latitude and the angle the shadow-cone makes with the earth's surface. At the equator, the speed may be only 1,000 miles per hour. In higher latitudes, especially near sunrise or sunset when the shadow-cone

is greatly slanted to the earth's surface, it may be 5,000 miles per hour.

c. The duration of the total part of a lunar eclipse is nearly two hours, the greatest possible duration of a solar eclipse at any one point on the earth's surface is 7 minutes and 30 seconds.

SERIES OF SOLAR ECLIPSES

Solar eclipses, too, occur in series, a complete series containing 70 or 71 eclipses and lasting about 1,260 years. The period of 6,585⅓ days between two successive eclipses in one series is identical in length to that of lunar eclipses.

The 70 or 71 eclipses of any solar series follow a pattern. The first one of a series is always a very small partial eclipse near one of the earth's poles. Subsequent ones are less and less partial and occur farther from the pole. The eclipses that occur near the middle of a series are of the "total eclipse" kind; their route on the earth's surface is farther and farther away from the pole at which the series first made its appearance. Toward the end of the series, the eclipses again become progressively partial, the last one of the series appearing at the opposite pole of the earth from which they entered.

Due to the time denoted by the fraction in the figure 6,585⅓, each member of a series appears farther west as compared with its predecessor. The change in longitude is nearly 120 degrees, as the earth has turned ⅓ of a revolution about its own axis during that time. After each three eclipses the trace returns to the original longitude. The latitude will be farther south or farther north, depending on whether the series had its start at the north or the south pole of the earth. See Fig. 222.

There is no need to wait almost 18 years (6,585⅓ days) to see a solar eclipse; at present, eleven solar series are producing eclipses. Two of these, known as numbers 6 and 7, are producing eclipses of particularly long duration. Series 5 is of special interest as its path is along easily accessible places and it is of moderate (2.5 minutes) duration.

The minimum number of solar eclipses in

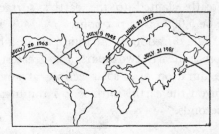

Fig. 222. Four Members of a series of Solar Eclipses.
Note: a) The period between successive eclipses in one series is nearly 18 years (6,585⅓ days).
b) Each member is located by ⅓ of a revolution west of its predecessor.
c) If the series started at the north pole, each successive member will be seen further south on the earth.

any calendar year is two. The maximum is five.

CATALOG OF ECLIPSES

The Austrian astronomer, T. Oppolzer, published a catalog in which are detailed descriptions of nearly 8,000 solar eclipses and 5,200 lunar eclipses between 1207 B.C. and 2162 A.D.; and the tracks of all the solar eclipses are shown on nearly 160 charts. Some follow:

Eclipses Visible in the United States Prior to A.D. 2000	Duration in minutes
July 20, 1963 Maine	1
Mar. 7, 1970 Florida	3
Feb. 26, 1979 Pacific Northwest	3

Eclipses of Long Duration Visible Outside the United States Prior to A.D. 2000	Duration in minutes
Feb. 5, 1962 Borneo, South Pacific	4
May 30, 1965 New Zealand, South Pacific, Peru	5
June 30, 1973 Guiana, Central Africa, Indian Ocean	7
Oct. 23, 1976 Congo, Indian Ocean, New Zealand	5
Feb. 16, 1980 Central Africa, India	4
June 11, 1983 Indian Ocean, Java, Coral Sea	5
July 11, 1991 Marshall Is., Central Mexico, Brazil	6
Nov. 3, 1994 East Indies, Australia, Argentina	4
Feb. 26, 1998 Central Pacific, Venezuela, Atlantic Ocean	4

The time of each eclipse can be predicted to within less than two seconds, and its path to within less than a quarter of a mile, based on complicated computations involving the positions and the motions of the moon and the sun. (In the United States, these calculations are made by the Naval Observatory, Washington, D.C.)

A DESCRIPTION OF A TOTAL SOLAR ECLIPSE

A total solar eclipse is many things to many people. To the primitive and the superstitious, it may cause great consternation and fright. Battles have been suspended and peace treaties signed in consequence of solar eclipses. For most of us, however, the total solar eclipse is simply a magnificent spectacle. The scientist is additionally interested since several important observations can be made only during the several minutes of totality, and so may travel halfway across the world to observe the phenomenon at totality.

The shadow-cone of the eclipse moves across the face of the sun from west to east, covering more and more of its western limb. Several important stages may be observed:

The first contact can be observed only by looking at the sun through smoked glass or overexposed photographic film. See Fig. 223A.

As the darkened western limb becomes larger, both the intensity and the quality of the sunlight change—it has less blue than the light from the center of the disk. See Fig. 223B.

In the last stages of the partial phase, the weird color of sunlight proceeding from the crescent is heavily accentuated, the dim, strange light seeming to affect both animals and plants: birds fly about, twittering; roosters crow; and dogs bark excitedly. See Fig. 223C.

Shortly before the phase of totality, fowl go to roost and many flowers close their blossoms, as they normally do at sundown. Images of the crescent sun appear in the shadows of tree leaves. See Fig. 223D.

Several minutes before the beginning of totality, ghostly shadow bands appear to be crossing over any exposed white surface. The

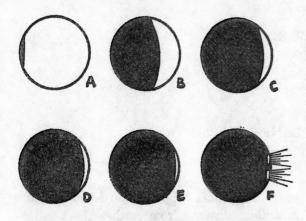

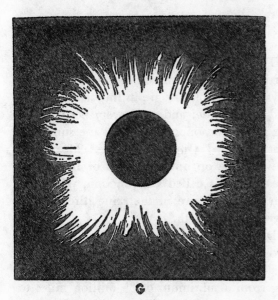

FIG. 223.

on display. The pearly halo surrounds the sun and, often, clearly defined streamers are seen emanating from the corona proper. Stars and planets make their appearance, adding greatly to the majesty of the scene. See Fig. 223G.

Totality may last as much as 7½ minutes. The uncovering of the sun then begins with the appearance of Baily's Beads on its western limb. All the phenomena that were seen at the eclipsing stage are repeated now in reverse order.

SCIENTIFIC INTEREST IN SOLAR ECLIPSES

Total solar eclipses offer unique opportunities to pursue several kinds of research:

a. The solar atmosphere can best be studied at the time of an eclipse; in particular, many photographs are taken of the flash spectrum, which is used to determine the exact thickness of the reversing layer, and in studies concerning the chemical elements constituting the layer.

b. A careful search is made in the immediate neighborhood of the sun for an intra-Mercurial planet—that is, for a planet closer to the sun than Mercury.

c. Contact times of the moon and the sun during eclipses serve as a check on the formulas used in determining the relative motions of these bodies.

d. Recent total eclipses were used to check the Einstein "bending." According to Einstein's General Theory of Relativity, light from stars should be slightly "bent" on passing close to the sun, due primarily to the effect of the gravitational pull of the solar mass on the rays of light. The values of the "bending," as forecast by Einstein's theory, correspond very closely to the ones found at the times of solar eclipses.

bands are atmospheric waves made visible by the narrow crescent of sunlight. See Fig. 223E.

A few seconds before totality, only several beams of sunlight reach the earth through the valleys on the moon's limb. (These are the so-called "Baily's Beads.") Those brilliant beads vanish almost at once and their disappearance marks the beginning of totality. See Fig. 223F.

At totality, the full beauty of the corona is

CHAPTER XIV

THE OUTER PLANETS

PART 1: THE PLANET MARS

BASIC DATA

Symbol: ♂
Diameter: 4,215 miles
Angular diameter: max. 24.5 seconds of angle
           min.   3.6 seconds of angle
Mass: 0.1 that of earth
Density: 3.9 that of water; 0.75 that of earth
Surface gravity: 0.38 that of earth
Velocity of escape: 3.2 miles/sec.
Period of rotation about axis: 24 hrs., 37 min., 22.6 sec.
Inclination of planet's equator to orbit: 25.2 degrees
    of angle
Distance to sun: mean 142,000,000 miles
Orbital velocity: 15 miles per sec.
Period of 1 revolution: sidereal, 687 days
                synodic, mean 780 days
Eccentricity of orbit: 0.09
Inclination of orbit to orbit of earth: 1.9 degrees of
    angle
Distance from earth: max. 247,000,000 miles
               min. 35,000,000 miles
Albedo: 0.15

INTRODUCTION

Because Mars is unique in many ways, it is doubtless the most studied planet. Lowell Observatory (near Flagstaff, Arizona) was designed for the express purpose of studying the planets in general and Mars in particular.

It is also the most controversial planet: facts submitted by some astronomers are strongly doubted by others—thus, for example, some claim to have seen artificial lines of irrigation which could only have been built by intelligent beings; others deny that such lines exist.

(The remote possibility that there is some form of life has been exploited by writers of pseudo-scientific fiction and producers of highly imaginary films and television shows.)

Mars is notable for its red color, and its variable brilliance—when close to earth, it is nearly fifty times brighter than when it is at maximum distance from earth.

THE ORBITS OF MARS AND THE EARTH

The orbit of Mars is just outside that of the earth. Once every synodic period (about 780 days) the two planets are in line with the sun and to one side; and once every period they are in line on opposite sides of the sun. **The first is called Opposition, when Mars and the sun are on opposite sides of the earth; the second is called Conjunction, when the sun and Mars are in the same direction as viewed from earth.**

Due to the eccentricity of Mars' orbit, the two planets do not follow equidistant tracks, the distance at opposition between them varying from a minimum of 35 million miles to a maximum of 63 million miles. They are closest near the point occupied by earth on August 25 (most distant during February). Oppositions on or near that date are called "favorable oppositions" and occur at intervals of 15 or 17 years—the next one is not due until 1971.

Most of our information about the planet is obtained during such favorable approaches. See Fig. 224.

The farthest Mars can be from earth is at Conjunction, when the distance is 247,000,000 miles, more than seven times farther than when at favorable opposition.

THE SURFACE OF THE PLANET

To the best of our knowledge, there are neither mountains nor valleys on Mars—the only markings are due to coloration:

a. reddish areas;

b. brown areas;

c. dark green areas; and

d. white areas.

The red, brown and the dark green areas are covered with a network of exceedingly

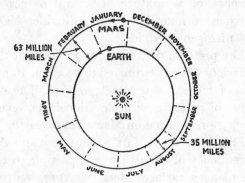

FIG. 224. The Orbits of Mars and Earth.

fine lines, at the junctions of which are minute black points.

The northern hemisphere of Mars differs greatly in appearance from the southern. The reddish areas are predominant in the northern hemisphere; the brown and green, in the southern. The white surfaces are found near both the north and the south poles of the planet.

All the surface colorations show marked seasonal changes; the most outstanding of these variations is the white area near the poles. The white cap appears at the beginning of winter when the particular pole is pointing away from the sun and very often disappears from view during the summer when the same pole points toward the sun. The north and south poles of the planet thus alternate in the possession of white cover.

The white cap builds up at a very rapid rate. In several days it may extend some 20° to 30° from the pole. This period is followed by a long period (the winter season) of stagnation, when it will remain essentially unchanged. With the advent of spring, it contracts greatly and breaks up into several small irregular white spots; these disappear altogether with the approach of summer.

The south polar cap generally becomes larger than the northern one; and it is also

the one most likely to disappear entirely during the summer in Mars' southern hemisphere.

A seasonal variation can also be observed in an interchange between the dark green and brown areas. The first is dominant during the spring and summer season; most of the green area changes to brown during the autumn and winter.

THE ATMOSPHERE OF MARS

Both theory and experiment show that a gaseous atmosphere exists on Mars. The theoretical consideration involves the velocity of escape, 3.1 miles per second, high enough to allow the planet to retain an atmosphere. Experimental evidence is manifold:

a. the existence of a twilight zone;

b. the albedo;

c. comparison of infrared and ultraviolet photographs;

d. the variation in size of the polar white caps; and

e. the occasional presence of clouds and mists.

a. **The Existence of a Twilight Zone.** Being an outer planet, Mars does not go through a complete series of phases as do the inner planets. One never sees a crescent of the planet, nor the quarter phase, but only the full and gibbous (slightly less than full) phases. At the gibbous phase, the presence of an atmosphere is observed. That part of the dark side of Mars which is turned toward the earth is slightly illuminated, and extends for about 8° beyond the part of Mars illuminated directly by sunlight. (It is called the Twilight Zone.) Light is derived from reflected sunlight, the reflection caused by the atmosphere of the planet, in a manner similar to the way that twilight reaches the earth.

b. **The Albedo.** Mars reflects sunlight better than an airless planet like Mercury. The albedo of Mars is nearly 15 per cent (i.e., 15 per cent of the incident sunlight is immediately reflected back into space), while that for Mercury is only 7 per cent.

c. **Comparison of Infrared and Ultraviolet Photographs.** Photographs taken of the planet through ultraviolet filters show it to be larger than do photographs taken with the aid of an infrared filter. The radius as computed from the two photographs differed by nearly 60 miles. The infrared picture seemingly corresponds to the solid disk of the planet; the disk appearing on the ultraviolet, to the outer surface of the atmosphere—in perfect agreement with physical theory. Red and infrared rays are transmitted by gases with little or no scattering; blue light is scattered greatly by any kind of a gaseous atmosphere. The infrared filter admits to the photographic plate the red and infrared light coming directly from the surface of the planet; while the ultraviolet filter admits the blue and ultraviolet rays scattered by the atmosphere. The difference in the two radii, i.e., 60 miles, is assumed to be the thickness of the atmosphere on Mars. See Fig. 225.

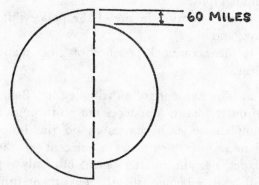

FIG. 225. Comparison of Infrared and Ultraviolet photographs of Mars. The left side was taken with a filter that lets through blue, violet, and ultraviolet light. The right side was taken with the aid of a filter through which red and infrared light passes. The difference in size is to be carefully noted. This difference indicates the thickness of the atmosphere that diffuses the blue and violet light.

d. **The Variation in Size of the Polar White Caps.** This variation is further direct proof of the existence of an atmosphere: the white caps are probably due either to snow or frost. In the absence of an atmosphere, the cycles of forming and melting would not be possible.

e. **The Occasional Presence of Clouds and Mists** is still further proof of the Martian atmosphere.

COMPOSITION

The composition of the atmosphere has not been definitely established, but it is probable that the abundance of carbon dioxide is twice that of the earth, and that the quantity of water vapor or oxygen is extremely low. Recent investigations seem to indicate the presence of a mixture of several oxides of nitrogen, primarily nitrogen dioxide, NO_2, and nitrogen peroxide, N_2O_4.

The pressure due to the atmosphere at the surface of Mars is estimated to be about 10 per cent of terrestrial sea-level pressure. The decrease of pressure with elevation is, however, much more gradual on Mars than on earth.

The thinness of Mars' atmosphere and the infrequency of clouds make it possible to see the planet's surface. Mars, Mercury, and, of course, the earth, are the only three planets whose surfaces can be clearly seen.

SEASONS AND CLIMATES ON MARS

The seasons on Mars are in some respects similar, and in others dissimilar, to those on the earth.

The similarities are:

1. The width of the climatic zones—due primarily to the inclination of the plane of the equator to the plane of the orbit—is similar on both planets. In the case of earth, this inclination is 23.5 degrees; for Mars, it is 25.2 degrees. The inclination of the axes is also responsible for seasons. Both planets have four seasons.

2. The variations in the period of daylight are similar on both planets. The period of one complete rotation of Mars about its axis is slightly more than 24½ hours, as compared with our 24 hours.

The dissimilarities are:

1. Each season on Mars is nearly twice as long as each season on earth. The length of the season depends upon the period of one revolution about the sun. Earth's sidereal period is 365¼ days; for Mars it is 687 days.

2. The average temperatures in each of the climatic zones on Mars are less than those of the corresponding zones on earth, because

Mars, on the average, is 50 per cent farther away from the sun than is the earth, so that the intensity of the sun's heat and light is diminished. The temperatures in the equatorial zone of Mars at noontime seldom rise above 70° F, while the early-morning and late-evening temperatures are well below the freezing point of water.

3. Summer on Mars' southern hemisphere is much warmer than summer on its northern hemisphere, due to the large eccentricity of the orbit, which is 0.09 as compared to the earth's 0.2. That is, the distance from Mars to the sun is closer by 20 per cent at perihelion than at aphelion. The difference in distance for earth is 3 per cent.

4. The changes in temperature from day to night are much greater on Mars than on earth, because of the thinness of Mars' atmosphere.

"LIFE" ON MARS

Is there any life on Mars? Do intelligent beings exist there? Do animals roam its surface? Is there any form of vegetable life? We do not know.

Some argue that the apparent structure of the canals on its surface could only be achieved by intelligent creatures, and add that the black dots at the junction point of the canals are reservoirs, and that the variation in color from dark green to brown are due to the annual change in color of highly developed vegetation in the Martian fields.

There are diametrically opposed views:

The canals are not irrigation ditches and are not straight. The markings are due to cracks formed when the planet was in the process of rapid cooling.

The changes in color from green to brown are due to a phenomenon known as efflorescence. Several chemicals on earth show similar changes in color (efflorescence) when exposed to water vapor.

RECENT INVESTIGATIONS

The discovery of several nitrogen oxides on Mars offers an entirely new explanation to current astronomical observations. According to this, the polar caps consist of the nitrogen oxides. Their whiteness is due to sunlight reflected by that gas. Similarly, the green and brown hues are sunlight reflected from mixtures of nitrogen oxides, the hue depending on the make-up of the mixture and its temperature.

SATELLITES OF MARS

Mars has two tiny satellites: Phobos (Fear) and Deimos (Panic) named for the two mythological companions of Mars, the god of war.

Phobos, the larger, has a diameter of about 20 miles, while the diameter of Deimos is only 10 miles. Both revolve about Mars in its equatorial plane in the usual counterclockwise fashion.

Phobos is 5800 miles from the center of its mother planet, and a mere 3700 miles from the surface. Its period of revolution about the planet is only 7 hours and 39 minutes, which is less than $\frac{1}{3}$ of the period of the rotation of Mars about its own axis.

Deimos is 4000 miles from the center of Mars. Its period of revolution about the planet—30 hours, 18 minutes—differs only slightly from the period of rotation of Mars about its own axis—24 hours, 37 minutes.

A TRIP TO MARS

At the time of the most favorable opposition, Mars is only 35,000,000 miles from the earth. For reasons of fuel economy, a space ship would follow a curved orbit and not a straight line. Along the greater part of the curved orbit to Mars, the ship would be able to coast and avoid the use of fuel.

An optimum orbit for a space ship to follow is indicated in Fig. 225A. The ship's orbit is an ellipse,

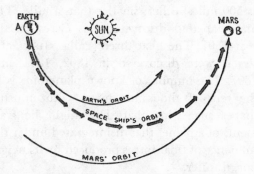

FIG. 225A. The orbit of the space ship is an ellipse with the sun at one of the foci. Point A is the perihelion (closest to the sun) of this orbit, and point B is the aphelion (point of the ellipse farthest from the sun).

with the perihelion at the time of the separation from the earth (point A), and an aphelion at the time it reaches Mars (point B).

To start the ship on its orbit, it would be necessary to supply it with a speed of about 27 miles per second, 20 miles per second to follow the required orbit, and 7 miles per second to escape from the earth's gravitational field.

Because of the velocity of the earth in its orbit around the sun, the ship has a built-in velocity of 18.5 miles per second. This means that the fuel would only have to supply a speed of 8.5 miles per second.

After coasting for much of the route, under the gravitational pull of the sun, the ship will arrive at point B (some 200 or more days after launching) with a speed of about 15 miles per second and come under the gravitational pull of the planet Mars, which would increase this speed by about 3 miles per second. Since the speed of Mars at its perihelion (point B) is about 16.5 miles per second, the relative velocities of the two bodies may amount to as much as 4.5 miles per second ($16.5 - 15 + 3 = 4.5$). It will be necessary to minimize the velocity before landing on the planet.

PART 2: PLANETOIDS

BASIC DATA

Total number: At least 50,000

Diameter: Smallest, a fraction of a mile; largest, 500 miles

Total mass of all planetoids: $\frac{1}{3000}$ that of earth

Mean distances to sun: 130 to 500 million miles

Periods: 2 to 12 years

Inclinations of orbit to ecliptic: 0 to 48 degrees

Eccentricities: 0 to 0.66

INTRODUCTION

One planet is missing. Theoretically, there should be a planet revolving in an orbit between Mars and Jupiter. No planet has ever been found there. Instead, there are a large number of small bodies, known either as minor planets, planetoids, or asteroids, the latter name indicating their resemblance to stars. Some fragments have diameters as large as 500 miles; others smaller than a mile. The first planetoid discovered was Ceres, in the year 1801. The next three (Pallas, Juno, and Vesta) were discovered in 1802, 1804, and 1807. The number of known planetoids is in the tens of thousands—many with unusual shapes suggesting that they might be fragments of a planet that disintegrated under the influence of tidal forces produced by its neighbor, Jupiter.

THEORETICAL "DISCOVERY"

As so often happens in Astronomy, the planetoids were first discovered in theory,

later in the sky. The "discovery" is based on Bode's Rule, named for the German astronomer, Johann Elert Bode.

Bode's Rule

a. List the planets in order from the sun

b. Write the number 4 under each planet

c. Write 0x3, 1x3, 2x3, 4x3, 8x3, and so on in proper order

d. Add the vertical columns and divide by 10

Mercury	Venus	Earth	Mars	?	Jupiter	Saturn
4	4	4	4	4	4	4
0	3	6	12	24	48	96
0.4	0.7	1.0	1.6	2.8	5.2	10.0

The last row of numbers corresponds very closely to the true distance of the planets from the sun, when expressed in astronomical units (1 astronomical unit is equal to the distance of the sun from the earth). The true distances are:

0.39 0.72 1.00 1.52 2.8 5.2 9.54

According to this rule, there should be a planet at a distance of 2.8 astronomical units from the sun. A systematic search for the "missing planet" along the belt of the zodiac, in which all the planets move, led to the discovery of a multitude of planetoids. The first planetoid (Ceres, for the guardian deity of Sicily) was discovered on January 1, 1801 by the Italian astronomer, Giuseppe Piazzi: its distance from the sun coincided very closely to the one assigned it by Bode's Rule.

NOTE 1: Uranus, Neptune, and Pluto had not been discovered when the Rule was published (1772). Uranus was discovered shortly after and was found to conform well to Bode's Rule—19.6 by rule, 19.2 by actual measurement. But Pluto and Neptune do not at all fit the Rule.

NOTE 2: Bode's Rule, known also as Bode's Law, is neither Bode's nor is it a law. The numbers are likely a coincidence with no particular significance or logical justification. The "law" was actually discovered by the astronomer Titius of Wittenberg, and Bode was instrumental only in publicizing it.

ORBITS OF THE PLANETOIDS

The vast majority of the planetoids move within orbits that lie between the orbits of Mars and Jupiter. The perihelia of some asteroids, among them, 433 Eros, 719 Albert, and 25 Procaea, lie within the orbit of Mars.

Planetoids are designated by a number—in order of their discovery—followed by a name. (E.g., 1 Ceres, 2 Pallas, 3 Juno, and so on.) The name is usually selected by the discoverer. In the beginning, feminine names were taken from mythology; later, names from Shakespearean plays and Wagnerian operas; many planetoids were named after wives, friends and even pet dogs and cats. Feminine names are used throughout except for the several planetoids that have unusual orbits; these were given masculine names.

There are a number of planetoids with aphelia outside the orbit of Jupiter: among them, 624 Hector, 659 Nestor, and 617 Patroclus.

The inclination of the planetoidal orbits to the ecliptic varies within wide limits, many of them moving in orbits that nearly coincide with the ecliptic; others, in highly inclined orbits. The orbit of Icarus is shown in Figure 226. Its orbit is inclined 21° to that of the earth about the sun.

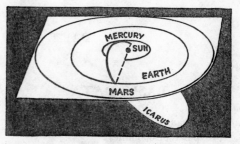

FIG. 226. The Orbit of Icarus is inclined 21 degrees to the orbit of the earth about the sun.

The orbit of largest inclination is that of Hidalgo, exceeding 42° of angle.

THE PERIODS OF THE PLANETOIDS

The periods of the planetoids vary greatly between a lower limit of two years and an upper limit of twelve years. There are, however, "forbidden" periods—i.e., no planetoids with periods $\frac{1}{2}$, $\frac{1}{3}$, or $\frac{1}{4}$ the period of Jupiter (11.86 years). This is a direct consequence of a physical phenomenon known as Gravitational Resonance. The gravitational attraction of Jupiter on planetoids moving in these orbits is cumulative, causing the small fragmentary masses to move on to other orbits.

OUR INTEREST IN THE PLANETOIDS

The primary interest in planetoids is in their close approaches to the sun and the earth. Icarus, discovered in 1949, passes closer to the sun than any other known body, attaining a maximum closeness exceeding that of Mercury by as much as 17 million miles.

Several planetoids have recently been discovered that pass within less than 10 million miles from the earth's orbit. The closest recorded approach, however, took place on October 10, 1937, when the small planetoid Hermes came within half a million miles of the earth. The planetoids are extremely useful in checking the motion of other heavenly bodies.

PART 3: THE PLANET JUPITER

BASIC DATA

Symbol: ♃

Diameter: equatorial, 89,000 miles
          polar, 82,800 miles

Volume: 1,309 times that of earth

Mass: 318 times that of earth

Density: 1.34 that of water

Surface gravity: 2.6 times that of earth

Velocity of escape: 37 miles per second

Period of rotation about axis: 9 hours, 54 minutes

Inclination of planet's equator to orbit: 3 degrees, 7 minutes

Distance to sun: mean 483,900,000 miles; 5.2 times that of earth

Orbital velocity: 8.1 miles per second

Period of one revolution: sidereal, 11.86 years
                         synodic, 398.9 days

Eccentricity of orbit: 0.05

Inclination of orbit to earth's orbit: 1 degree, 18 minutes

Albedo: 0.5

Surface temperature: —200° F

INTRODUCTION

Jupiter, with Saturn, Uranus, and Neptune, forms the group of Major Planets—distinguished by their large volumes, large masses and low densities.

Jupiter is the most voluminous: it could accommodate within the space occupied by itself, all the other planets. Its mass, too, is enormous. More than 300 spheres as heavy as the earth would be needed to balance Jupiter.

And only one star, Sirius, exceeds Jupiter in brightness. Among the planets, only Venus, and at times Mars, is brighter. For nearly six months of every year Jupiter is in full view every night, a brilliant planet moving slowly in a field of stars.

THE ATMOSPHERE

Its surface has never been seen and, possibly, no distinct solid surface exists there. Telescopic observations show only its outer atmosphere, which is assumed to be of a thickness between 300 and 500 miles.

An analysis of the spectrum of light from Jupiter indicates the presence of ammonia and methane in the atmosphere. (Ammonia is the strong-smelling substance often used as a household cleaning agent. Methane, CH_4 is known as "fire damp" and is the main constituent of the gases that cause explosions in coal mines.)

In addition to ammonia and methane, there is probably a great deal of hydrogen in the atmosphere, but this cannot be ascertained by spectographic studies. At the low temperatures (—200° F) prevailing at its outer surface, the hydrogen absorption bands occur only in the ultraviolet, and are therefore completely obscured by the opacity of the earth's atmosphere to this region of the spectrum.

At the prevailing temperature of —200° F, the ammonia present is probably in the form of tiny solid crystals—on earth, it freezes at a temperature of —108° F, and cannot exist as a liquid at much lower temperatures.

The ammonia crystals are probably afloat in the gaseous envelope consisting of methane and hydrogen.

The pressure due to these gases and crystals increases rapidly with depth below the outer surface of the planet—probably, at depths of several hundred miles, the gases, under the terrific pressure of the overlying layers, turn into liquids. The consistency of the atmosphere there is probably similar to that of a thick soup—solid particles of ammonia suspended in liquid.

Telescopic observations of the planet show prominent belt markings—either red or brown on a bright creamy white background. These currents within the extensive atmosphere of the planet resemble somewhat the trade wind zones on earth.

The equatorial belt is light in color and varies from 12,000 to 15,000 miles in width—on each side, alternate dark and light belts assume parallel courses. While maintaining their general outline the belts vary greatly with time—in location, in color and in form.

At times, bright spots appear on the dark belts, and at times dark spots appear on the bright belts; one—known as the Great Red Spot—has made astronomical history. It appeared fairly suddenly in 1878, occupying a region on the outer surface of Jupiter 30,000 miles long and nearly 7,000 miles wide. Soon after its appearance, it began to fade, at first rapidly, then gradually, and now only a bare outline remains.

ROTATION OF JUPITER ABOUT ITS AXIS

The period of rotation is determined from observations of the semi-permanent markings on the outer surface of the planet, no two of which are of the same period. The mean is about 9 hours, and 54 minutes.

The period varies with latitude—shortest at the equator (9 hours and 50 minutes); and longest in latitudes far from the equator (9 hours and 56 minutes). Variation of period with latitude does not increase uniformly, but rather is quite erratic. To complete the confusion, the periods of like latitudes in the northern and southern hemispheres of Jupiter are not equal to one another, nor do the periods remain constant for any long interval of time.

The mean period of rotation, 9 hours and 54 minutes, and the radius of the planet, 44,500 miles, imply immense speed for matter located near the planet's surface—in fact, 30,000 miles per hour; the corresponding figure for the earth is about 1,000 miles per hour.

The high speed of rotation of Jupiter is no doubt responsible for its considerable equatorial bulge; the polar diameter is shorter by nearly 6,000 miles than the equatorial diameter.

THE SATELLITES

Twelve moons revolve about Jupiter. The first four—described as the "Galilean satellites"—were discovered by Galileo in 1610, and are known either by the names Io, Europa, Ganymede, and Callisto, or simply as JI, JII, JIII, and JIV. The fifth satellite, JV, was discovered in 1892 by the eminent American astronomer, Edward Emerson Barnard; the twelfth satellite was discovered at the Mount Wilson Observatory in 1951. The twelve satellites divide naturally into three groups: (a) the Inner; (b) the Intermediate; and (c) the Distant.

a. **The Inner Group.** This group comprises satellites one through five, that is, the Galilean ones, and the one discovered by Professor Barnard.

The Galilean satellites move in nearly circular orbits at distances varying from 260,000 to 1,160,000 miles with periods varying from 1¾ days to 16⅔ days. All four are large enough to show perceptible disks in a telescope and were it not for the overpowering brilliance of the mother planet, they could be observed by the naked eye. At times, all four are on the west side of the planet; at other times, only three, two, one, or none are there, the others being on the east side. Frequently, one of the satellites is in eclipse (passing behind the planet) or in transit (passing in front of the planet).

The fifth satellite is closer to Jupiter than are the Galilean ones, its distance from the center being only 110,000 miles, and from its outer surface, only about 66,000 miles. The period of revolution about the mother planet is less than 12 hours; the orbital velocity, therefore, is 17 miles per second, or nearly 60,000 miles per hour.

b. **Intermediate Group.** JVI, JVII, and JX belong to this group. They are all small in size, having diameters less than 100 miles; and are at an average distance of 7 million miles from Jupiter. Their period of revolution is estimated to be about 270 days.

c. **The Distant Group.** This group comprises JXII, JXI, JVIII, and JIX. It is characterized by:

1. great distance from the mother-planet, estimated to be close to 15 million miles;

2. long period of rotation, all four exceeding two years; and

3. motion of all four is retrograde, that is, they revolve in a direction opposite to the one which all planets, and most other satellites move. A vertical view taken from above the

North Pole of Jupiter would reveal the satellites moving in their orbits in a clockwise direction.

THROUGH A TELESCOPE

With a power of 120 or better, the following are visible:

a. the elliptical shape of the planet;

b. the principal belts, and if seeing conditions are particularly favorable, the color of these belts;

c. the rapid rotation of the surface (the moving panorama of the diverse markings is one of the greatest pleasures to be derived from a small telescope);

d. the change in position of the satellites (this can be detected in several hours of observation);

e. eclipses and transits. The transits themselves are often difficult to follow; however, the shadows they produce on the surface of Jupiter are very clear and can be followed even with fairly small telescopes, when good "seeing" conditions prevail.

PART 4: THE PLANET SATURN

BASIC DATA

Symbol: ♄
Diameter: equatorial, 75,000 miles
 polar, 67,000 miles
Volume: 735 times that of earth
Mass: 95 times that of earth
Density: 0.7 that of water
Surface gravity: 1.2 times that of earth
Velocity of escape: 22 miles per second
Period of rotation about axis: 10 hours, 12 minutes
Inclination of planet's equator to orbit: 26 degrees, 45 minutes
Distance to sun: 887,000,000 miles, 9.54 times that of earth
Orbital velocity: 6 miles per second
Period of one revolution: sidereal, 29.46 years
 synodic, 378 days
Eccentricity of orbit: 0.056
Inclination of orbit to earth's orbit: 2 degrees, 29 minutes of angle
Albedo: 0.63
Surface temperature: −240° F

INTRODUCTION

Saturn is the planet with rings—one of the major planets, large in dimension and massive; second in size to Jupiter. Its mass is 95 times that of the earth. Like the other major planets, its density is low—less than that of water, that is, it could float on water. (Its mean value of density is 0.72 that of H_2O.)

Also typical of major planets, it rotates at high speed about its own axis completing one rotation in approximately 10½ hours. This period is not constant for the whole planet as with Jupiter, it is shorter at the equator and lengthens toward the poles. The accepted mean value for one complete rotation at the equator is 10 hours, 14 minutes, and close to the poles, about 10 hours and 38 minutes.

The values of rotation refer to the planet's outer atmosphere, the top of which because of its opacity is the only "surface" visible to us.

Saturn's uniqueness is due to the system of three surrounding rings—first seen by Galileo in 1610, and first clearly described by the Italian-French astronomer, Cassini (1625–1712).

THE ATMOSPHERE

It is supposed that the depth of Saturn's atmosphere is 15,000 miles.

As with Jupiter, spectroscopic studies of its reflected light show the presence of ammonia and methane; but on Saturn it is the methane, CH_4, that predominates, since at its low temperature (less than −240° F) most of the ammonia is in solid form, and does not affect materially the reflected sunlight. Also as with Jupiter, most of the atmosphere is probably composed of hydrogen, ammonia, and methane constituting only a small part.

The top of Saturn's atmosphere is belted, but not as conspicuously as Jupiter. Photographs taken with color filters reveal a gradual change in color of the dark belts. Those close to the equator are yellowish; those at the poles have a distinct greenish hue. As with Jupiter, it is assumed that the belts are due to atmospheric currents.

At times, spots appear on the planet's image—an outstanding one appeared in 1933, and was named the Great White Spot. In several months it elongated into a white band around the planet. The spots are probably due to large-scale disturbances in the planet's atmosphere, concerning which very little is known.

ROTATION OF SATURN ABOUT ITS AXIS

The period of rotation is determined from observations of spots, which are then checked with values obtained from spectroscopic analyses: it is shortest at the equator (10 hours and 14 minutes) and longest near the pole (10 hours and 38 minutes).

With this information, and the diameter of the planet's equator (75,000 miles), the velocity of matter at that equator is determined to be about 22,000 miles per hour.

This rapid rotation naturally produces a considerable equatorial bulge for which the fact that the atmosphere makes up a sizeable part of the volume is partly responsible. The equatorial diameter is nearly 8,000 miles longer than the polar diameter.

RINGS

There are three distinct rings (denoted by letters A, B, and C), separated by gaps. Their dimensions and those of the gaps, are given on Figure 227.

They differ materially in brightness: the middle ring (the B ring) is the brightest of the three; the outer ring (the A ring) is next; and the innermost (the C ring) is least bright. The innermost is often called the Crepe ring; it is rather faint, and is difficult to see.

The gap between the middle and outer rings is known as the Cassini Division, in honor of its discoverer.

The rings are remarkable for thinness: a cross-section would be an extremely thin rectangle—that of the outer ring, for example,

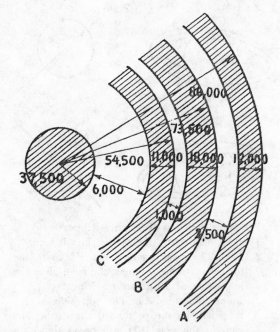

FIG. 227. The Rings. A top view of Saturn shows clearly the three rings, as well as the gaps between them.

The widths of the rings are 11,000, 18,000, and 10,000 miles, respectively.

In brightness they vary in order of B, A, C; the C is by far the dimmest.

The 2,500-mile gap between A ring and B ring is known as the Cassini Division.

would be a rectangle 10,000 miles long and only 5 or 7 miles wide.

The rings are exactly in the plane of the planet's equator, the latter being inclined about 27 degrees to the plane of the ecliptic. Since the axis of Saturn maintains a fixed orientation in space (that is, the axis always points to the same spot on the celestial sphere), terrestrial observers can see the rings at different inclinations. This is shown in the several parts of Figure 228.

Part 1 is the view of the rings in 1957—the lower side of the rings is in our line of sight. Part 2 is the view of 1965—the rings are sideways and give the impression of a straight line going through the planet. In 1971 (part 3), the upper side will be in view; the view in 1980 is shown in part 4.

A cycle of the ring phases is completed once every 29.5 years, this being the period of one revolution of Saturn about the sun.

The rings are composed of countless small

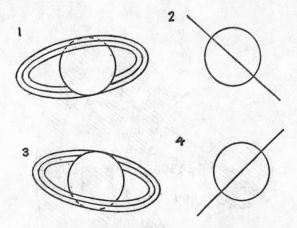

Fig. 228. Four Positions of Saturn's Rings.
1) 1957. The south side of the rings is seen.
2) 1965. The rings are now seen sideways. Due to their extreme thinness, the edge gives the impression of a thin straight line.
3) From 1965 to 1980. The top side of the rings will be turned toward the earth. The view in the year 1971 will be as shown in part 3.
4) In 1980 the edge of the rings will again be in line of sight for terrestial observers. Its inclination, though, will be different from the one in 1965.

Thus in a little less than 30 years a complete cycle of views of these rings is exhibited.

particles, the size of sand or thin gravel. This supposition is based on two facts: (a) The rings are semi-transparent; occasionally a star can be seen shining through. (b) The inner part of each revolves about the planet in less time than the outer part: if the ring were solid or liquid, the period of rotation for each would be constant.

The gaps between the rings are due to "gravitational resonance" (see discussion of Planetoids). Here, the resonance is between the satellites of Saturn and the revolving sand or gravel. The small particles remain outside orbits in which the period of revolution would be a simple fraction of the period of the satellite. No particles move in the gap between rings A and B because the period of such motion would be exactly half the period of Mimas, Saturn's closest satellite.

It is now believed that the rings are due either to a satellite that was torn asunder by the tidal forces of the mother planet, or to a satellite that was never quite created: for the former, it is assumed that a satellite extremely close to Saturn was torn to fragments by tidal forces; for the latter, it is assumed that material about to form a satellite was prevented from doing so by the same tidal forces.

Mathematical analysis supports these assumptions, demonstrating that no satellite can exist closer to a planet than 2.44 times the planet's radius, or within a distance of 1.44 from the planet's surface. The figures are known as Roche's Limits, for the scientist who discovered them in 1850.

THE SATELLITES

Saturn is attended by nine satellites—the nearest, Mimas, is at a distance of 117,000 miles from the center of the planet. The most distant, Phoebe, is more than 7,000,000 miles away from the mother planet.

The periods of the satellites vary from 23 hours for Mimas to 550 days for Phoebe, all, with one exception, revolving about Saturn in the normal direction. Phoebe alone shows retrograde motion, thus adding greatly to its orbital stability. Mathematically it can be shown that a distant satellite, whose direction of motion is normal, can more easily be withdrawn from the planet than one whose motion is retrograde.

The diameters of the satellites are fairly small—the largest is that of Titan (about 2,600 miles), and the smallest that of Hyperion (about 300 miles).

The satellites appear to rotate with a period equal to that with which they revolve, thus keeping the same face toward the primary (i.e., the mother-planet) and accounting for their observed variation in brightness. The periods of these variations in brightness are identical with the periods of revolution—the brightness of one satellite, Iapetus, changes by a factor of five from minimum to maximum for each revolution.

THROUGH A TELESCOPE

Saturn is second to Jupiter in interest to the amateur observer, for these reasons:

a. Elliptical appearance of the planet;

b. the belts on the surface;

c. the rings' clear visibility—the gap between the two brighter rings, the Cassini Division, can be seen under favorable conditions with a small telescope;

d. the largest satellite, Titan, and the next largest, Iapetus, are easy to observe; three other satellites (Rhea, Tethys, and Dione) can be seen under particularly favorable conditions.

PART 5: THE PLANET URANUS

BASIC DATA

Symbol: ♅

Diameter: 31,000 miles

Volume: 59 times that of earth

Mass: 15 times that of earth

Density: 1.3 times that of water

Surface gravity: 0.9 that of earth

Velocity of escape: 13 miles per second

Period of rotation about axis: 10 hours, 49 minutes

Inclination of planet's equator to orbit: 82 degrees

Distance to sun: 1,785,000,000 miles; 19.2 times that of earth

Orbital velocity: 4.2 miles per second

Period of one revolution: sidereal, 84.0 years
synodic, 369.7 days

Eccentricity of orbit: 0.05

Inclination of orbit to earth's orbit: 0 degrees, 46 minutes

Albedo: 0.6

Surface temperature: −300° F

INTRODUCTION

Uranus' apparent magnitude is 5.7—it is thus barely visible to the unaided eye when seeing conditions are particularly favorable. Its faintness is due both to its great distance from the sun, which illuminates it, and from the earth.

It moves in the same path as do the other planets, but its apparent motion is relatively slow, completing one revolution about the sun in nearly 84 years. Its progress from the western terrestrial horizon toward the eastern is about 4 degrees per year.

The planet greatly resembles the other major planets, Jupiter, Saturn, and Neptune. Its atmosphere, too, very likely consists of a combination of ammonia, methane and hydrogen, the percentage of the ammonia being fairly low as compared with the methane and the hydrogen.

Like Jupiter and Saturn, it is encircled by belts lying parallel to its equator—the difference in color between the dark and the light belts, however, is less marked than for Jupiter or Saturn.

Uranus is unique on several counts:

a. It was the first planet to be discovered with the aid of a telescope;

b. it was discovered by accident;

c. it rotates about its own axis "backwards";

d. its equatorial plane is almost at right angles with the orbital plane—the exact value of the angle between the two planes is 82°.

THE DISCOVERY

The planet was discovered by William Herschel, a professional musician and amateur astronomer, on March 13, 1781, with a small 7-inch reflecting telescope of his own construction. It appears in such a telescope as a very small disk, little differing from a point of light typical of a star. This slight difference in size, however, was sufficient reason for Herschel to suspect that the object was **not** a star; and his data confirmed that a new planet revolving about the sun, at a distance of 19 astronomical units, had been discovered.

THE SPINNING OF THE PLANET ABOUT ITS AXIS

The spin is "backward" or retrograde, in contrast to the other planets, which move about the sun counterclockwise and spin similarly about their own axes. Uranus describes the orbit about the sun in the normal counterclockwise manner; but the rotation about its own axis is clockwise, the equator of the planet being inclined 82° to its orbit about the sun. An alternate way of describing the rotation is often used. This states that the equator of the planet is inclined 98 degrees with its orbit. The original north and south poles are thus reversed, and the direction of spin about the axis is normal, not retrograde.

For a clearer picture of the effects of these large angles, either 82° or 98° for Uranus, the results of large inclinations on the earth may be studied.

Suppose that the earth's equator is inclined, not 23.5 degrees but 90 degrees to its orbit, that is, the axis of the earth would lie in the plane of its orbit.

At one time, the present north pole would be closest to the sun; six months later, the south pole would most directly receive the sun's rays. The concept of climatic zones, as we know it, would no longer apply. See Fig. 229.

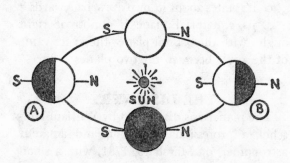

FIG. 229. Effect of Large (hypothetical) Inclination of Earth's Axis. If the earth's axis were inclined by 90° (and not 23.5° as in reality) to the axis of its orbit, then at one time during the year the North Pole would be the warmest place on the earth (Position A).

Six months later sunlight would shine most directly at the South Pole, and it would be the warmest place on earth (Position B).

Suppose then that the angle is still further increased, say, to 100 degrees. The original north pole would be below the ecliptic; the United States would be in the Southern Hemisphere; California would be on the East Coast; and a vertical view taken from above the

ecliptic would show the earth to spin in a clockwise fashion, i.e., in retrogade motion. See Fig. 230.

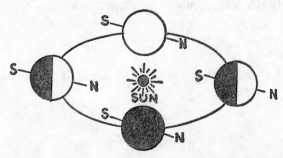

FIG. 230. If the earth's axis were rotated still further from its present inclination of 23.5° to, say, 100°, the poles would interchange their identities. The "north" pole would now be below the plane of the ecliptic and would therefore be known as the south pole. The U.S. would now be in the Southern Hemisphere. An observer looking down at the new north pole (the erstwhile south pole) would see the earth rotating clockwise. Clockwise rotation is the normal direction for the earth's south pole.

THE SATELLITES

Uranus has five satellites: Miranda, Ariel, Umbriel, Titania, and Oberon, all revolving in the plane of the mother-planet's equator, hence, at nearly right angles with the orbit in which the planet moves. All five have retrograde motion, consistent with the planet's spin about its own axis.

The satellites range in size from about 400 to about 1,000 miles in diameter. The radii of their orbits range from 76,000 miles for the satellite closest to the planet to 364,000 miles for the farthest.

THROUGH THE TELESCOPE

Uranus can be seen very clearly through a 3-inch telescope—easily identified as a planet as it does not show the diffraction ring which always encircles a star image in a good telescope. The planet is too remote to show any surface details, except with very powerful telescopes.

PART 6: THE PLANET NEPTUNE

BASIC DATA

Symbol: ♆
Diameter: 33,000 miles
Volume: 72 times that of earth
Mass: 17 times that of earth
Density: 1.2 times that of water
Surface gravity: 0.9 times that of earth
Velocity of escape: 14 miles per second
Period of rotation about axis: 15 hours, 45 minutes
Inclination of planet's equator to orbit: 29 degrees
Distance to sun: 2,797,000,000 miles; 30.1 times that of earth
Orbital velocity: 3.5 miles per second
Period of one revolution: sidereal, 164.8 years
synodic, 367.5 days
Eccentricity of orbit: 0.009
Inclination of orbit to earth's orbit: 1 degree, 47 minutes
Albedo: 0.73
Surface temperature: −300° F

INTRODUCTION

Because of its great distance, Neptune is invisible to the naked eye. Telescopic observations rank its brightness as equal to that of an 8th magnitude star. It requires nearly 165 years to complete one revolution about the sun. Its drifting among the stars, eastward is slightly more than 2 degrees of angle per year.

There is little variety of season: the mean temperature is −300° F, summers not much warmer than winters.

It is unique, in that it was discovered *first* by mathematical computations, *then* by actual observation.

THE DISCOVERY

Astronomers were first alerted because Uranus moved strangely in its orbit. By 1845, the discrepancy between its computed and observed positions was 2 minutes of angle, an "intolerably large quantity" in Astronomy. One explanation was that the motion of Uranus was disturbed by an unknown planet beyond its orbit, which, when ahead, pulled on Uranus, thus increasing its speed; and when behind, acted, by its gravitational pull, as a brake on its motion.

John Couch Adams, then an undergraduate at the University of Cambridge (England), and a young French mathematician, Leverrier, each independently, computed the orbit of the hypothetical planet, both arriving at the same results. Within an hour after the telescopic search began, the planet was found in the exact position indicated by the mathematical calculation.

THE SATELLITES

Two satellites have been discovered: the first, Triton, within a few months after the planet's discovery; the second, more than a century later, in 1949.

Triton is unique in being the only satellite close to its mother-planet having retrograde motion. Its distance from the mother-planet is 220,000 miles, almost the same as the distance between our moon and earth. Triton's retrograde motion may be a direct result of the following two events: *a.* Triton and the ninth planet, Pluto, were at one time satellites of Neptune, both moving in a direct way. *b.* A close encounter between them caused the ejection of Pluto (which became an independent planet) and a reversal in the direction of Triton.

Triton has a diameter of about 2,200 miles; a mass about 1/15 that of the earth; and revolves about Neptune once every 5 days, 20 hours, in an orbit inclined 37 degrees to the plane of the ecliptic.

The second satellite, Nereid (a mythological sea nymph-attendant of Neptune, God of the Sea), moves about its mother-planet in a direct way. Its sidereal period is 360 days and its orbit is inclined about five degrees to the ecliptic.

Nereid is unique for two reasons:

a. It is too faint to be seen even with great telescopes. Observations of this satellite are made primarily by photography.

b. The large eccentricity of its orbit (0.79). Its distance from Neptune varies from 730,000 miles at its closest point to 7,000,000 at the farthest point on its orbit.

THROUGH THE TELESCOPE

Through the telescope, Neptune appears as a minute disk without any definite markings, faint bluish in color.

PART 7: THE PLANET PLUTO

BASIC DATA

Symbol: ♇
Diameter: 3,700 miles (uncertain)
Mass: Slightly less than that of earth
Density: Similar to that of earth
Distance to sun: 3,670,000,000 miles or 39.5 times that of earth
Orbital velocity: 3 miles per second
Period of one revolution: sidereal, 248 years
                            synodic, 366.7 days
Eccentricity of orbit: 0.25
Inclination of orbit to earth's orbit: 17 degrees, 9 minutes
Surface temperature: −350° F

INTRODUCTION

The ninth and most distant known planet is Pluto, named for the mythological god of Hades. Its distance from the sun is nearly four thousand million miles—thus the benefits from it are minute, receiving only 1/1600 the amount of heat and light the earth does. The pale light from the distant sun probably helps make the frozen wastes of the planet's surface appear more frightful and unreal than it otherwise would.

Pluto appears even to the most powerful telescope as a minute yellowish point of light —except to the 200″ telescope on Mount Palomar, which shows Pluto's apparent disk.

As with Neptune, its fame is connected with its discovery—for which Percival Lowell of Flagstaff, Arizona; W. H. Pickering of Harvard; and Clyde Tombaugh, then a student-assistant in the Flagstaff Observatory, are responsible. The search for the planet occupied more than twenty years. An announcement of its discovery on March 13th, 1930, coincided with Professor Lowell's birthday, and the anniversary of Herschel's discovery of Uranus. Its symbol is ♇ (P and L, the initials of Percival Lowell).

Again the search for Pluto was provoked by a deviation from computed motions of Uranus and Neptune.

Pluto is outstanding in several respects: (See Fig. 231).

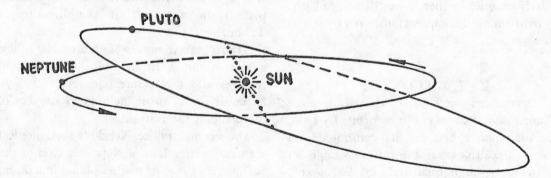

FIG. 231. The orbits of Neptune and Pluto. Neptune, and all the other planets, move in orbits that are only slightly inclined to the ecliptic. The only exception is Pluto. The large inclination of Pluto's orbit as compared with Neptune's is shown here.

a. The orbit has the highest inclination of any of the planets (17°).

b. The orbit has the highest eccentricity of any of the planets (0.25).

c. Pluto may have the highest value, among the planets, for average density.

With the discovery of Pluto, the motions of Uranus and Neptune were fully explained.

Any planets which may exist beyond Pluto will have little effect on the known planets.

PART 8: SOLAR SATELLITES

A solar satellite is a satellite placed in orbit around the sun. Because a solar satellite's orbit is similar to the orbits followed by the planets, it is sometimes called a planetite or an artificial planetoid.

The first solar satellite, Lunik I, was launched by the U.S.S.R. on January 2, 1959. It weighed 3,245 pounds, carried instruments weighing 795 pounds, and took 15 months to complete one revolution around the sun.

The first American solar satellite, known as Pioneer IV, weighing 134 pounds, was launched on March 3, 1959. The orbits of both Lunik I and Pioneer IV are between the earth and Mars. See Fig. 231A.

The second artificial planetoid launched by the United States—on March 11, 1960—was called Pioneer V. An aluminum sphere, it weighs 95 pounds and has a diameter of 26 inches. It has a 150-watt transmitter designed to permit communication with the earth at distances up to 50,000,000 miles. The transmitter was designed to radiate for only 5 minutes during every 5-hour period. The measurements obtained during the silent periods were stored in a miniature memory device for transmission during the active 5-minute period.

Although Pioneer V's launching speed was nearly 25,000 miles per hour, its speed was reduced to 8,000 miles per hour several hours after take-off by the earth's gravitational pull. Its speed was increased as it was influenced by the sun's gravitational pull. In orbit around the sun, its estimated average speed is 70,000 miles per hour.

The scientific information obtained from Pioneer V included: (a) measurements of the intensity of magnetic fields in space (b) action of plasma—electrified gaseous clouds that float in interplanetary space (c) the number and velocity of micrometeorites (d) information on high-energy radiation hurled into space by solar disturbances, and (e) help in providing more exact data on the distances between planets.

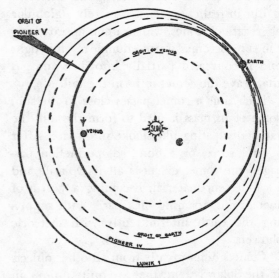

FIG. 231A. Orbits of Several Artificial Planetoids. The orbit of Pioneer V is inside the earth's orbit. Pioneer IV and Lunik I are farther away from the sun than the earth. The orbits are not all in the same plane. The orbit of Venus makes an angle of 3.4° with the orbit of the earth.

CHAPTER XV

COMETS AND METEOROIDS

PART 1: THE COMETS

INTRODUCTION

Comets are perhaps the most remarkable objects in the Solar System, their appearances differing greatly from what they really are.

In appearance, a bright comet is a large illuminated moonlike disk, often visible in broad daylight, followed by a tail hundreds of millions of miles long, moving like a planet about the sun, in a rather elongated ellipse.

But in reality, a comet is merely a globular aggregate of stones, which, upon approaching the sun, becomes warm enough to emit light and is converted partially into dust and gas that leave the comet to form the tail.

Each time a comet passes close to the sun, some of its mass is used to form the tail, the latter dissipating like smoke into space. After several score, or a hundred, perihelion passages, the comet exhausts all its volatile and incandescent material, becoming a swarm of meteoroids roaming in space and supplying the earth intermittently with meteoric showers.

Comets differ greatly from all other objects in the Solar System: they are quite unique in size, in mass, in density, and in behavior.

The length of a typical comet is approximately 100 million miles; and it may reach a length of 500 million miles. The width and thickness of a comet are also of colossal proportions; 100,000 miles is a typical figure for either one of these dimensions.

Disproportionately, the mass is insignificantly small, too small to disturb the motion of even the smallest satellites on close encounter: the mass of a large comet is estimated at one millionth that of our earth.

Large volume and small mass make for very low mean density—probably not more than a millionth that of air at sea level. (Comets have been described as "the nearest thing to nothing that anything can be and still be something.") This low density is one reason that it is semi-transparent, so that stars can be observed through it.

Notwithstanding the low density and the minuteness of its mass, a comet, when visible, is an imposing object. It may rival the brightness of Venus; it may stretch across half the sky from zenith to the horizon.

The vast dimensions of some comets, together with their remarkable brilliance, are no doubt responsible for the many superstitions historically associated with their appearances. The appearance of a bright comet was believed to be "ominous of the wrath of Heaven, and harbingers of war and famine, of the dethronement of monarchs, and the dissolution of empires." Myth is further provoked by their characteristic sudden appearances.

Actually, very few bright comets have been recorded: one in a lifetime is the average. The last great comet appeared in 1882, was observable for nearly nine months, and was conspicuous for several weeks. No truly spectacular comet has appeared in the present century. Two that appeared in 1910 (one, a return of Halley's Comet; the other, the 1910 I Comet), and the far southern comet of December, 1947, were only "fairly" great comets.

The frequency of faint comets is, of course, much greater than that of great or "fairly" great ones.

About eight new comets are discovered every year, most of them too faint to be seen by the unaided eye.

There are approximately a thousand known comets.

Comets are known by the name of their discoverer (e.g., Donati's Comet) or by the name of the astronomer who made the comet an object of scientific attention (e.g., Halley's Comet).

Now they are usually designated by the year of their first observed passage near the sun, together with a Roman numeral to indicate the order in that year (e.g., Comet 1910 I, or Comet 1882 III. Donati's Comet is also known as 1858 VI).

THE STRUCTURE OF A COMET

A comet usually consists of: a. a head, called Coma, near the center of which is b. a nucleus, usually quite small but much brighter than the rest of the head, and c. a tail that gives the appearance of streaming from the Coma. The tail is always much dimmer than the head, although there is no sharply defined boundary separating them. See Fig. 232.

Individual comets show great variations from the norm—some may be without tail, or nucleus, or both.

a. **The head.** Most comets have globular heads, varying greatly in size. The diameter may be less than 10,000 miles or may exceed 200,000 miles.

Nor is the size of the head constant. The dimensions are usually largest just after perihelion, with a secondary maximum just before reaching the nearest point to the sun. Thus the diameter of Halley's Comet, when it was about 300 million miles from the sun, was a mere 14,000 miles, increasing to 220,000 miles before reaching perihelion, decreasing to 120,000 miles at perihelion. It increased again to 320,000 after perihelion and finally decreased to 30,000 miles as it moved farther from the sun.

The head is very likely composed of solid stones of a great variety of sizes, beginning with very thin dust. Some stones are probably composed of iron and nickel; others are similar in composition to terrestrial stone.

b. **The nucleus** is the central bright spot of the head, fairly small, rarely exceeding a

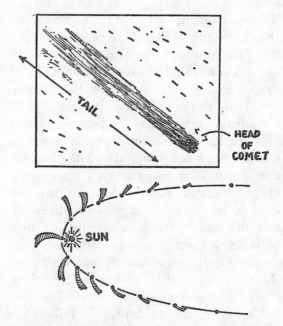

Fig. 232. The Structure of a Comet. The head, or Coma, forms the front of the comet, the nucleus being the central part of it. The main bulk of the comet is taken up by the tail. This is a negative of the view, the bright objects appearing black in it.

The tail makes its first appearance when the comet is within several astronomical units distance from the sun. It is longest at perihelion, and disappears when the comet is again at a great distance from the sun. Because of the pressure of sunlight the tail at all times points away from the sun.

diameter of 10,000 miles. (The common figure is between 500 and 1,000 miles.) The nucleus differs from the rest of the head only in density: its matter is much more concentrated than elsewhere in the coma.

c. **The tail** of the comet is transient in nature, bearing a great similarity to chimney-smoke, first appearing as the comet approaches perihelion and disappearing after the comet has completed its U-turn about the sun and is moving away. The gases composing the tail probably result from the tremendous heat to which the solid particles of the coma are exposed upon approaching the sun. The volatilizing of the surfaces of these solids produces that large elongated cloud of gas known as the "tail" of the comet. A spectroscopic analysis indicates the presence of iron, nickel, carbon, nitrogen, as well as several other substances in gaseous form.

While a length of a hundred million miles

is fairly common, the tail of the Great Comet 1843 I was estimated to have been more than 500,000,000 miles long. This large spread is due to the fact that radiation pressure caused by sunlight greatly overcomes the gravitational pull of the coma on these gases.

Radiation pressure, as the term implies, is pressure due to radiation. Its value on terrestrial objects is insignificantly small—the pressure due to solar radiation on a square mile of the earth's surface is slightly less than two pounds. Its effect on the gases volatilized inside the coma, as well as on the fine dust particles, is great. Radiation pressure easily overcomes the gravitational pull acting on these particles, and is thus able to eject them from the coma to great distances. The propelling force due to this pressure follows the particles along their route. Their speed upon leaving the head is approximately 0.5 miles per second; farther along the tail, velocities of 50 miles per second are quite common.

Another result of the pressure due to the sun's radiation is that the tails always point away from the sun, trailing the comet as it approaches the sun and preceding it when the latter recedes.

THE ORBIT OF COMETS

a. Elliptical Orbits

Of the thousand known comets, nearly a hundred are known to move in elongated ellipses, most famous among these, Halley's Comet. Halley, a contemporary of Sir Isaac Newton, was the first to suggest that the comet observed in 1682 was the same that was seen 75 years and 151 years earlier; and predicted its next visit early in the year 1759. He did not live to see his prediction come true; but the comet appeared as forecast in April, 1759, and made two subsequent appearances on schedule. See Fig. 233.

b. Other Orbits

The orbits of the other 900 comets have not been definitely ascertained. It is possible that these too move along elongated ellipses; or, they may move along parabolic or hyperbolic curves.

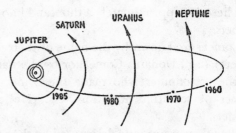

Fig. 233. The Orbit of Halley's Comet as Seen Against the Background of the Orbits of the Planet. In 1960 the comet will be past its aphelion and on its way to the sun. 1970 will find it at a distance about one third of the way between the planets Uranus and Neptune. The actual orbit is inclined about 17° to the plane of the ecliptic.

Figure 234 indicates the three types of curves. It is of the utmost importance to be able to ascertain the route followed by a

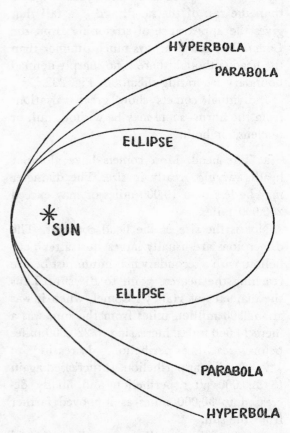

Fig. 234. Possible Orbits for a Comet. An ellipse is a closed orbit; comets moving on it return time and time again to perihelion, and can thus be seen by terrestrial observers. Both the parabola and the hyperbola are open orbits; the two ends of each never meet. Any object moving in such an orbit comes from infinite space, makes one appearance at perihelion, and disappears never to be seen again.

comet. Comets that move in elliptical orbits return repeatedly to perihelion. Comets that move on either of the other two orbits appear only once to terrestrial observers. They probably come from space, and after making a 180° detour about the sun, return there.

Regrettably, it is impossible to ascertain the orbits of many comets.

When the comet is close to the sun, the curvature of the three orbits is nearly identical, making it almost impossible to distinguish among them. At great distances from the sun, when the orbits diverge from one another, the comets are too faint for observations.

Many astronomers believe that all comets move in elliptical orbits with periods varying from a low value of 3.3 years for Encke's Comet to a high value of many hundreds of years, at speeds varying from a fraction of a mile per second when remote from the sun to nearly 300 miles per second when at perihelion.

Orbits of comets are often changed by close approaches to one of the major planets. Thus, in 1886, comet Brooks passed within about 55,000 miles of Jupiter's surface and suffered a change in period from over 29 years to slightly more than 7 years.

The orbits of the hundred or more comets that are known to have elliptical orbits lie wholly within the Solar System—more than fifty have their aphelia (point farthest from the sun) near the orbit of Jupiter. These are known as "Jupiter's Family of Comets." Others have their aphelia near Saturn, Uranus, and Neptune, and are known as the "families" of the respective planets. Halley's Comet is a member of Neptune's "family."

LIFE AND DEATH OF A COMET

A study of long-period comets indicates that at a distance of between 25,000 and 150,000 astronomical units from the sun, there is a "Comet Cloud" containing as many as a hundred billion individual comets. Due to perturbation of neighboring stars, some of these are occasionally injected into the domain of the Solar System, beginning their stay in the Solar System as long period comets, moving along greatly elongated ellipses.

During their stay in the Solar System, both their orbit and their content may be greatly changed.

The orbit is affected during close approaches to one of the major planets. Such an encounter may change the comet's aphelion from thousands of astronomical units to a distance of tens of astronomical units from the sun; and the period from hundreds of years to tens of years.

A comet's content is changed each time it passes near the sun—part of its mass forming the tail, which eventually diffuses into space.

A comet may also split into two or more parts during a perihelion passage, or when passing close to one of the major planets. Heavy tides formed at such close passage are primarily responsible for the splitting.

Roche's limit indicates that a comet passing within 90 million miles of the sun, or 9 million miles from Jupiter, or 2 million miles from the earth, should disintegrate as a result of the tides produced in it. The theoretical predictions are verified by observation. The 1947 XIV comet (the fourteenth comet in 1947) passed within 10 million miles of the sun and was split in two.

Even if the comet does not split, its lifetime is limited to about a hundred perihelion passages. Towards the end, the comet has lost all the gases that could have been volatilized from it; the remaining debris continues along its normal orbit, colliding occasionally with the earth's atmosphere to produce meteoric showers.

New comets, however, are continuously being injected from the gigantic comet cloud to provide us once in a lifetime with the unforgettably brilliant spectacle.

PART 2: METEOROIDS (METEORITES)

(NOTE: A revised terminology to describe meteoric phenomena was approved in 1961 by the International Astronomical Union. These new terms are used here. Meteoric terms used prior to 1961 are given in parentheses.)

INTRODUCTION

Meteoroids are tiny solid objects (the size of sand particles) traversing through space, mostly along orbits formerly occupied by comets.

It is believed that many of these meteoroids are the remnants of comets that have lost a great deal of their mass on successive passages near the sun, the gravitational attraction of the remaining mass being too weak to keep the particles together. Soon after the "demise" of the comet, **the particles form a closely packed group, well described as a "flying gravel pile"; such a group is known as a swarm.** With time, there is a great deal of scattering both along the elliptical orbit and sideways; **an elongated pile of such particles, which may extend all around the orbit, is known as a stream.**

The earth, moving along its orbit, is continuously colliding with some of these scattered solid particles, the vast majority of which do not survive the clash. Upon entering the earth's atmosphere at a fairly great speed (25 miles per second), they are incinerated by the white heat produced by the compression of the air in front of the object, and by the friction between the air and the sides of the meteoroid. Meteoroids first appear at heights of 60 to 90 miles; most vanish at heights of 30 to 50 miles.

The light phenomenon which results from the entry into the earth's atmosphere of the meteoroid is called *meteor* or *shooting star*.

Shooting stars are extremely common: The number of those visible each day is approximately 20 million; the number of fainter meteors that can be observed only with the aid of a telescope is thought to be between 5 and 10 billion.

The dust resulting from the incineration settles slowly towards the earth, increasing the mass of our planet annually by hundreds of tons.

Occasionally, a large meteoroid collides with the earth's atmosphere and survives, in part, the tremendous heat engendered in its passage. Such a meteoroid is called a *meteorite*. Meteorites can be seen on exhibit in various museums, many of them several feet in each dimension.

Twice, to our knowledge, the earth was hit by truly gigantic meteorites—one, on June 30, 1908, of 40,000 tons. Luckily, it fell in a deserted spot in northern Siberia, with immense damage to forestland.

The other gigantic meteorite left its imprint in the desert of northeast Arizona, near Canyon Diablo. The crater formed by the impact is nearly 4,000 ft. across, and is surrounded by a rim which stands about 140 ft. above the surface of the surrounding limestone plain; the bottom of the crater is nearly 600 ft. below the rim. Geological estimates based on a study of the rocks within the crater indicate that the collision between that meteorite and the earth occurred about thirty or forty thousand years ago.

FREQUENCY

The frequency of observable meteors varies with:

a. the time of day,

b. the season of the year, and primarily,

c. whether the earth collides with some stray meteoroids that were scattered far from the path of an extinct comet, or whether the earth collides with a stream or swarm of meteoroids that still follow the elongated elliptical orbit.

a. Frequency is greatest in the hours after midnight. On the average, twice as many meteors can be seen in the hours between midnight and sunrise than in a similar interval before midnight, since during the former period, the observer is on the front side of the earth as it moves along its orbit, and sees both meteors that are overtaken by the earth

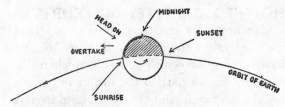

FIG. 235. Frequency of Meteors after Midnight. Nearly twice as many meteors can be seen in any region of the sky after midnight, as compared to before midnight.

Between midnight and sunrise a terrestrial observer is "riding" on the front part of the earth and can see both "head on" and "overtaken" collisions between meteors and the earth's atmosphere.

and those that are met head on. See Fig. 235.

b. There is also a seasonal variation. Because of the inclination of the earth's equator to its orbit, the frequency of meteors is greatest, for observers in northern latitudes, in the fall.

c. Enormous increase in the number of meteors occurs when the earth goes through a "swarm" or a "stream," at which time their number may be in the hundreds of thousands in any small region, as compared to the hundred or so that are normally seen. **A large number of visible meteors is called a "Meteoric Shower."**

Naturally, meteoric showers are much more spectacular when the earth goes through a swarm ("flying gravel pile") than when the earth goes through a stream, in which the particles are distributed throughout the orbit.

On the other hand, passages through streams are much more frequent than passages through swarms. The former occurs annually when the earth, moving in its own orbit, crosses the orbit of the stream. See Fig. 236. For a meteoric shower due to a swarm to occur, both the earth and the swarm must be

at the point of intersection at the same time. See Fig. 237. For some swarms, this occurs once in 33 years; for others, at various intervals.

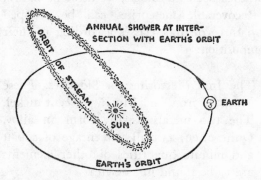

FIG. 236. Meteoric Showers due to a Stream. These showers are annual events. They can be seen each time the earth is close to the stream of meteoroids.

The meteors in a shower move in parallel paths. Due to perspective, these paths appear to an observer to converge at a point on the celestial sphere. This point is known as the radiant.

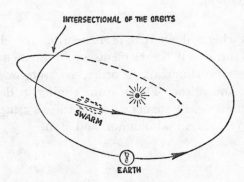

FIG. 237. Meteoric Showers Due to a Swarm. These showers are much more spectacular. They occur every time that the earth and the swarm are simultaneously at the point of intersection of their orbits.

For some swarms this may be once every few hundred years.

METEORIC SHOWERS

Name	Date	Comet	Period of Comet	Remarks
Lyrids	April 20–21	1861 I	415 yrs.	A few *every* year.
Aquarids	May 3–6	Halley's	76.6 yrs.	A few *every* year.
Perseids	August 9–12	1862 III	120 yrs.	Many every year.
Orionids	October 19–22	?	?	Many every year.
Leonids	November 14–17	Tempel's	33.3 yrs.	Swift meteorites.
Geminids	December 11–12	?	?	Dependable showers.

Each shower is named after the constellation in which its particular radiant is located —Lyrids, Perseids, etc.

Several of the principal meteoric showers, and the associated comets, are listed on p. 173.

Recoverable meteorites can be grouped into three distinct classes according to their composition:

a. The Iron Meteorites, or Siderites. These consist of iron, and 5 to 15 per cent nickel. The two metals usually form an alloy. Quite often, a small percentage of cobalt and minute quantities of other elements are to be found in siderites.
b. The Stony Meteorites, or Aerolites. These largely resemble terrestrial stones, although they are usually denser than the earthly variety.
c. The Stony Iron, or Siderolites. These meteorites usually consist of an iron-nickel frame sponge, containing the stony material in the interstices. The metals and the stones are mixed in about equal proportion.

A chemical analysis of meteorites reveals that nearly all the elements occur in them. The most abundant, in order, are iron, oxygen, and silicon. This is quite similar to the most abundant elements in the earth's crust: oxygen, silicon, aluminum, and iron.

HOW TO IDENTIFY METEORITES

Siderites. The iron meteorites or siderites are the easiest to identify. Siderites usually have a glossy brownish appearance when discovered, due in part to the fusion which the metal underwent while in the air, and in part to normal rusting on the ground.

To obtain final proof of the meteoritic origin of a siderite, the following procedure may be followed:

a. Cut off a piece of the meteorite.
b. Polish the freshly exposed surface.
c. Etch the polished surface with diluted nitric acid.

The etching brings out a crystalline design that is characteristic of iron meteorites.

Aerolites. The stony type of meteorite greatly resembles terrestrial rocks and is therefore much more difficult to identify. Two aids often used to identify aerolites involve the following procedures:

a. Pulverize a small piece of the suspected stone. If the powder contains glistening flakes of metallic material (nickel, in particular), it is fairly safe to assume that the stone came from outer space.
b. Put a small section under a microscope. If small round particles (called chondri) are embedded in the bulk of the specimen, you can be quite sure that the specimen has an extraterrestrial origin.

CHAPTER XVI

ARTIFICIAL EARTH SATELLITES

An **artificial earth satellite** is an object revolving about the earth in a circular or nearly circular (elliptical) orbit. The first satellite, called Sputnik I, was launched by the U.S.S.R. on October 4, 1957. Sputnik I was a sphere that weighed 184 pounds and

had a diameter of 13 inches. It circled the earth in an elliptical orbit with a perigee of 155 miles and an apogee of 580 miles, completing a trip around the earth in 96 minutes. During its lifetime, from the time of its launching until it disintegrated into the atmosphere, Sputnik I traveled 37 million miles.

To launch a satellite, it is necessary:

(a) to raise it to the proper height above sea level

(b) to orient it in the proper direction

(c) to give it the proper speed.

The satellite must be elevated several hundred miles so as to minimize the effect of atmospheric friction on its orbital motion.

It must be given a velocity perpendicular (90°) to the earth's radius if a circular orbit is desired. If an elliptical orbit is desired, the satellite must be given a velocity slightly different from perpendicular. The satellite must also be placed in the proper angle with the meridian. The proper angle is a compromise between making the best use of the "built-in" velocity caused by the earth's rotation about its axis and the best range of latitudes on the earth's surface for observation of the satellite.

To use most advantageously the velocity caused by the earth's rotation on its axis, the satellite should be launched at the equator and pointed in an easterly direction, where this "built-in" velocity is at a maximum, about 1,000 miles per hour. Any object at the equator has this velocity relative to space by virtue of the earth's completing one rotation (circumference 24,000 miles) in 24 hours. Such a satellite could only be seen by observers located at or near the equator. The satellite would only provide information about the 0° latitude.

To be seen by all terrestrial observers as well as to provide the maximum supply of information, a satellite should be set in a north-south direction. This would, however, negate the use of the "built-in" velocity.

The proper horizontal velocity is between 18,000 and 25,000 miles per hour or between 5 and 7 miles per second. Five miles per second is for very small orbits and 7 miles per second is for very large ones. If the horizontal velocity was less than 5 miles per second, the satellite would not go into orbit but would fall back to the earth. If the velocity was more than 7 miles per second, the object would not go into orbit around the

earth but would escape from the earth's gravitational field.

The three tasks involved in launching a satellite are usually combined. The satellite is usually put into orbit by a multi-stage rocket. The primary purpose of the initial stage is to get the satellite through the thick part of the atmosphere, following the shortest route (i.e., straight up) and obtaining the optimum velocity (to minimize the effect of friction). The other stages turn the satellite toward the horizontal and bring its velocity up to the desired speed.

Before take-off, each stage is properly loaded with the correct amount of fuel, either solid or liquid, which is discarded as soon as its mission is accomplished.

A typical rocket used to launch a satellite may consist of three stages and a nose cone. See Fig. 237A. The nose cone is put in front of the satellite to streamline it.

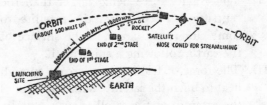

FIG. 237A.

Once placed in an orbit, a satellite will continue there indefinitely, as the forces acting on a satellite cancel out, leaving a net force of zero.

Well above the earth's surface, there are only two forces acting on a satellite; these forces are:

a. Force of Gravity.

$$F_{grav.} = 6.7 \times 10^{-8} \frac{Mm}{r^2}$$

where M is the mass of the earth, m the mass of the satellite, and r the distance between the center of the earth and the center of the satellite. This force exerts a pull on the satellite, tending to bring it toward the earth.

b. The centrifugal force $F = \dfrac{r}{mv^2}$, where m is the mass of the satellite, v is the velocity along its orbit, and r is the distance of the satellite to the center of the orbit. This is a repelling force tending to increase the distance between the satellite and the earth.

For a proper value of velocity, these two forces are equal in magnitude and opposite in direction. Hence they cancel out one another. A satellite with the proper speed will thus continue to move in its orbit, there being no force to remove it from its established path.

Within the earth's atmosphere, the friction between the atmosphere and the satellite upsets the equilibrium between the gravitational and centrifugal force. The force due to friction slows down the forward speed of the satellite and starts the following chain of events:

I. The decrease in speed causes a decrease in centrifugal force.
II. The gravity force being larger than the centrifugal force causes the satellite to come closer and closer to the surface of the earth, following a spiral path.
III. The force of friction may create enough heat to burn the satellite before it reaches the ground, or the satellite may actually reach the ground the way large meteoroids often do.

The best time to visually observe a satellite is either at dawn or at dusk. At these times, the sun is below the horizon, the observer is in the region of darkness, while the satellite, several hundred miles up, is receiving and reflecting light from the sun.

The orbit followed by the satellite is fixed, except for some minor perturbations, in space while the earth inside that orbit is rotating once every 24 hours. See Fig. 237B.

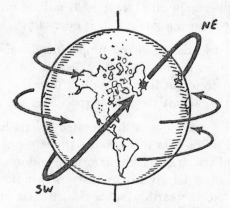

Fig. 237B. Motion of the Satellite. The heavy line forms a hoop along which the satellite moves.

Thus an observer in New York may view the satellite traveling from southwest to northeast, and 12 hours later he may see the same satellite in another part of its orbit moving from northwest to southeast.

A great deal of knowledge about outer space has been acquired with the aid of satellites; the most important single item is the fact that the earth is surrounded by at least three radiation belts (called the Van Allen belts, after their discoverer).

Some of the satellites that have been placed in orbit are designed to perform specific functions. These include:

a. Tiros I, and others in this series, that are designed to obtain meteorological data that can be of great use to the weather forecaster.
b. the Transit series of satellites that is expected to form a network of satellites that will serve as radio beacons to provide a global, all-weather navigational system for both airplanes and ships.
c. the "eye in the sky" series that is designed to give early warning of the possible launching of enemy missiles.

CHAPTER XVII

THE ORIGIN OF THE SOLAR SYSTEM

INTRODUCTION

It is now generally believed that the members of the Solar System belong to three gen-

erations. The sun is the only first generation member, born about four billion years ago. The planets, planetoids and most of the other units of the system came into being at a slightly later date, and form the second generation. Satellites—the third generation—are the offspring of the planets, of still more recent date. It is generally assumed that the masses of all these bodies were derived from matter originally belonging to the sun.

Several hypotheses attempt to explain the manner in which, say, the planets were created. Chief among these are:

a. The Centrifugal Force Hypothesis
b. The Tidal Hypothesis
c. The Collision Hypothesis
d. The Double Star Encounter Hypothesis
e. The Turbulence Hypothesis.

THE CENTRIFUGAL FORCE HYPOTHESIS

This hypothesis is usually referred to as the Nebular Theory of Laplace, after the great French mathematician and astronomer, Pierre Simon Laplace, who first proposed it in 1796. According to this theory, the sun was once a slowly rotating vast disk-shaped mass of hot gas, extending well beyond the orbit of the outermost planet. The birth of the planets resulted from the following chain of events:

I. The sun cooled.

II. As a result, the gas contracted, the radius of the disk becoming smaller.

III. The decrease in radius caused an increase in rotational velocity, thus increasing the centrifugal force.

IV. When the centrifugal force, acting on the outermost regions of the sun, exceeded in value the force of attraction, a ring was separated from the main body of the sun.

V. This gaseous ring gradually condensed into a sphere which became one of the planets.

The sun continued to cool, and this process repeated itself to produce the other planets.

Criticism of the Laplace Theory. While, at first glance, the theory seems reasonable, further thought shows it to be completely untenable, as it is inconsistent with several fundamental principles of mechanics. Two of these inconsistencies are:

a. It can be shown that the rings, after being separated from the sun, could not coalesce to form a single body, nor even a few bodies. Instead, physical theory shows that most of the material in these rings would evaporate, molecule by molecule, into space; the remainder, due to tidal effects from the sun on the ring, would become a multitude of gravel-sized, or smaller, particles.

b. It can be shown that planets thus created should rotate and revolve much more slowly than they actually do (or that the sun should rotate much faster). Otherwise stated, the sun should possess most of the angular momentum of the solar system, while all the planets and planetoids together—very little.

The physical quantity used to describe the momentum of a body due to circular motion, is called Angular Momentum. By definition, the angular momentum of a body of mass m, velocity along its orbit v, and distance from the center r, is the product of these three quantities, namely $m.v.r.$

The facts contradict this theory badly: the sun, with 99.9% of the mass of the Solar System, has only 2% of the rotational momentum, while all the other members of the solar system combined have .1% of the mass, but 98% of the angular momentum.

Thus, according to theory the nebula, while cooling, should concentrate and retain the major portion of this angular momentum in its central mass (the sun), and endow the departing rings with only a minute fraction of this rotational inertia—the fact is, however, that the sun possesses only 2% of the momentum.

THE TIDAL AND THE COLLISION HYPOTHESES

a. The **Tidal Hypothesis,** also known as the **Encounter Hypothesis,** maintains that the planets were created as a result of enormous tides raised on the sun by a passing star. The dense gases drawn out of the sun were also endowed with a sideward motion in the direction in which the passing star was moving. Part of the matter thus raised would very likely follow the star; another part would presumably return to the surface of the sun. Still another would be acted upon with a centrif⋯

gal force large enough to overcome gravitational attraction and would form the several planets. This hypothesis, suggested by Moulton and Chamberlin of the University of Chicago in 1900, was originally known as the planetesimal theory, the term "planetesimal" meaning "little planet." This diminutive suggests that the immediate result of the tidal action was only small planets; these grew in size by picking up neighboring scattered material to form the system of the nine known planets.

NOTE: Recent (1960) computations by Professor Woolfson, using the Manchester (England) University computer, show that a passing star could form the planets and cause them to take positions in accordance with Bode's Law. According to Professor Woolfson's method, the star set up tides on the sun and pulled solar material away at regular intervals of six and three quarter years. Venus was formed first, then the other planets, out to Pluto. Mercury does not fit well in these computations and a suggestion has been made that Mercury did not start its present course around the sun at the same time as the other planets. According to this theory, the asteroids resulted from a collision between two planets that were once occupying the space between Mars and Jupiter.

b. The **Collision Hypothesis** differs from the tidal hypothesis in that it assumes that the encounter between the sun and the visiting star took the form of an actual collision.

Criticism. Computations, based on fundamental formulas of Physics, show that neither hypothesis is acceptable. Again the primary difficulty has to do with the observed distribution of angular momenta, namely, that the sun has only 2%, while the planets have close to 98% of the rotational momentum. Professor Henry Norris Russell of Princeton University concluded that under no reasonable assumption relating to an encounter could as much as 10% of the known angular momentum per ton of planet be possible.

THE DOUBLE STAR ENCOUNTER HYPOTHESIS

This hypothesis, introduced by the English astronomer, R. A. Lyttleton, has the enormous advantage over the preceding ones in that it does not contradict the observed facts of rotational momentum. Lyttleton's hypothe-

sis supposes that the sun was originally a double star, and that a passing star collided with the sun's companion. The events that followed this collision, which may have lasted about an hour, were:

I. The colliding stars (the intruder and the companion of the sun), after the rebound, drew out a ribbon of material, large enough to produce all the planets, satellites, etc.

II. The two stars (like billiard balls after a collision) proceeded along their courses, carrying away the parts of their "ribbon" that were under immediate influence of their respective gravitational fields.

III. The various members of the solar system came into being from the central part of that withdrawn matter; the angular momentum of the matter in this central part could conceivably correspond to the observed values.

Criticism. Computations show that 94% of the ribbon would be taken along by the two colliding stars, while the 6% of the central portion would follow the intruder and the sun's companion for some time before returning to the sole influence of the sun. The probability that planets would be formed from this 6% of the matter is extremely slight. It is infinitely more likely that tidal effects from the intruder and the companion tore this part of the ribbon into shreds that eventually were scattered into neighboring space.

THE TURBULENCE HYPOTHESIS

The most promising theory is the work of the contemporary German physicist von Weizsäcker. The point of departure of his hypothesis, published in 1945, is similar to that of Laplace. Von Weizsäcker's theory assumes that at one time in its development, the sun was surrounded by a slowly rotating disk-shaped cloud of gas. The diameter of the disk was of the order of magnitude of the diameter of the present Solar System, and the temperature at various distances from the central sun corresponded to the temperatures now prevalent on the nine planets located at the same distances (e.g., the temperature of the gases in the disk at the distance of the earth is assumed to be equal to the earth's present temperature). The mass of the nebula is assumed to be 100 times larger than the combined masses of the planets, equal approximately to 10% of the sun's mass; and consisting primarily (99%) of hydrogen and helium and only 1% of the heavier elements. The following chain of events presumably followed this initial state:

Ia. In 200 million years, the molecules of hydrogen and helium were dissipated into space, diminishing the mass of the gases from the original 10% to the present value of slightly more than .1% of the sun's mass, but leaving the angular momentum of the nebula basically unchanged, thus accounting for its present large value.

Ib. In those 200 million years, due to the differences in speed between parts of the nebula close to the sun (great speeds), and those farther from it (small speeds), turbu-

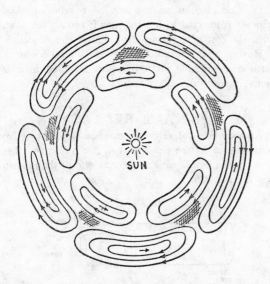

FIG. 238. The Turbulence Hypothesis. Due to differences in speed in the various parts of the nebular turbulence cells were formed.

Five such cells are shown at the outer boundary, as are five neighboring cells.

Each one of these cells spins in a clockwise direction, while the center of the cells proceeds in a counterclockwise direction about the sun.

Large masses of matter formed in the regions between the cells; several of these are shown shaded in the diagram.

According to von Weizsäcker's theory these lumps eventually formed the planet at that particular distance from the sun.

lence cells were formed. The matter in each cell moved in a clockwise direction, while the cells themselves (see Figure 238) moved counterclockwise. The planets, according to this hypothesis, formed in the dead-end region between the cells. These regions, due to the conflicting currents at its boundaries, are most active in accretion of material from the neighboring cells, and are thus instrumental in building up great quantities of matter rotating in a counterclockwise direction. Five such equidistant quantities eventually join in the formation of the planet at the given distance.

Criticism. Much that we know about the Solar System can be explained on the basis of von Weizsäcker's hypothesis. Many questions, however, still remain unanswered.

The hypothesis explains, for example:

(a) the fact that the planets, as well as the planetoids, revolve in nearly a common plane;

(b) the fact that the sun's equatorial plane nearly coincides with the orbital planes of the planets;

(c) the fact that the planets possess nearly all of the angular momentum of the whole system; and

(d) the fact that the spacing of the planets follows a regular pattern, as described in Bode's Law for planetary distances.

The number of questions that are still unanswered are many. Among these are:

(a) How did the droplets and particles form the lumps?

(b) By what process did the several lumps unite to form a single planet?

(c) Why does Uranus rotate about an axis that is almost perpendicular to the axis of its orbital plane?

(d) How were the satellites created, and why do a few of them move in retrograde motion?

The solutions to these problems and to countless others will no doubt eventually be formulated by the dedicated men who devote their lives to a better understanding of the universe we live in.

HOME-BUILT TELESCOPES

INTRODUCTION

Excellent telescopes are being designed and constructed by an evergrowing number of amateur astronomers, using rather simple "ingredients" and a great deal of devotion and "elbow grease."

Some homemade telescopes are of simple construction; others approach in complexity instruments produced in professional shops. In all cases, many decisions have to be made in the course of production.

The very first decision that has to be made is whether to build a refractor (the objective-a lens) or a reflector (the objective-a mirror). The relative merits to be considered are:

a. For a Refractor

I. Of the two, the percentage of light transmitted to the eyepiece by a lens objective is slightly higher—a lens of 5-inch clear diameter being the equal of a mirror of 5½-inch clear diameter.

II. Surveys of large portions of the sky are much more efficiently carried out with refractors. The field of a reflector is limited to a fraction of a degree.

III. Upkeep is small for any telescope; it is slightly less for a refractor. The aluminum coating on the mirror deteriorates and has to be renewed every few years. A refractor does not deteriorate with time; its adjustments, once made, are permanent.

b. For a Reflector

I. A mirror is perfectly achromatic, while a lens, even when corrected, has a residual color defect.

II. To reduce the residual color defect to a tolerable minimum, the ratio $\frac{focal\ length}{diameter}$ of the objective lens has to be large,* say 15 or 20; while in the case of a mirror objective, chromatic aberration is nonexistent and the focal length is usually designed to be 3 or 4 or 5 times the size of the diameter. Small

---

* The larger the ratio $\frac{focal\ length}{diameter}$ in a lens, the less objectionable is its color aberration. The focal length of an achromatic objective with tolerable color aberration is given to fair accuracy by the formula $f = 5d^2$, where f is the focal length in inches and d is the diameter in inches.

---

ratios imply short telescopic tubes which are easier to mount and easier to transport from place to place. Also, long focal ratio refractors are too slow for photographic work. Mirror objectives are much more efficient in photographing both individual objects and clusters of stars.

III. The probability of success is larger, especially for a beginner, with a reflector. A beginner is much more likely to construct a good concave mirror, which has to have the proper curvature only on one side, than a good achromatic lens with exact curvatures on four surfaces, two of which have to fit together.

IV. Cost, too, is on the side of a reflector. The expense connected with a reflector is usually less than 50% the cost of a refractor of similar size objective.

Having weighed all these factors, most amateur astronomers decide on a reflector. Detailed instructions for both follow.

HOME-MADE REFRACTOR

An astronomical refractor consists of an objective lens, housed in the front part of the objective tube; and an eyepiece housed at the rear end of the mounting. See Fig. 239.

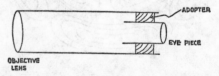

Fig. 239. An Astronomical Refractor. The front lens points toward the object and is known as the Objective or Objective Lens.

The eyepiece is used to magnify the (First) image produced by the objective.

The diameter of the eyepiece mounting is usually smaller than the diameter of the objective tube: an adapter made of wood or other material is used to fill the gap.

1. The Objective Lens

A beginner would do well to acquire a ready-made

objective and forego the desire to produce one himself. Good assortments of perfect or nearly perfect war surplus "large diameters," "achromatic," "large f-number," "coated" lenses are available at reasonable prices and should be used in the first attempt to design a refractor.

Such a lens, 3¼-inch diameter, achromatic, coated, 40 inches focal length, and an f-number equal to 12.3 will be used as an example in what follows. General formulas will be given which can be used with other objective lenses.

The meanings of the various terms are given elsewhere in the book and are briefly summarized here.

"Achromatic lens" usually means that it consists of two components cemented together to form a unit, free of most color defect.

"Coated" usually means that the surfaces of the lens have been covered with a coating of magnesium fluoride to eliminate reflection of light at these surfaces. This coating is extremely thin; its thickness equals a quarter of a wavelength of yellow-green light.

"Focal length" means the distance between the center of the lens and the focus. This distance can easily be checked by placing the lens perpendicularly to solar rays, finding on a screen the focus, and measuring the distance F. See Fig. 240.

FIG. 240. Focal length F is the distance between the center of the lens and the focus. It is usually stated either in inches or in millimeters.

"f-Number," also known as "focal ratio," is simply the ratio between the focal length and the diameter of the lens. In the example under consideration, the f ratio is $\frac{40}{3\frac{1}{4}} = 12.3$. This ratio is of particular importance in photographic work. Small values of ratio correspond to great photographic speeds; large values correspond to slow speed, i.e., require large exposure times.

2. Tubing for Objective

Cardboard tubing, the kind used for mailing charts and calendars, is quite satisfactory. Aluminum tubing is better. The inside of the tube should be well covered with flat black lacquer.

Aluminum tubing with inside diameter 3.281" and outside diameter 3.406 inches, will exactly accommodate a 3¼-inch diameter lens.

The length of the objective tube should be larger by an inch than the focal length of the objective. A piece of tubing 41 inches long will serve for a f = 40" lens.

3. Mounting of Objective in Tubing

There are many ways to attach the objective to the tubing; the goal always is to produce a firm attachment, without covering much of the lens surface (the "clear" diameter of the lens should be as close as possible to its "real" diameter).

An aluminum tubing mounting can be made from two narrow (say ¼ inch) rings, from which small segments are cut (see Fig. 241), so that the remainder

FIG. 241. One of the two narrow rings with small segments missing that are used to mount the objective in the tube.

will just fit inside the objective tubing. The rings may be attached to the tubing with two or three small machine screws. See Fig. 242.

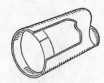

FIG. 242. The rings minus the segment just fit inside the tubing (only one ring is shown here). The lens is placed between the two rings.

4. The Eyepiece

The three (Huygenian, Kellner, and Orthoscopic) common types of eyepieces were earlier described. These descriptions, with particular attention to the merits of each type, should be carefully reviewed before acquiring this part of the telescope. Let us assume that a Kellner ½" focal length, coated, 40° apparent field of view eyepiece has been selected for the 3¼-inch diameter objective; the eyepiece is mounted in a piece of tubing, the outside diameter of which is 1¼".

5. Calculations

Given the optical data about the objective, and the optical data of the eyepiece, many of the properties of their combination (i.e., the telescope) can be computed:

A. Magnification = $\dfrac{\text{Focal length of Objective}}{\text{Focal length of Eyepiece}}$

For the objective and eyepiece on hand,

Magnification = $\dfrac{40}{\frac{1}{2}}$ = 80 times.

B. True Field of View =

$\dfrac{\text{Apparent Field of View of Eyepiece}}{\text{Magnification}}$

In the example being worked out, the apparent field of view of the eyepiece is 40°, the magnification is 80X. Hence,

True Field of View = $\dfrac{40}{80}$ = $\frac{1}{2}$°.

This answer implies that $\frac{1}{2}$ a degree (about the size of the angular diameter of the moon) of the sky is seen through a telescope made of this objective and eyepiece. See Fig. 243.

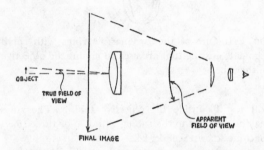

FIG. 243. Apparent Field of View is the angle subtended at the eye by the final image. True Field of View is the angle subtended by the object at the eye.

C. Resolving Power of Telescope.

Resolving Power = $\dfrac{5}{\text{Diameter of Objective}}$

A telescope having a $3\frac{1}{4}$-inch objective has a resolving power of

$\dfrac{5}{3\frac{1}{4}}$ = 1.5 seconds of angle;

that is, two stars at an angular distance of 1.5 seconds of angle will be seen as two distinct points of light. See Fig. 244.

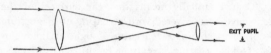

FIG. 244. Resolving Power is the smallest angle that two distant objects may subtend and still be seen as two distinct units.

D. Size of Exit Pupil

Exit pupil is, by definition, the diameter of the cylindrical beam of light emerging from the eyepiece.

This diameter should never be larger than the diameter of the pupil of the human eye (say 1/6 of an inch) or smaller than, say 1/64th of an inch. The value of the exit pupil is computed from the formula:

Exit Pupil = $\dfrac{\text{Diameter of Objective}}{\text{Magnification}}$

For a $3\frac{1}{4}''$ diameter lens, and a magnification of 80 times, the exit pupil is equal to:

$\dfrac{3\frac{1}{4}}{80}$ = $\dfrac{13}{320}$ = $\dfrac{26}{640}$ = $\dfrac{2.6}{64}$ inches

This value is well within the limits prescribed for the diameter. See Fig. 245.

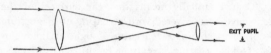

FIG. 245. Exit Pupil is the diameter of the cylinder of light leaving the eyepiece.

E. Radius of Image produced by Objective.

The size of the first image, i.e., the image produced by the objective alone, depends on (a) the true field of view, and (b) the focal length of the objective. The formula is:

Radius of Image =

$\dfrac{\text{True Field of View} \times \text{Focal Length of Objective}}{57.3}$

The 57.3 in the denominator is a conversion factor from angles in degrees to angles in terms of radians. For an objective lens of 40 inch focal length and $\frac{1}{2}$ degree of angle field of view, the radius of the first image is:

$\dfrac{.5 \times 40}{57.3}$ = $\dfrac{20}{57.3}$ = .35 inch.

6. Mounting of the Eyepiece

The outside diameter of eyepiece mountings (standardized to $1\frac{1}{4}''$ diameter) is usually materially smaller than the inner diameter of the draw tube; and an adapter has to be used between the mounting and the tube. Such an adapter, in the form of a hollow cylinder, may be made of wood or any other convenient material. The outside radius of the hollow cylinder would have to fit inside the objective tube (say $3\frac{1}{4}''$ diameter); the inner radius would have to accommodate the $1\frac{1}{4}''$ eyepiece mounting. The adapter should not be too thick, so as not to interfere with the light going from objective to eyepiece.

It is important to make sure that when the eyepiece mounting is fully inserted, the field lens (the lens in the eyepiece close to the objective) is close to the focus of the objective, and that the mounting can be pulled out half an inch or so without becoming detached from the objective tubing. The focus of the eyepiece is just a little ahead of the field lens.

7. Layout

In the case of a 3¼″ objective and the ½″ Kellner eyepiece, the simplest arrangement would be as shown in Figure 246.

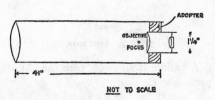

FIG. 246. Layout of Telescope. The focus of the eyepiece is just ahead of the field lens, the ½″ being measured from the "center" of the eyepiece.

8. Image Stop and Glare Stop

An image stop is placed in the focal plane of the objective in order to cut out weak edge rays and thus obtain a sharp well-defined image. The stop consists of a round disk of blackened cardboard or other convenient material, with a central hole of radius equal to the radius of the image formed by the objective. In the case of the 3¼″ lens, this radius was computed (see Calculations) to be equal to .35 inches.

Two or three glare stops are often inserted in the objective tube to eliminate stray radiation which enters the telescope from outside the field of view. These, too, are round disks, with a central hole, usually made of the same material as the image stop.

The stops are placed so that they divide the distance between the objective and first image in equal parts. The size of the hole is determined from a drawing showing (to scale) the objective, the first image, and two lines (such as AC and BD) joining the ends of same.

A typical stop placed at a distance of 13″ from the objective should have a diameter KL; this would permit the full cone of light from objective to proceed toward image, but will eliminate stray radiation. See Fig. 247.

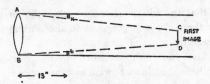

FIG. 247. Diameter of Stop. A stop at the distance of 13″ would have a diameter of KL, K and L being points on the lines AC and BD that include the full cone of light proceeding from the objective to the image.

HOME-MADE REFLECTOR

An astronomical reflector consists of a concave aluminized mirror, usually spherical or paraboloidal in shape, mounted at the bottom of an open tube, a plane mirror (known as a flat or as a diagonal), and an eyepiece. See Fig. 248.

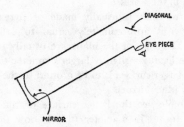

FIG. 248. A reflector consists of a concave mirror, a diagonal (flat mirror) or a prism and an eyepiece.

Light from the object under study passes down the tube to the mirror, which reflects it back up to form the first image (the action of the mirror in the reflector is thus similar to the action of the objective lens in the refractor). The small plane mirror (or diagonal, or "flat") intercepts the reflected rays just before their focal plane and diverts them at right angles towards the side of the upper end of the tube. The first image formed by these rays is viewed by the eyepiece located in this upper tube. See Fig. 249.

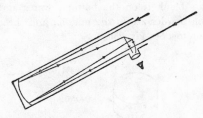

FIG. 249. Path of Light in a Reflector. Rays of light from object pass down the tube to concave mirror, the first image (the action of the mirror in the reflected rays are intercepted (before image was formed) by plane mirror and diverted towards the side of the tube. The image formed there is magnified by the eyepiece.

Eyepieces have been described earlier; the same types can be used for both reflectors and refractors.

It is assumed that both the eyepiece and the diagonal will be acquired ready-made.

The following description will deal primarily with the grinding, polishing, and testing of the mirror.

MIRROR GRINDING

Ready-made mirrors of various sizes and perfections are now available in the stores. But there is no substitute for the satisfaction of having a mirror of one's own making.

The starting point is extremely simple—two glass disks (blanks): one for the mirror, one for the "tool"; a supply of a few kinds of abrasives used in glass grinding; the final result may very well be a mirror that excels in definition and perfection the best obtainable in the stores.

The mirror disk is usually made of pyrex glass; its thickness is approximately equal to 1/6th the diameter. The sides of the blank are usually tapered, one surface having a slightly larger diameter than the other (the larger surface is to be ground to the proper curvature of the mirror).

For example, let the larger surface of the mirror disk be 6 inches in diameter (this is now the most popular size, many thousands of these were made in recent years). Let the desired focal length of the finished product be 48 inches.

The tool is usually ordinary plate glass of the same diameter as the mirror and of thickness equal to or slightly less than the mirror blank.

The first abrasive used in the grinding process is usually carborundum #80. Carborundum, a synthetic abrasive consisting of silicon carbide, is considerably harder than emery and many times more efficient. The 80 indicates that it just goes through a mesh having 80 strands per inch. The second abrasive is usually carborundum #220; this is followed by three or four successively thinner abrasives to complete the grinding process.

The working set-up resembles a sandwich. The plate glass blank is on the bottom; water and carborundum powder are in the middle; and the pyrex blank is on top. See Fig. 250.

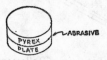

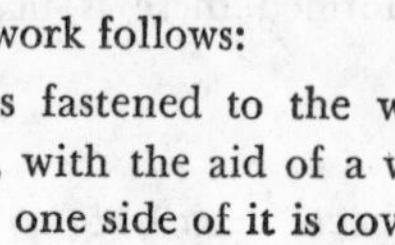

FIG. 250. The Working Setup. The plate glass flat cylinder is on the bottom; the pyrex blank to be ground is on the top; the abrasive is in between.

The order of work follows:

1. The tool is fastened to the working platform, usually a barrel, with the aid of a wooden base. The glass is warmed; one side of it is covered with turpen-

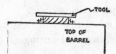

FIG. 251. The tool is glued (pitch is used) to the wooden base. The wooden base is bolted firmly to the top of the barrel.

tine. Melted pitch is poured on the wooden base and then the wet face of the blank is pressed tightly against the pitch-covered wood. See Fig. 251.

2. A handle is attached to the pyrex disk. To do this, the back of the mirror is warmed, the center of it is wet with turpentine, upon which warm pitch is poured, and the handle is then firmly pressed on. See Fig. 252.

FIG. 252. A handle is attached, with the aid of pitch, to the pyrex blank.

3. The abrasive is introduced. Carborundum #80 is sprayed on the tool; the face of the mirror is dipped in water and the grinding begins.

4. Three motions are followed simultaneously during the grinding. I. A to-and-fro motion (center over center) of the pyrex disk over the tool; II. rotation of the pyrex blank about its own center; and III. slow walk of worker around the barrel, so as to cover the whole circumference of the stationary tool.

The first of these three motions is the all-important one. The length of the stroke determines the shape of the mirror. To produce a spherical shape (usually a perfect spherical shape is produced first; the parabolic correction is added later) the length of the stroke should be about ⅓ the diameter of the disk, that is, the center of the top blank is moved 1/6th one way and 1/6th the other way over the center of the stationary blank. Parabolizing is accomplished by increasing the length of the strokes to ½ or even a larger fraction of the diameter.

Note that while the upper disk is becoming concave (hollow), the lower disk (the tool) is becoming convex. This is due partly to the increased pressure between the disks, when only part of them are in contact. See Fig. 253.

FIG. 253. The pyrex disk becomes concave as the tool becomes convex.

Note that in this overhang position the pressure between the disks is larger than in the normal sandwich position.

Note also that both surfaces become spherical in shape; spherical surfaces remain in continuous contact at every point when moved over each other in any direction.

5. When the abrasive ceases to cut, the mirror is lifted and the tool is sprayed anew with carborundum.

This grinding, known as rough grinding, continues until the radius of the mirror is about 10 inches longer than the one aimed for. In the example under study, the aim is a 96-inch radius (or 48-inch focus; the radius of the mirror is twice its focal length). The rough grinding will continue until the radius is about 106 inches; the excess will be taken care of by the next grinding stage.

A quick determination of the radius of the mirror is obtained by:

a. placing the mirror in a vertical position,

b. placing the eye on level with center, and

c. holding in one hand a candle, moving it back and forth at right angles to the axis of the mirror and noting the direction of motion of the candle's reflection in the mirror.

If the reflection moves in the same direction as the candle, the eye is closer to the mirror than its center of curvature. If the reflection moves the opposite way from that of the candle, the eye is farther from the mirror than its center of curvature.

By moving the eye closer to or farther from the mirror, its center of curvature can be ascertained within an accuracy of several inches.

6. The fine grinding brings the radius to within ½ or ¼ of an inch of its ultimate radius; the process of polishing usually shortens the radius of the curve by ¼ or ½ an inch.

Carborundum #220 is used in the first stage of this fine grinding. Care should be taken to remove, by thorough washing and rinsing, every last trace of the carborundum #80 that was used in the rough grinding process.

Usually seven or eight charges of the #220 are sufficient for this stage. Each charge (known as a "wet," because the carborundum has water added to it) lasts about 5 minutes before it ceases to cut; this whole stage of fine grinding takes about 40 minutes.

Fig. 254. Setup for Foucault Test. Light from the point source is reflected by the mirror (only the beginning and the end of the path of light is shown) towards the eye.

7. The fine grinding process is then repeated by three or four successively thinner abrasives (say abrasive numbers 320, 400, and 600), care again being taken to remove the coarse abrasive before the finer one is applied. Again six "wets" (charges) are usually sufficient for each stage.

8. Testing the spherical shape of the mirror is the next job.

There are several tests to ascertain whether the mirror has a perfectly spherical shape—the best known

of these we owe to the Frenchman Foucault (of the Foucault pendulum experiment-fame).

The equipment for the test consists of a point source of light; (a small hole in a metal chimney containing an electric light usually serves as the pinhole); and a knife edge.

The point source of light is placed several inches to one side of the center; the eye is placed an equal distance on the opposite side. See Fig. 254.

If the curvature of the mirror is spherical, then

I. The light reflected by the mirror will meet at *one* point.

II. A knife edge "cutting" that point will cause the mirror:

A. to darken *evenly* all over;

B. look flat; and

C. a slight movement of the knife edge across that point will cause no moving shadow in the mirror. See Fig. 255.

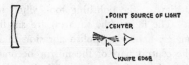

Fig. 255. Test for Spherical Shape. If the face of the mirror is perfectly spherical all the reflected rays will meet at one point. A knife edge placed at that point will block these rays from the eye.

The mirror seen in the light of starry radiation will appear evenly dark. (Only the end of the paths of the light is shown.)

If the mirror is not spherical, none of these characteristics will be present, e.g., slight movements of the knife edge at right angles to the axis of the mirror will cause its shadow to move one way across the mirror's face.

9. The polishing of the mirror can be done with either fine optical rouge (Fe_2O_3), Cerium oxide (CeO_2), of Barnesite (a mixture of several rare earth oxides). Cerium oxide is two to three times as efficient as rouge. Barnesite probably yields the most superior polish of the three.

The arrangements for the polishing include:

I. Cover the tool with a layer of pitch.

II. Cut out channels, usually of a V cross-section. These serve as reservoirs for the liquid mixture of water and polishing agent. See Fig. 256.

The polishing consists of moving the mirror over the pitch-covered tool with a ⅓ diameter stroke center over center, and should be continued until all the pits (which may be seen through a magnifying glass) are removed from the mirror. The rotational motions used in grinding (rotation of the mirror and walking about the tool) are used in polishing as well.

10. The job of changing the spherical into a parab-

FIG. 256. Polishing Setup. The tool is covered with a layer of pitch in which channels are cut.

oloidal shape is known as "figuring." It will be recalled that paraboloidal shape is superior to spherical as it converges all the paraxial (parallel to axis) rays entering the telescope to meet in a single point (the focus).

FIG. 257. View of the polishing tool, when used for "figuring." The facets (the squares) are smaller near the perimeter; hence less polish abrasion takes place there. The central part of the mirror becomes more curved than the outlying zones, typical of the paraboloidal shape.

One of the ways to "figure" a spherical mirror is known as "Parabolizing by Graduating Facets." In this method, the channels are widened progressively from center to edge, thus decreasing the area of the facets and the resulting rate of polish abrasion. The center of the mirror is thus deepened faster than its edges; the cross-section acquires the curvature typical of a parabola. See Fig. 257.

A perfect cross-section is obtained when the radius of the peripheral zones, such as AB, is longer than the radius at the axis, CD, by an amount $\frac{r^2}{R}$, where r is the radius of the face of the mirror and R is the average radius of the curvature. See Fig. 258.

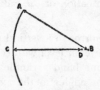

FIG. 258. A parabola is more curved at its center than at the edges, hence the radius CD is smaller than the radius AB.

In the example under consideration, the radius is 3", and the radius of curvature is approximately 96" (twice the focal length of 48"); hence, AB should be longer by $\frac{32}{96} = \frac{9}{96} = 0.09$ inches, or approximately 0.1 inches than CD.

11. The equipment used in the Foucault test for spherical shape can be used for testing the paraboloidal shape of the mirror. The latter consists at the edges; hence the radius CD is smaller than the polishing continues until such time as the difference between these is $\frac{r^2}{R}$. When AB is measured, the central part of the mirror is covered with non-reflecting material, the light being reflected towards the eye from the peripheral zones only. When CD is measured, the peripheral zones are made non-reflecting.

12. The aluminizing of the mirror has to be performed under vacuum and is best done in shops specializing in that kind of work.

GLOSSARY

Absolute Magnitude. The magnitude that would be assigned to a star, if it were placed at a distance of 10 parsecs from the observer. Stars closer to us than that distance would appear fainter. Stars farther from the Solar System would appear brighter.

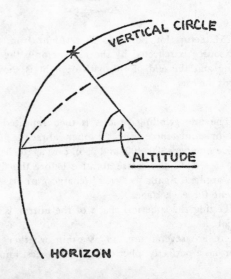

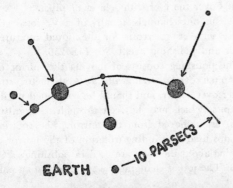

Achromatic Lens. A lens that transmits white light, without dispersing it into a color spectrum. It usually consists of two component parts, cemented together to form one unit.

Albedo. Percentage of light reflected by a body, such as a planet, to amount of light falling on it.

Altitude. Angular distance between horizon and a given object, measured along a vertical circle.

Annular Eclipse. An eclipse of the central portion of the solar disk; an outer ring shows.

Aphelion. Point on planet's orbit farthest from the sun.

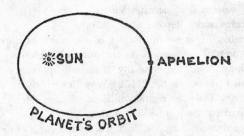

Apogee. Point on the moon's orbit farthest from the earth.

Artificial Satellite. A man-made object placed into an orbit about the earth or about another celestial body such as the sun or the moon.

Binary Star. Two close stars held together by a gravitational force and revolving like a dumbbell about a common center of gravity. The center is closer to the more massive star.

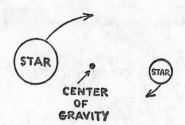

Celestial Sphere. An imaginary sphere of infinite radius surrounding the earth and serving as a screen against which all celestial objects are seen.

Cepheid. A star the brightness of which varies periodically. The periods range from several hours to 50 days.

Chromatic Aberration (also called color defect). Blurring of image due to the separation of colors by a lens. A point of white light in the object appears as a complete spectrum of colored points in the image.

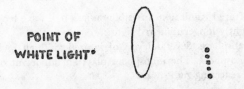

POINT OF
WHITE LIGHT

Collimator or Collimating Lens. A lens whose function it is to make rays of light parallel.

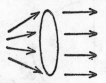

Colure, equinoctial, also known as the Prime Hour Circle. The hour circle that goes through the First Point of Aries. The hour angles (same as longitude on earth) are measured from the equinoctial colure.

Conjunction. Apparent line-up of sun, earth, and a planet. Inferior conjunction is when the planet is between the earth and the sun.

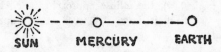

Superior conjunction is when the planet is on the opposite side of the sun.

Constellation. A group of stars apparently close together in the sky. Modern astronomy recognizes 88 such groups (e.g., Cassiopeia, Leo, etc.). Actually, the individual stars of a constellation may be great distances apart and moving in different directions one from the other.

Copernican System. The system that assumes that the sun is at the center, and the earth and the other planets move around it.

Culmination. The position of a celestial body when it is on the meridian. A star is said to be at its "Upper Culmination" when it has reached its highest point for the day.

Declination. Angular distance of an object from the celestial equator, measured in degrees, minutes and seconds. Analogous to latitude in geography.

Diffraction of Light. A phenomenon exhibited by light on passing through a narrow slit or a small aperture. The light is modified to form alternate dark and bright fringes.

Discrete Source. A small area in the sky—almost a point—from which very intense electromagnetic waves of radio frequency reach the earth. These points were formerly called radio stars.

Doppler Effect. Change in frequency of light due to relative motion between observer and source of light.

Eccentricity. Eccentricity indicates the degree of flatness of an ellipse, or its departure from a circle.

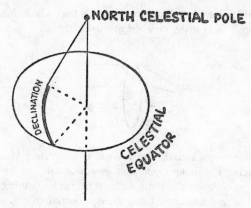

It is denoted by e; its value is obtained from the formula $e = \dfrac{2c}{2a}$, when $2c$ is the distance between the foci, and $2a$ is the length of the major axis. When e is small (e.g., 0.05), the ellipse approaches a circle in shape; when it is large (e.g., 0.8), the ellipse is elongated.

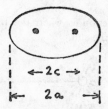

Eclipse

1. *Solar.* The sun's light is cut off by the moon's interposition between the sun and the earth.

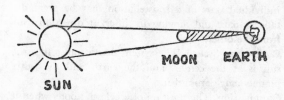

2. *Lunar.* The moon darkens because the earth intercepts the sunlight on its way to the moon.

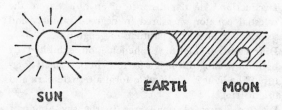

Ecliptic. Two equivalent definitions are possible.
A. The great circle on the celestial sphere formed by the intersection of that sphere with the plane of the earth's orbit.
B. The path described on the celestial sphere by the sun during its apparent annual motion around the earth.

Elongation. Angular distance from the sun, measured in degrees, minutes and seconds of angle.

Ephemeris. A book of tables showing computed daily positions of heavenly objects.

Equinox. One of the points of intersection between the ecliptic and the celestial equator. When the sun is at one of these two points, the length of day and night are equal everywhere on the earth. The sun is at these points every year on or about March 21st and September 23rd.

Escape Velocity. See Velocity of Escape.

Evening Star. (This is not a star; it is a planet.) A planet, especially Mercury, or Venus, when seen in the western sky just after sunset.

Extragalactic. Beyond Our Galaxy.

Faculae. Areas on the surface of the sun that appear brighter by comparison to surrounding regions.

Galaxy. A large community of stars in space, such as "Our Galaxy," or the "Milky Way," to which the sun belongs. Galaxies contain billions of stars. Many are shaped in the form of a spiral.

Granules. Smallest visible units on the sun's surface. Granules or granulations have diameters hundreds of miles long. They change in size and in structure continuously.

Hour Angle, analogous to longitude in geography. Angle between the local celestial meridian and the hour circle of a given object in the sky, measured westward from the meridian. It may be given in units of time (hours, minutes and seconds). 1 hour = 15 degrees of angle. Hour angles are easily visualized as either arcs along the celestial equator, or angles at the celestial poles.

Hour Circle (similar to meridian in geography), a great circle passing through the two celestial poles.

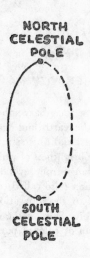

Infrared Radiation. Invisible radiation of wave length slightly longer than red light.

Ionosphere. Several layers of ionized air high in the atmosphere. The ionosphere plays an important part in reflecting radio waves.

Libration. Apparent "rocking" or "nodding" of moon or the planet Mercury. Due to this oscillation, some of the usually hidden sides are exhibited to the terrestrial observer.

Light Year. A unit of distance, not of time. The distance that light travels in one year.

Magellanic Clouds. (These are not clouds; they are galaxies.) Two nearby galaxies, of irregular shape, named after Magellan.

Magnitude (or Apparent Magnitude), a number indicating the apparent brightness of a star. Bright stars are designated by small numbers (magnitude 1, say) while dim stars are designated by large numbers (e.g., magnitude 15).

Main Sequence Stars (not White Dwarfs, or Red Giants), stars that fit in the diagonal of the Russell Diagram. The position on the diagram depends, of course, on the spectral type and brightness of the star.

Meteor. (Same as shooting star.) A meteorite during the time it is giving off light.

Meteorite. A body too small (often size of a pin head) to be called a planetoid.

Micrometeorite. A tiny meteorite, too small to become incandescent during its passage through the atmosphere. Average size is about $\frac{1}{1000}$ of an inch in diameter.

Milky Way. A luminous band across the sky. The light is due to the fact that the vast majority of stars in our (disk-shaped) galaxy are located along this narrow band on the celestial sphere.

Morning Star. (A planet, not a star.) A planet, e.g., Mercury, when seen in the eastern sky just before sunrise.

Neap Tides. The lowest tides of the month.

Nebula. A vast cloud of gas, or gas and dust in space.

Node. A point of intersection of one orbit (say, the moon's) with the plane of another orbit (say, the earth's).

Nova. A star that suddenly increases greatly in brightness.

Occultation. Eclipse of a star or a planet by the moon. The term "occultation" also applies to a satellite passing behind its primary.

Parallax. Apparent shift of position of an object with respect to its background due to a shift in position of the observer. An observer at A sees the star in region a of the sky. An observer at B sees the same star in region b.

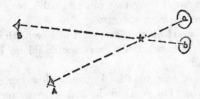

Parsec. The distance BD in the triangle ABD.

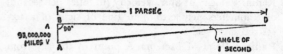

One parsec is equal to 19.2 million million miles.

Penumbra. The outer and lighter part of a shadow cast by a planet or satellite, as in regions A and B.

Perigee. Point in orbit (of moon, say) nearest Earth (as point A).

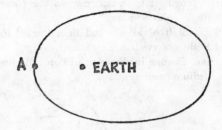

Perihelion. Point in orbit nearest sun. (Point A.)

Photosphere. The visible surface of the sun or star. Below it is the interior of the sun; above it, the atmosphere.

Planet. One of the nine bodies revolving about the sun in almost circular orbits. Planets are made visible by reflected sunlight.

Planetary Nebula. A nebula resembling a planet in shape.

Planetoid. Same as asteroid; same as Minor Planet. A small irregularly shaped solid body revolving about the sun.

Poles, Celestial. Points of intersection of extension of earth's axis and the celestial sphere.

Precession. The slow change in direction of the earth's axis due to the gravitational pull of the moon on the bulge at the earth's equator. The slow change in the axis causes the westward motion of the equinoxes among the constellations.

Proper Motion of Star. The angular velocity (in seconds of angle per year) of a star in a direction perpendicular to the line of sight of a terrestrial observer.

Radial Velocity of Star. Velocity (in miles per second, or kilometers per second) in line of sight of a terrestrial observer.

Radiant Point of Meteors. A point in the sky from which meteors seem to come.

Radio Astronomy. The branch of astronomy that deals with the electromagnetic waves emitted by various celestial bodies as well as the theory of their emission.

Radio Star. See **Discrete Source.**

Radio Telescope. An instrument used for examination of celestial objects by means of the radio waves emitted by these objects.

Radio Window. The atmosphere is transparent to radio waves that range between 0.25 cm. and 30 meters in length. The transparency to these waves is often called "radio window."

Red Shift. Shift of all spectral lines toward longer wave lengths observed in all galaxies.

Refraction. Change in direction of light on entering a new medium (such as glass).

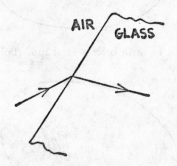

Resolving Power of Telescope. Power to separate two close points into two distinct units.

Retrograde Motion. Apparent backward (westward) motion of a planet.

Reversing Layer. The lowest of the three solar atmospheric layers; it is responsible for most of the dark lines in the solar spectrum.

Right Ascension. (Analogous to longitude in geography.) Angular distance from the prime meridian measured eastward along the celestial equator from 0° to 360°, or from 0 to 24 hours.

Rocket. A tube, designed to move through space, that derives its thrust by ejecting hot, expanding gases—known as jet—that have been generated in its motor. The rocket contains within itself all the material needed for the production of the jet.

Saros. The interval (about 18⅓ years) between two successive eclipses of the same series.

Satellite. (e.g., the moon) A body revolving about one of the planets.

Sidereal Period. Time required to make one revolution (as seen from one of the fixed stars).

Solar Constant. 1.94 calories per minute reach every square centimeter, at the earth's mean distance.

Solstice. The point of maximum declination on the ecliptic. The solstices are half way between the equinoctial points. The summer solstice occurs when the sun is farthest north from the equator; the winter solstice, when the sun is farthest south.

Spectroscopic Binary. A system of two stars that can be detected only with the aid of a spectroscope.

Spherical Aberration. Shape defect of lens. Light passing a spherical lens near its edge is converged more than light passing the center of the same lens, causing the image to blur.

Spiral Nebula. A galaxy of stars (*not* a nebula) in the form of a spiral.

Star. A large globe of intensely hot gas, shining by its own light (e.g., the sun).

Supernova. A star that quite suddenly increases (a million times) in brightness. It is similar to a nova, but its increase is vastly greater.

Synodic Period. Interval of time for a planet (or the moon) to complete one revolution, as seen from the earth.

Terminator. Boundary between the illuminated and dark portion of the moon or a planet.

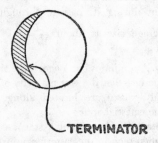

Transit. Motion of a small body (e.g., Mercury) across the face of a larger body (e.g., the sun).

Tropical Year. The ordinary year. The year used in everyday life.

Umbra. The dark shadow cast by a planet or a satellite.

Velocity of Escape. The velocity that an object must acquire in order to escape from the gravitational pull exerted upon it by another body. The velocity of escape at the earth's surface is seven miles per second. Any terrestrial body that can reach this velocity will permanently leave the earth.

White Dwarf Stars. White stars of low luminosity.

Zenith. The point on the celestial sphere directly overhead.

Zodiac. A belt in the sky containing twelve constellations. The sun, moon and planets appear to travel within that belt.

The ecliptic divides it in two.

INDEX